THE CLASSICAL COUNTRY HOUSE

THE CLASSICAL COUNTRY HOUSE

FROM THE ARCHIVES OF COUNTRY LIFE

◎ ◎ ◎

DAVID WATKIN

AURUM PRESS

For
Paul Robert Aidan Doyle

First published in Great Britain 2010 by Aurum Press Limited
7 Greenland Street, London NW1 0ND
www.aurumpress.co.uk

Text copyright © 2010 David Watkin
Photographs © *Country Life* Picture Library

All rights reserved. No part of this book may be reproduced or utilised in any form or by any means, electronic or mechanical, including photocopying, recording or by any information storage and retrieval system, without permission in writing from Aurum Press Limited.

A catalogue record for this book is available from the British Library.

ISBN 978 1 84513 593 5
10 9 8 7 6 5 4 3 2 1
2014 2013 2012 2011 2010

Design by James Campus
Originated, printed and bound in Singapore by C S Graphics

Frontispiece: *Mereworth Castle, Kent, by Colen Campbell, c.1720–25, viewed from the loggia of the east pavilion.*

Front endpaper: *Wilton House, Wiltshire, approached through the Corinthian Triumphal Arch built by William Chambers on a hill in the park in 1759 and brought here by James Wyatt in 1809.*

Rear endpaper: *Chiswick House, Middlesex, designed by Lord Burlington c.1725–29, and guarded dramatically by rusticated piers with neo-antique Greek key friezes.*

THE COUNTRY LIFE PICTURE LIBRARY

The *Country Life* Picture Library holds a complete set of prints made from its negatives, and a card index to the subjects, usually recording the name of the photographer and the date of the photographs catalogued, together with a separate index of photographers.

It also holds a complete set of *Country Life* and various forms of published indices to the magazine. The Library may be visited by appointment, and prints of any negatives it holds can be supplied by post.

For further information, please contact the Library Manager, Justin Hobson, at *Country Life*, Blue Fin Building, 110 Southwark Street, London SE1 0SU (*Tel*: 020 3148 4474).

ACKNOWLEDGEMENTS

I would like to express my gratitude to Jeremy Musson for proposing the subject and the title of this book and for inviting me to write it.

LIST OF ARTICLES

This is a list of *Country Life* articles on the houses in this book. The photographer's name is given in brackets, if known.

Ashfold House, Sussex: 7 November 2001 (June Buck).

Beach House, Sussex: 29 January 1921.

Belsay House, Northumberland: 5 and 12 October 1940.

British Embassy, Washington DC: 14 and 21 January 1939; 30 November 2006 (Ian Bradshaw).

Brodsworth Hall, Yorkshire: 3 and 10 October 1963; 8 June 1989 (Michael Cyprien); 29 June 1995 (Paul Highnam/English Heritage).

Cairness House, Aberdeenshire: 28 January and 4 February 1971; 20 August 2008.

Chiswick House, Middlesex: 9 and 16 February 1918; 28 August 1926; 18 July 1947.

Coleshill House, Berkshire: 26 July and 2 August 1919.

Ferne Park, Dorset: 5 and 12 May 2010 (Will Pryce and Andrew Lawson).

Gledstone Hall, Yorkshire: 13 and 20 April 1935 (A. E. Henson); 31 December 1981 (Alwyne Gardner).

Gosford House, East Lothian: 2 September 1911; 21 October and 4 November 1971 (Tom Scott).

Grange Park, Hampshire: 8 and 15 May 1975.

Henbury Hall, Cheshire: 28 February 2002 (Tim Imrie-Tait).

Holkham Hall, Norfolk: 24, 31 January, 7 and 14 February 1980 (Alex Starkey); 7 and 21 August 1980 (correspondence).

Kedleston Hall, Derbyshire: 26 January, 2 and 9 February 1978 (Alex Starkey).

Kingston Lacy, Dorset: 17 and 24 April, 5 and 12 June 1986 (Alex Starkey).

Manderston, Berwickshire: 20 January 1917; 29 May 1969 (Jonathan M. Gibson); 14, 22 February and 1 March 1979 (Jonathan M. Gibson).

Mereworth Castle, Kent: 12, 19 and 26 June 1920.

Merks Hall, Essex: 7 July 1998 (Tim Imrie-Tait).

Millichope Park, Shropshire: 10 and 17 February 1977 (Jonathan M. Gibson); 10 September 2008 (Val Corbett).

Monticello, Virginia: 17 January 1963.

Nashdom, Buckinghamshire: 31 August 1912.

Nuthall Temple, Nottinghamshire: 28 April and 5 May 1923 (Ward).

Packington Hall, Warwickshire: 9, 16 and 23 July 1970 (Jonathan M. Gibson).

Pitzhanger Manor, Middlesex: 22 February 1911; 10 September 1953; 20 April 1989 (Michael Boys).

Prestwold Hall, Leicestershire: 16, 23 and 30 April 1959 (Alex Starkey).

Sheringham Hall, Norfolk: 30 January and 7 February 1957 (A. E. Henson).

Solar House, Sussex: 21 June 2001 (June Buck).

Stoke Bruerne Park, Northamptonshire: 23 July 1953 (Alex Starkey); 29 September 2005 (Paul Barker).

Tusmore Park, Oxfordshire: 30 July and 6 August 1938; 8 December 2005 (June Buck).

Villa Verde, Algarve: 3 September 1987 (Mark Fiennes).

Villa Vizcaya, Florida: 10 and 17 January 1980 (Frank Boran and W. W. Willard).

Wardour Castle, Wiltshire: 10 October 1968 (Alex Starkey).

West Wycombe Park, Buckinghamshire: 1 and 8 January 1916; 6 and 13 May 1974 (Gill); 20 and 27 June 1974 (Alex Starkey); 6 September 1990 (Julian Nieman).

Wilton House, Wiltshire: 21 and 28 January 1944; 9, 16 and 23 May 1963 (Alex Starkey); 26 September and 3 October 1968 (Alex Starkey); 15 September 1988; 30 January 1992; 15 July 2009 (Will Pryce).

Wivenhoe New Park, Essex: 22 July 1965 (Jonathan M. Gibson).

Recent Houses in the USA and the Bahamas: 11 October 2001 (Paul Barker); 8 February 2007 (Scott Frances, Tim Aylen).

PICTURE CREDITS

The photographs on the following pages are reproduced by kind permission of: English Heritage, National Monuments Record: 90–91, 92, 93; Monticello/Thomas Jefferson Foundation, Inc., photograph by Mary Porter: 16; The Trustees of Sir John Soane's Museum: 82, 84–85.

CONTENTS

*

Introduction

6

I

THE SEVENTEENTH CENTURY:
The Birth of Classicism on English Soil

18

II

THE EIGHTEENTH CENTURY:
From Palladio to Pompeii

42

III

THE NINETEENTH CENTURY:
Back to Greece and Forward to Rome

88

IV

THE TWENTIETH CENTURY:
Pre-War Varieties of Classicism

122

V

INTO THE TWENTY-FIRST CENTURY:
Classicism Reborn: 1960 to the Present Day

154

Bibliography

190

Index

192

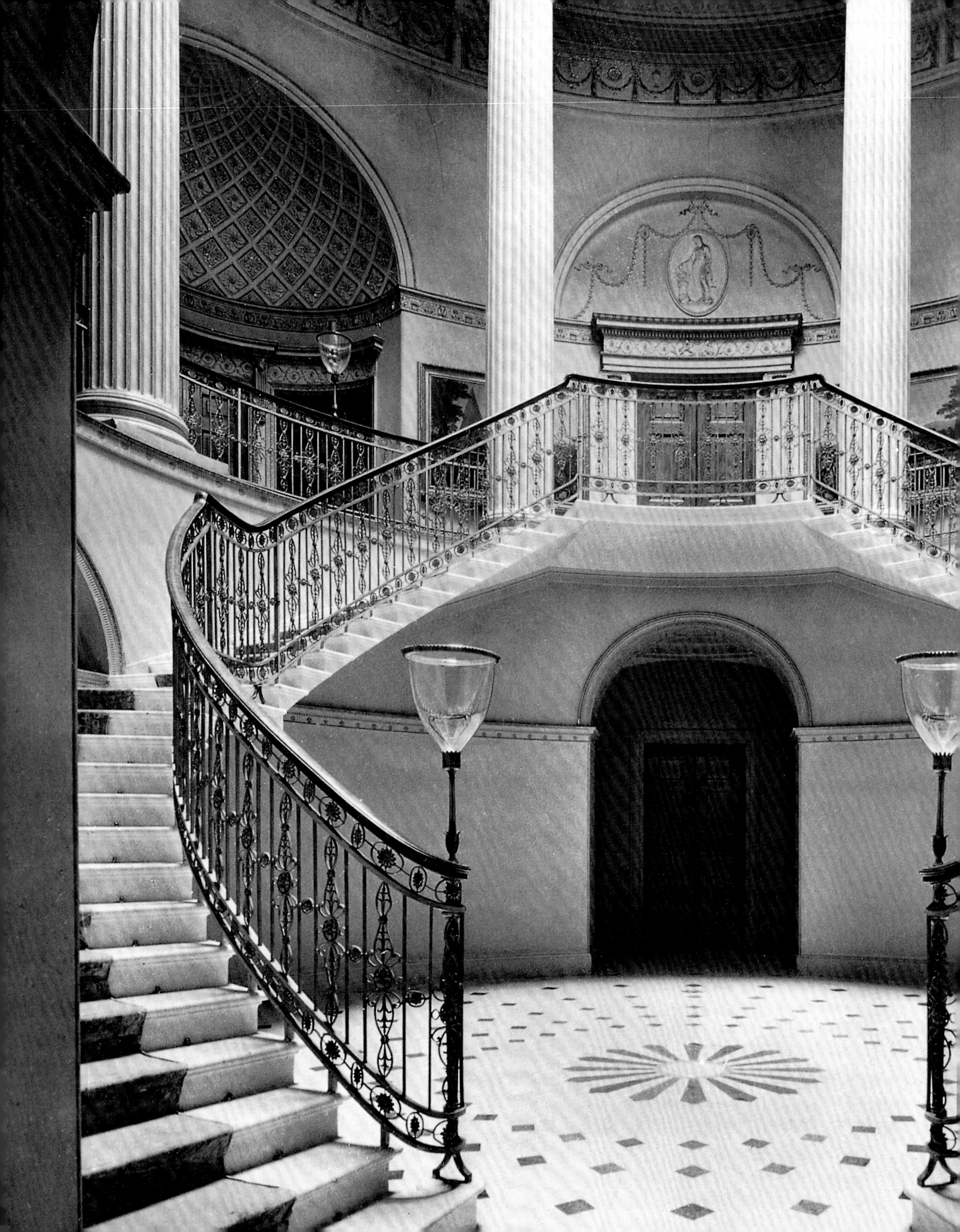

THIS BOOK takes a fresh look at country houses by isolating for the first time the history of one major theme – Classicism – from the beginning of the seventeenth century to the twenty-first. The Classical houses described here derive from three beliefs: first, that the roots of the architecture of western civilization lie in Classical antiquity, second, that they were uncovered and revived in the Renaissance, and finally, that they should form once more the basis of modern architecture. The resulting houses are bold and clear statements of Classical Order and symmetry, and incorporate the correct use of the Orders. They were often designed in opposition to current styles, which their patrons and architects found lacking in Classical propriety. Thus, in the seventeenth century Inigo Jones reacted against Jacobean excess in form and decoration, while the next century saw Lord Burlington similarly opposing what he and Colen Campbell in *Vitruvius Britannicus* (vol. 1, 1715) viewed as the rich and 'licentious' forms of Baroque.

It was the Earl of Arundel and Inigo Jones who, travelling together in Italy in 1613–14 to study ancient and modern buildings and works of art, may be said to have initiated the Grand Tour, a method of gaining knowledge about the Classical ideal, which remains with us in various forms to the present day. Jones was hailed as early as 1606 as a genius 'through whom there is hope that ... all that is praiseworthy in the elegant arts of the ancients, may one day find their way across the Alps to our England.' One of the reasons why this was considered necessary in the seventeenth century was that the breach with Rome at the Reformation under Henry VIII had cultural as well as religious consequences. In other words, the arrival of Renaissance art and architecture, which had already begun under Henry VIII, had been brought to an abrupt halt. Even Jones's attempts to catch up with the Renaissance culture of Continental Europe were interrupted by the Civil War.

This book ties together threads dating from antiquity and the Italian Renaissance through Inigo Jones to the present day, and evokes an architecture suffused with resonance and memory, like that of the Ancient Romans with their wise reverence for the architecture and sculpture of the Ancient Greeks. Characteristic of this story are the connections made in this book between Peruzzi's Palazzo Massimo, Rome (*c.*1532), an attempt to recreate the Ancient Roman house with its atrium courtyards, and houses as superficially different from it as Burlington's Chiswick House (*c.*1726) and Lutyens' Nashdom, (*c.*1908). Moreover, links are forged between several houses analyzed here, which date

WARDOUR CASTLE, WILTSHIRE *The magnificent, domed columnar staircase by James Paine of 1770–76.*

VIEW
FROM THE HOUSE
LOOKING SOUTH.

from 1650 to 2005: Coleshill, Kingston Lacy, Gosford, and Tusmore. Kingston Lacy in Dorset was believed by its owner, William Bankes, to be the work of Inigo Jones, so when remodelling it in 1835–55 he urged his architect to seek inspiration from Coleshill, also then attributed to Jones. Coleshill was needlessly demolished in 1952, but its balustraded roof flat surmounted by a cupola, as well as its gate piers, were echoed by Quinlan Terry at Merks Hall, Essex, in 1984–86. The superb marble staircase hall created at Kingston Lacy for Bankes was hardly equalled until that at Gosford of 1883–91, while Bankes said that his staircase was surpassed by James Paine's domed columnar staircase of 1770–76 at Wardour Castle, Wiltshire. Much later, it inspired that by William Whitfield at Tusmore Park (2003–05) in Oxfordshire.

In this narrative the patrons are as important as their architects for they were also men of single-minded passion. A typical relationship is that summarized by the Earl of Wemyss in relation to the work carried out for him at Gosford House, East Lothian, in the 1880s by the architect, William Young: 'He has designed, I have planned,' Lord Wemyss observed. Patrons have had an almost obsessive attention to detail from domes down to doorknobs. For example, William Bankes complained that his restorers had disfigured doors he had bought from the Vatican by adding 'oak knobs in a room where there is gilding!!', while Edward Knoblock spoke of 'not resting till every moulding and door-knob in the place [Beach House, Sussex, c.1920] was of the correct period,' adding that as a result 'the place ended by my not possessing *it* but by its possessing me.' Robert Adam and Quinlan Terry, both of whose work is investigated in this book, have found patrons with equally discerning eyes: the Duke of Northumberland urged Adam in 1764 to have ornamental details for Syon returned for re-carving since they had not come up to his high standards, while Lyn Muse at Quinlan Terry's Highland Park House, Dallas, discarded a number of Ionic capitals for the same reason on arrival on site in 2002.

All good houses are linked to gardens, a practice to which Ancient Roman houses were no exception. We should note that the patrons in this book were mostly familiar with the letters of the younger Pliny, who described the enchanting relation of his villas to their gardens with terraces, walks, avenues, seats, fountains and banqueting houses. Though the walks were formally laid out, the garden layouts were not entirely formal, for some areas were left deliberately naturalistic,

WILTON HOUSE, WILTSHIRE Above: *The Palladian Bridge of 1736–37, designed for himself by Henry Herbert, 9th Earl of Pembroke, with assistance from Roger Morris.*
SHERINGHAM HALL, NORFOLK Left (above): *Built in 1813–19 by John Adey Repton to harmonize with the park designed by his father, Humphry Repton;* (below): *The park, including on the left the deliberately retained wheat field, seen from the dining room windows, drawn by Humphry Repton for the Red Book of 1812.*

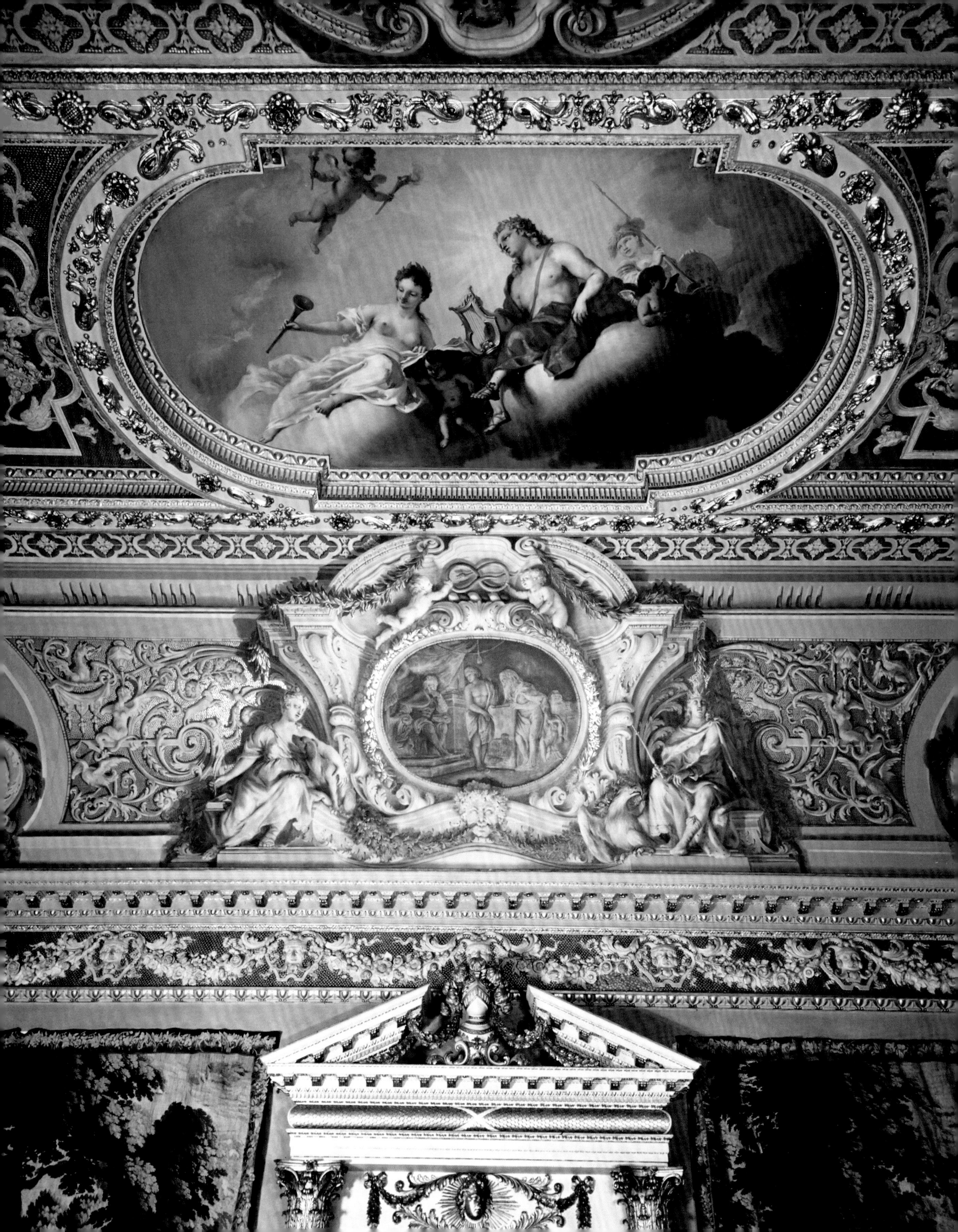

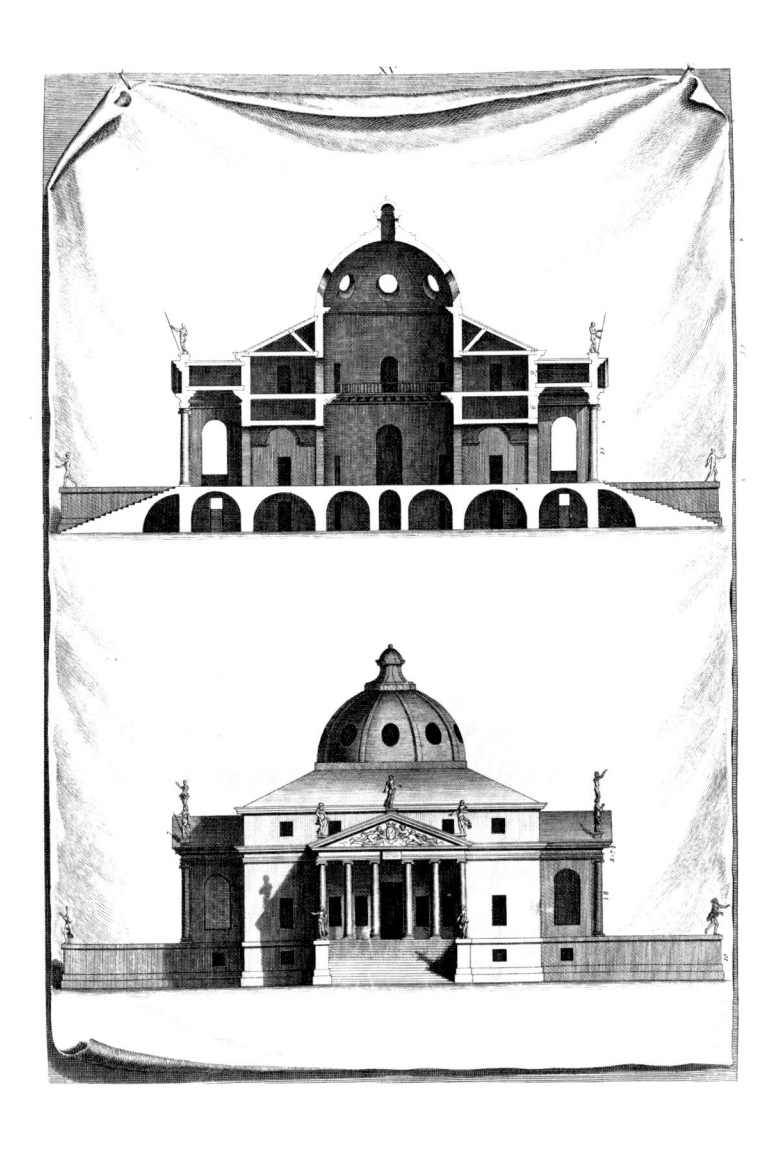

VILLA ROTONDA, VICENZA Top: *Elevation and section of Palladio's seminal work of c.1566–69.*

NUTHALL TEMPLE, NOTTINGHAMSHIRE Above: *Built from 1754–57 (demolished 1929), from designs by Thomas Wright, astronomer, landscape gardener and architect, its portico* in antis *is inspired by Scamozzi's Villa Rocca Pisani.*

MEREWORTH CASTLE, KENT Top right: *Built by Colen Campbell c.1720–25, Mereworth is closely based, except in plan, on Palladio's Villa Rotonda but larger in all dimensions. On the right is one of the twin flanking pavilions, each a perfect cube.* (left): *The deep cove of the gallery is enriched with sumptuous illusionistic paintings, signed and dated by the Venetian painter, Francesco Sleter in 1732.*

incorporating views of the rural landscape. Pliny described a combination of villa and farm with vineyard, orchards, streams, cornfields, and meadows containing sheep, horses, and cows. A late and beautiful example of such a landscape is that at Sheringham Hall, Norfolk, where Humphry and John Adey Repton designed the house and park together in 1812 as a single unit, retaining in the view from the house a wheat field next to the parkland. This was to echo the 'accidental' character of the already partly wooded slopes and to break with the bland parks of Humphry Repton's predessor 'Capability' Brown.

Apart from Pliny, there were few sources available to those who sought to recreate the character of the gardens of the ancient world, for no guidance could be found in Palladio or Inigo Jones, neither of whom had designed gardens. Conveniently, Alberti in *De re aedificatoria* (1486), translated by Leoni as *The Architecture of L. B. Alberti* (3 vols, 1726–29), had brought together references to gardens in Pliny and in all other Classical texts. Like Pliny, Alberti saw gardens in architectural terms as an extension of the house, his most important point being that the garden is the province of the architect. This idea did not reach England for many years though, as we shall see, it was eventually taken up enthusiastically by architects as varied as William Kent and Edwin Lutyens.

The architects and patrons in this book also drew on Henry Wotton's *The Elements of Architecture* (1624), the first architectural treatise written in English. In what was effectively a guide for the English gentleman wishing to create a Classical country house and garden, Wotton drew for guidance on Alberti and on Daniele Barbaro's commentary on Vitruvius, illustrated by Palladio. Like his readers, Wotton believed that the Renaissance gardens of Italy with their Classical statues, cascades, temples and grottoes reflected the gardens of antiquity.

Such opinions were expressed in various ways at houses illustrated in this book, such as Chiswick, West Wycombe, and Wilton, where Roger Morris and Henry Herbert, 9th Earl of Pembroke, a gifted and prolific amateur architect, were responsible for the gracious Palladian bridge of 1736–37. With its open columnar loggia, flanked by arched and pedimented end bays, this was inspired by Palladio's design for the Rialto bridge in Venice, which he published in *I Quattro Libri dell'Architettura* (1570), claiming that it echoed Hadrian's Pons Aelius, today the Ponte Sant'Angelo, Rome. The bridge at Wilton was so much admired that it

INTRODUCTION · 11

was imitated at Stowe, Prior Park, Hagley Hall, Amesbury Abbey, and by Catherine the Great at Tsarskoe Selo. Palladio's Rialto bridge remained unexecuted so, once again, it was his British followers who, as at Wilton, realized some of his ambitions. The increasing wealth of Britain enabled it to catch up with the revived Classical language of the Renaissance during the eighteenth century, in a process that led to houses such as Wilton and Holkham being regarded by contemporaries as virtually Grand Tour destinations in themselves.

Lord Burlington's Palladian house at Chiswick was echoed in three country houses which were similarly inspired by, though not copies of, Palladio's Villa Capra and Scamozzi's Villa Rocca Pisani: Mereworth Castle, Kent (c.1720–25), by Colen Campbell, larger than the Villa Capra, and with a long gallery inspired by Wilton; Nuthall Temple, Nottinghamshire (1754–57; dem.1929), by Thomas Wright, architect, astronomer and landscape architect, with Rococo plasterwork by Thomas Roberts; and Foots Cray Place, Kent (c.1754; dem.1950), probably by Isaac Ware. In the Classical Revival of the late twentieth century in British and American architecture, the ever-intriguing Villa Capra has once more returned as a source of inspiration in two houses of very different character from each other. The one closest to Palladio's model is Henbury Hall, Cheshire, based on a painting of 1982 by Felix Kelly, which was worked up first in a design by Quinlan Terry and then, as built in 1984–87, in further designs by Julian Bicknell. A freer, simpler, but in some ways more inventive design is that by David Hicks for Villa Verde, Algarve, Portugal. Crowning a high hill overlooking the sea, this was built in 1987–88 with two great porticoes in an Order which is part Greek Doric, part Tuscan.

Links between Italy and England were not always one way in the eighteenth century, for architects arrived in England from Italy, including Giacomo Leoni, Giovanni Battista Borra, Alessandro Galilei and Joseph Bonomi, while the Adam brothers imported Italian artists, craftsmen and decorators. These were expert in the creation of the stuccoed and painted neo-antique interiors, which had been familiar in Italy from the time of Raphael, Vasari and Giovanni da Udine, in the early sixteenth century, but had scarcely arrived in England. We shall see the fruits of this tradition in the eighteenth century at Robert Adam's Kedleston Hall, Derbyshire, and James Wyatt's Packington Hall in Warwickshire.

A dazzling example is the Roman Catholic Chapel at Wardour Castle, Wiltshire, the fruit of close cooperation for many years from 1774 between three discerning figures: the 8th Lord Arundell of Wardour (1740–1808), who had made his Grand Tour of Italy from 1758–60, Fr John Thorpe, a Jesuit priest and antiquarian, resident in Rome, and the Italian architect, Giacomo Quarenghi, who was influenced by Piranesi. Thorpe recommended Arundell to employ Quarenghi because he 'has always made his studies upon Palladio and the best models of antiquity' and was, in addition, an amenable architect ready to 'alter his sketches as he is desired.' The fine staircase at Wardour Castle was built from designs by James Paine for Lord Arundell, but the sumptuous, free-standing altar in the chapel was designed by Quarenghi and made of a variety of deep, glowing marbles. The hanging, gilt-bronze sanctuary lamps were designed by Luigi Valadier in Rome in 1774.

Just as Italian architects and craftsmen arrived in England, so British architects who feature in this book now spent formative years studying in Italy, notably Gibbs, Kent, Talman, Burlington, Stuart, Chambers, Adam, Mylne, Dance, Wyatt, Soane, Cockerell and Barry. Many of these became, as it were, honorary Italians, by being elected to the academies, which were the product of Renaissance Italy but hardly reached England before the foundation of the Royal Academy in 1768.

The eighteenth century also saw an increasing understanding of the inventiveness of ancient architecture, thanks to the rise of archaeology,

MERKS HALL, ESSEX Above: *Built from designs by Quinlan Terry in 2000–2002, its cupola over a balustrade flat or belvedere echoes that of Coleshill House by Sir Roger Pratt.*

VILLA VERDE, ALGARVE Top left: *A fresh look at the tradition of the Villa Rotonda by David Hicks of 1987–88.*

HENBURY HALL, CHESHIRE Right: *A closer version of the Villa Rotonda built in 1984 in an existing landscaped park.*

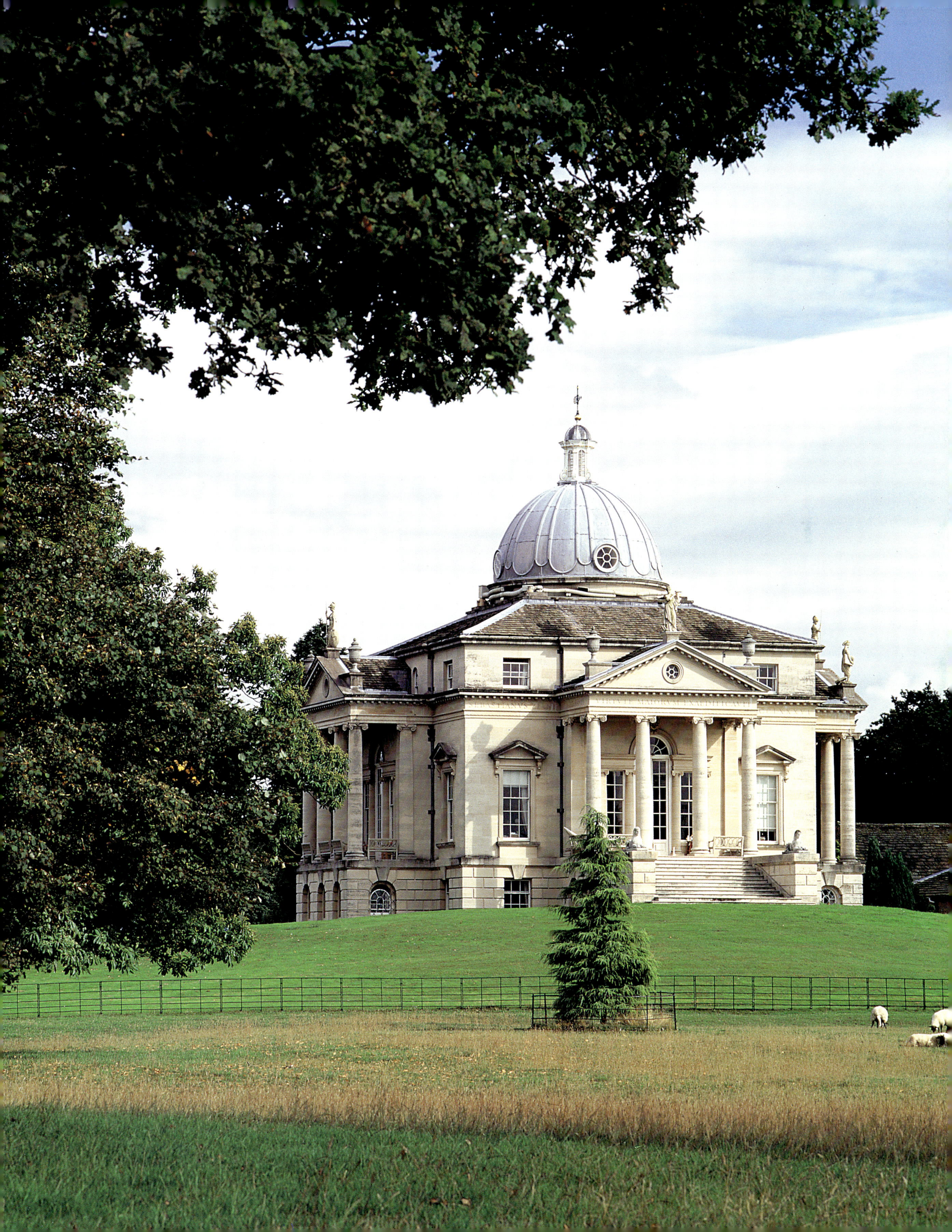

Hampshire, and Millichope Park, Shropshire. However, their austere forms, together with their somewhat cold and undomestic interiors, gradually fell out of fashion in the nineteenth century. In reaction, the richer languages of the Italianate Renaissance revival and the Gothic Revival came to be favoured, as can be seen at Brodsworth Hall, Yorkshire, built in the 1860s from designs by an Italian architect, who sent his drawings to England from Lucca. A fine Italianate mansion, it was effectively a sculpture museum, like many eighteenth-century houses.

A new phase of the Classical country house was introduced from the early twentieth century by Sir Edwin Lutyens whose sense of the poetry of mass and space pervaded all his designs, whether Classical or Arts and Crafts. His mastery of the Classical language is seen here in two very different but spectacular houses by him: Nashdom and Gledstone. Christopher Hussey, writing about Gledstone in *Country Life* in 1935, had been influenced by Geoffrey Scott's *The Architecture of Humanism* (1914, rev. ed., 1924). Scott had devised a rhetorical language which enabled Robert Byron, A. S. G. Butler, and Hussey himself, to make Lutyens' extraordinary achievement sound plausible and comprehensible to a modern English audience. In a development from the account by Vitruvius of the anthropomorphic origin of the Classical Orders, Scott claimed that 'The whole of architecture is, in fact, unconsciously invested by us with human movement and human moods ... *We transcribe architecture into terms of ourselves.*'

Among the many houses illustrated in *Country Life* that could have been described more fully in this book is Thomas Jefferson's Monticello, near Charlottesville, Virginia, designed for himself by one of the founding fathers of the American Republic and author of the Declaration of Independence. In its first phase from 1768–82, Monticello was Anglo-Palladian with a two-storeyed portico from Palladio's *Quattro*

which meant that architects no longer had to see Ancient Roman buildings through the eyes of Palladio, as they had since the time of Inigo Jones. A telling expression of the growing desire to replace romantic speculation with physical excavation is the reaction of Horace Walpole to Joseph Addison's *Remarks on Several Parts of Italy* (1705) which, going into many editions, had been used as a guide by countless Grand Tourists. Coining the phrase 'classic ground', Addison recounted descriptions by Ancient Roman authors, known to his readers, of sites such as Tivoli and Frascati. However, Walpole complained in 1740 that Addison had 'travelled through the poets and not through Italy; for all his ideas are borrowed from the descriptions and not from reality.'

This new insistence on the reality revealed by archaeological excavation, and the widening bounds of what was thought Classical, led to a thorough-going Greek revival from the late eighteenth century of which Cairness House, Aberdeenshire, is one of the most spectacular examples. It was built in 1791–97 for Charles Gordon by James Playfair (1755–1794), one of the most brilliant of all architects of international Neo-Classicism until his career was cut short by his premature death. Its powerfully rusticated cyclopean arches and primitive Doric columns show that Playfair must have seen the work of Ledoux during his stay in Paris in 1787. While in Italy in 1791–93, he met Canova and Flaxman and drew the Greek Doric temples at Paestum, and his library included a French translation of Winckelmann's pioneering *History of the Art of the Antiquity* (1764), in which a column at Paestum was illustrated.

Though used more frequently for public buildings, the Greek Revival produced other striking country houses, as we shall see at Grange Park,

CAIRNESS HOUSE, ABERDEENSHIRE Above: *A detail showing the use of primitive Doric columns on the striking Neo-Classical house of the 1790s by James Playfair.*

MILLICHOPE PARK, SHROPSHIRE Top left: *Built in 1834–50 by Edward Haycock for a wealthy clergyman, the house has a giant hexastyle portico in the Greek Ionic Order, perfectly reflected in the serpentine lake.*

WARDOUR CASTLE, WILTSHIRE Right: *The Roman Catholic chapel, begun by James Paine in 1776 was lengthened by John Soane in 1788. The free-standing altar of rich marbles was designed in Rome by Giacomo Quarenghi.*

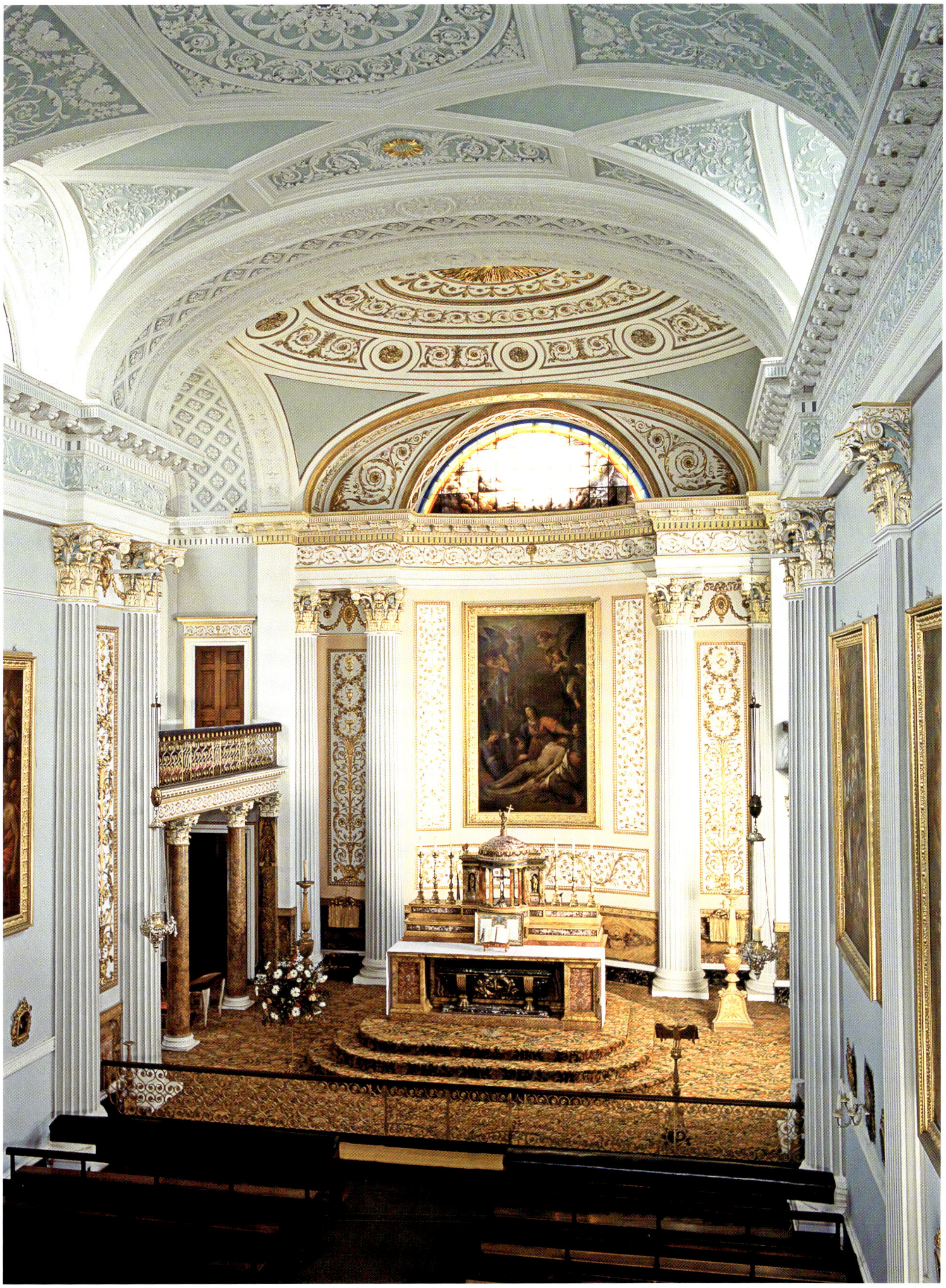

Libri (1570), and a plan inspired by one in Robert Morris's *Select Architecture* (1755). However, in its second phase of building from 1796–1809, after Jefferson's return in 1789 from five years as Second American Minister to Paris, it emerged as an attempt to echo the antique villa, indebted to stylish works such as the Hôtel de Salm, Paris (1782–85), by Pierre Rousseau. At the same time, Monticello featured an octagonal dome over a portico as at Chiswick House.

An American house featured in Chapter IV of this book, Villa Vizcaya, Florida, built in 1913–15 for James Deering, was perhaps the most extravagant and romantic of all reactions to Italian Renaissance and Baroque architecture and gardens. It was closely related to the intellectual and cultural world of Anglo-American society in Florence, and thus to figures as varied as Bernard Berenson, Henry James and John Singer Sargent, who painted both it and James Deering in 1917.

The rise of Modernism from the 1930s led many to believe that the Classical Orders would never again feature in contemporary architecture. Though the 1960s was the worst decade for anyone wanting to practise the Classical language of architecture, Raymond Erith now built Wivenhoe New Park, Essex, as a programmatic Palladian statement. At the centre of an agricultural estate like the villas of Palladio, which it partly echoes with its long, low service wings, it recalls Palladio's advice in *Quattro Libri* that: 'The covered buildings for items belonging to the farm should be built for the produce and animals and connected to the owner's house in such a way that he can go everywhere under cover so that neither the rain nor the blazing summer sun would bother him as he goes to supervise his business.' He added engagingly, 'besides which these porticoes are extremely attractive.' With pantiled roofs over walls of pale red brick, Wivenhoe has the economical plan and construction of the farmhouses and villas in the Veneto area of Northern Italy, though its austerity is partly due to the client of whom Erith said, 'He liked everything as plain as could be and hated anything to be what he called Rolls Royce'.

Ferne Park, Dorset, by Erith's partner and eventual successor, Quinlan Terry, is a contemporary country house where, as with numerous examples being built today, patron and architect work together to renew the Classical ideal – in a manner not dissimilar to that of the earlier programmatic counter-revolutions led by Jones and Burlington.

MONTICELLO, VIRGINIA Above: *The novel Palladian villa designed for himself by Thomas Jefferson in two phases between 1768 and 1809.*

WIVENHOE NEW PARK, ESSEX Right (above): *The linocuts by Quinlan Terry, made when a pupil of Erith, resemble a page from Palladio's* I Quattro Libri. *They were exhibited at the Royal Academy in 1963;* (below): *An early attempt to revive the Classical tradition at a time of Modernist dominance in 1962 by Raymond Erith.*

MR GOOCH'S NEW HOUSE NEAR WIVENHOE PARK

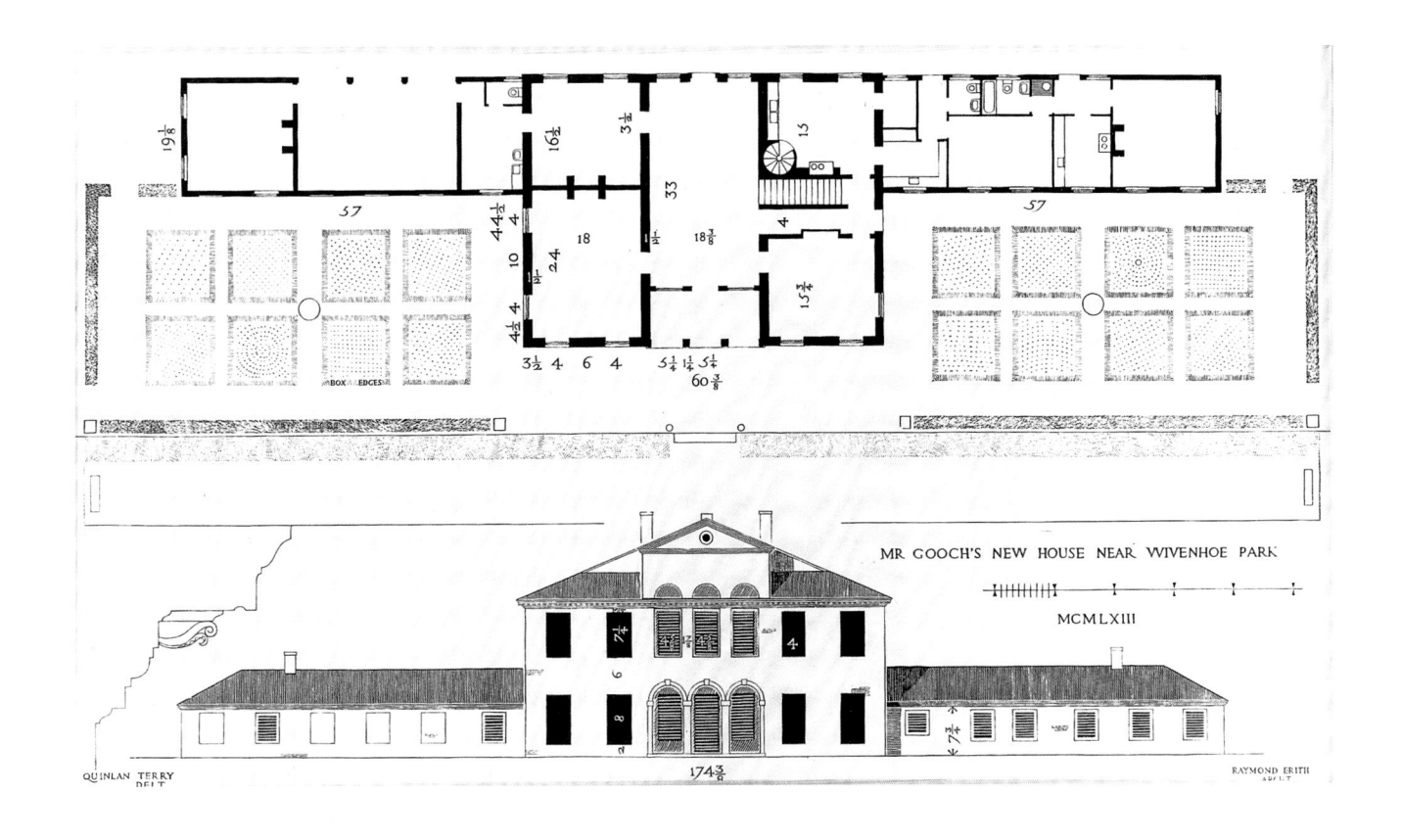

MCMLXIII

QUINLAN TERRY DELT

RAYMOND ERITH ARCH.T

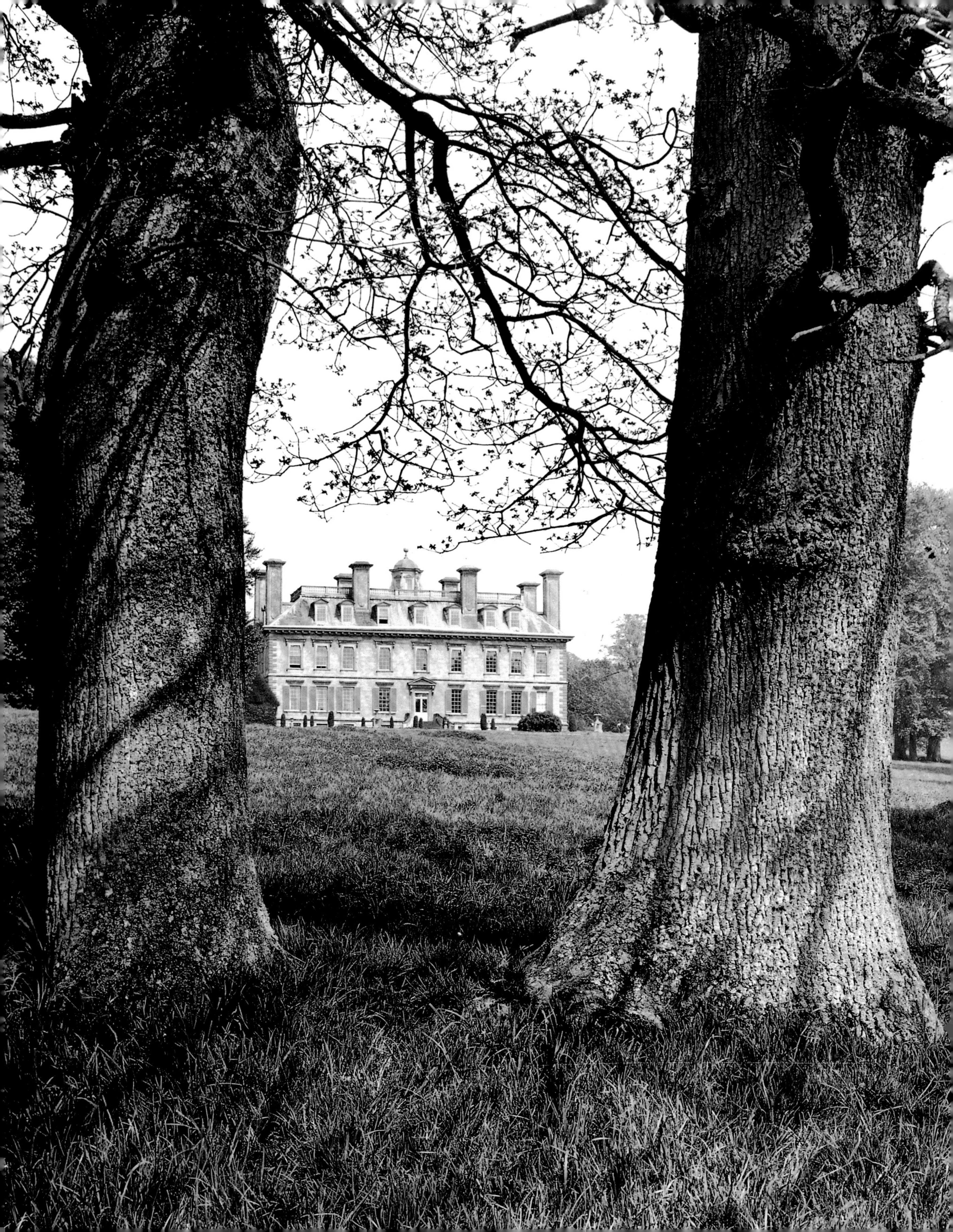

I
THE SEVENTEENTH CENTURY: THE BIRTH OF CLASSICISM ON ENGLISH SOIL

※

The houses discussed in this chapter followed the Elizabethan and Jacobean period, which produced some of the most glorious houses in English architecture, including Audley End, Blickling, Bramshill, Burleigh, Castle Ashby, Cranborne Manor, Hardwick Hall, Hatfield House, Longford Castle, Longleat, and Wollaton. Enchanting though they are, they are not included in this book. Why? One answer is that the Classical language of these houses was not conceived as a totality governing the architecture of the whole building, its exteriors and interiors. By contrast, the Classical contribution to Tudor and Jacobean houses often took the form of fashionable decoration, based on illustrations in Flemish, German, Italian and French pattern books.

The admiration of the Elizabethans for their Gothic past also led them to create gate towers, oriels and fantastic skylines, while a mania for glass produced lantern houses unlike anything previously built in England or elsewhere. At Wollaton Hall, Nottinghamshire, the three Orders (Doric, Ionic, Corinthian), run all the way round its four façades, yet the finer detail is the rampant Flemish Mannerism of Vredeman de Vries, and the building is crowned by medievalizing

COLESHILL HOUSE, BERKSHIRE *A perfect house of the mid-seventeenth century, designed by Sir Roger Pratt as a model of Classical balance and harmony, but now tragically destroyed.*

turrets. This is not to criticize such houses: we should not see them as Holkham or Kedleston *manqués*, for they have merits enabling them to stand alone, not as harbingers of future developments.

This chapter is dominated by Inigo Jones, who was the first fully Classical architect in England, no longer a surveyor or mason but a Renaissance *uomo universale*. His visit to Italy in 1613–14 with the Earl of Arundel effectively established the Grand Tour, which helped shape architecture during the eighteenth century. He was transformed by his investigation of Ancient Roman buildings in Italy, where he met the leading disciple of Palladio, Vincenzo Scamozzi, whose treatise, *L'Idea dell'Architettura Universale* (1615), greatly influenced him. Jones thus came to believe that architecture 'ought to be solid, proportionable according to the rules, masculine and unaffected', as in his Banqueting House in Whitehall and in the unpedimented portico he added to old St Paul's Cathedral, the largest portico north of the Alps.

Jones's vision of Italy as the modern transmitter of the ancient world's cultural ideals has been shared by most of the architects and patrons in this book. Though Jones built comparatively little, and few of his contemporaries understood him, his importance, as Mark Girouard has remarked, came from his 'laying a series of time bombs which were to explode in subsequent centuries.' In the next chapter we shall explore what we might call the fall-out of these explosions.

WILTON HOUSE, WILTSHIRE

Inigo Jones (1573–1652), less than ten years younger than Shakespeare, might be regarded as the most important figure in our story for it was he who introduced pure Italian Classicism into English architecture. His friend, the Cambridge antiquarian, Edmund Bolton, hailed him in 1606 as a genius 'through whom there is hope that ... all that is praise-worthy in the elegant arts of the ancients, may one day find their way across the Alps to our England.' The first of the arts Jones practised was that of masque design, beginning with employment in 1605 in the service of King James I's queen, Anne of Denmark. During the next thirty-five years he staged over fifty masques, plays and other entertainments, all with scenery and costumes inspired by those of performances at the Medici court in Florence.

This theatrical aspect of Jones's career is often underestimated in accounts of his architectural career in which he was inspired by studying buildings when in Italy, and by following the precepts of the Renaissance architects and theorists, Serlio, Palladio and Scamozzi. In travelling abroad with the Earl of Arundel, a patron and collector, he virtually invented the Grand Tour, which coloured much of English culture for at least two centuries. We begin this book by investigating Wilton House where the famous south front, begun in 1636, has long been associated with his name. Thanks to Jones, it seemed to visitors as though Italy and the Classical past had been transported to England: 'Wilton is become tramontane Italy', according to the antiquarian, William Stukeley, in 1776, while John Dodd observed of Wilton in a letter of 1785 that 'To describe this Place would be to write the Greek and Roman History.'

The patron of Inigo Jones at Wilton was the 4th Earl of Pembroke (1584–1650), a connoisseur of the arts at the court of Charles I. He was educated at Oxford and became a great holder of public offices, including those of Lord Chamberlain, High Steward of the Duchy of Cornwall, Lord Lieutenant of Kent, and briefly Chancellor of the University of Oxford in the 1640s. Lord Clarendon explained in his *History of the Rebellion* (1702–1704) how Lord Pembroke had been taken up by King James I thanks to the 'comeliness of his person ... [which] drew the King's eyes towards him with affection.' As a result, the King created him Earl of Montgomery at the age of twenty-one. He was a man of an irascible and choleric disposition of whom his friend, the antiquarian John Aubrey, observed in his *Brief Lives* that he 'did not delight in books or poetry; but exceedingly loved painting and building, in which he had singular judgement.' After Charles I, he was Van Dyck's greatest patron.

Lord Pembroke succeeded his brother as 4th Earl in 1630, and soon after began to consider employing Inigo Jones, Surveyor of the King's Works, to replace the Tudor courtyard house of Wilton. This had been built out of the ancient nunnery of Wilton Abbey, which was given to one of Pembroke's predecessors by Henry VIII. Jones had a long

There has been much debate about the roles of Inigo Jones, Isaac de Caus and John Webb in the design of this celebrated house, conceived as a setting for royal visits by Charles I and Henrietta Maria.

THE BIRTH OF CLASSICISM ON ENGLISH SOIL · 21

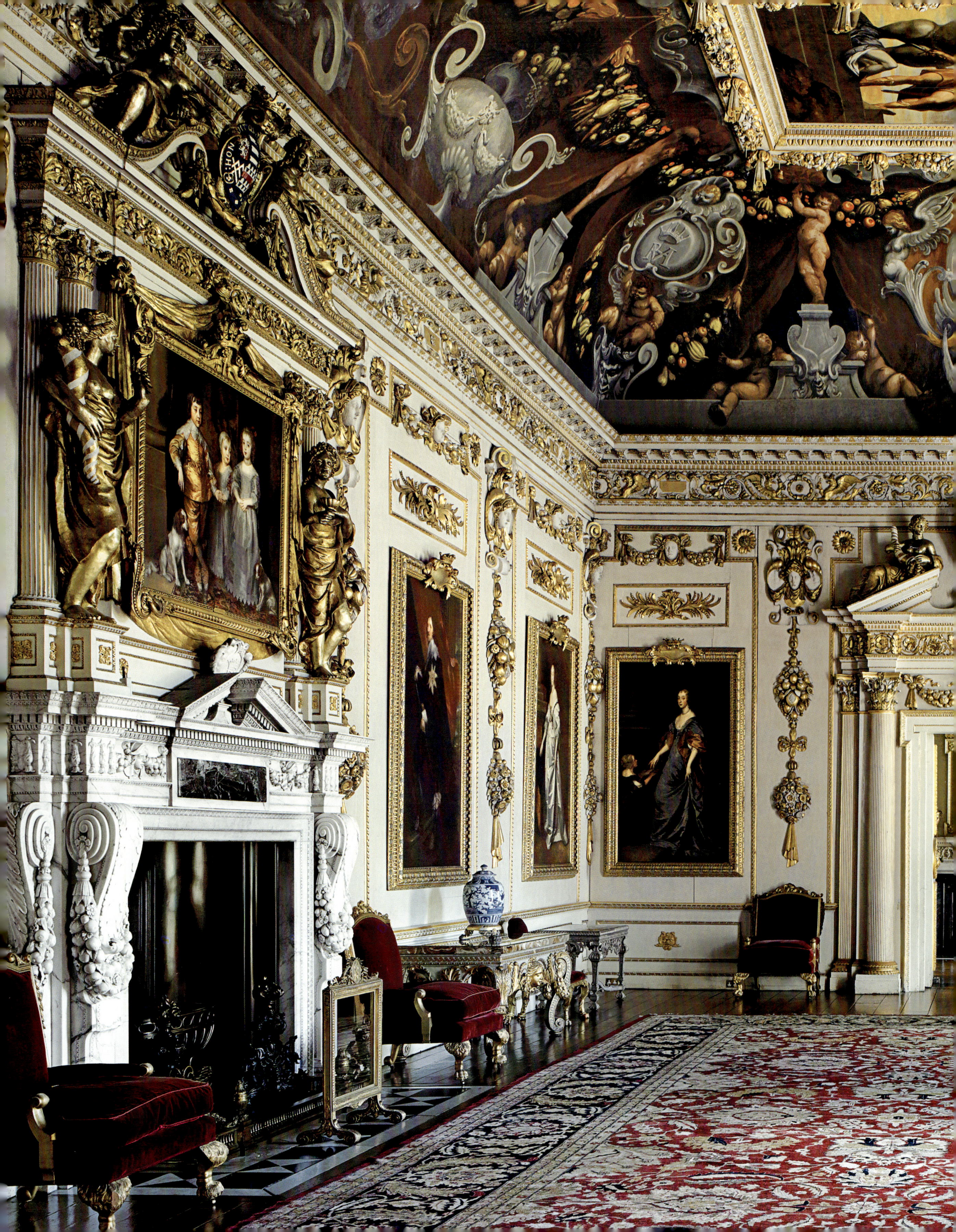

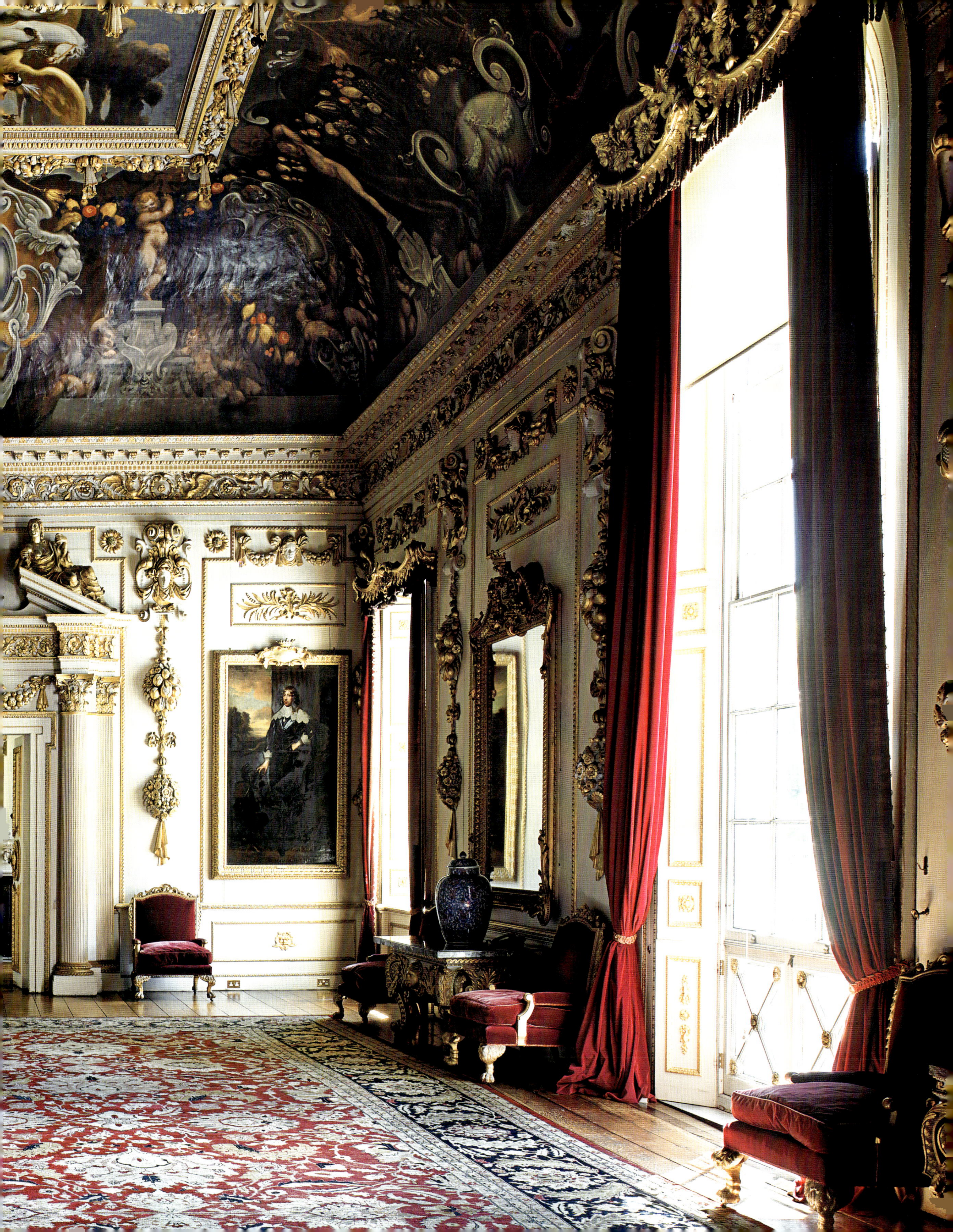

connection with Wilton, going back to the 3rd Earl in the reign of James I who had included the house on his first itinerary through his kingdom in 1603, when, according to one tradition, Shakespeare appeared in a command performance of *As You Like It*. In July 1615, Jones's patron, Lord Arundel, wrote that James I would be dining at Wilton and that Lord Pembroke wished Jones to be there. In 1620, Jones was asked by the King, who was staying at Wilton, to explain the history of Stonehenge, which is about ten miles from the house. He concluded that it was in fact the remains of a Roman temple.

Charles I, a key figure in the history of Wilton House, was a monarch of advanced aesthetic sensibility, profoundly conscious of how the arts could shape his image, and a great collector of pictures, notably the Gonzaga collection from Mantua. Aubrey observed that:

He did love Wilton above all places, and came thither every summer. It was he that put Philip ... Earle of Pembroke upon making this magnificent garden and grotto, and to new build that side of the house that fronts the garden, with two stately pavilions at each end, all al Italiano. His Majesty intended to have it all designed by his own architect, Mr Inigo Jones, who being at that time, about 1633, engaged in his Majesties buildings at Greenwich, [i.e. the Queen's House] could not attend to it; but he recommended it to an ingeniouse architect Monsieur Salomon de Caus, a Gascoigne, who performed it very well; but not without the advice and approbation of Mr Jones.

Aubrey meant not Salomon de Caus but his son or nephew, Isaac de Caus, from Dieppe not Gascony, a French hydraulic engineer who was primarily a designer of gardens and waterworks. He built a grotto for Charles I in the basement of Jones's Banqueting House, Whitehall,

24 · THE SEVENTEENTH CENTURY

in 1623–24, and another for the Queen in the garden at Somerset House in 1630–33. He was at work on constructions in the gardens at Wilton for the 4th Earl in 1632–35 and published a book on his waterworks in 1644.

Above: The Double Cube Room with Van Dyck's largest English portrait, 17-foot long, of the 4th Earl of Pembroke with his wife and their children, with those who had died depicted as cherubs in the sky above.

Previous pages: Created c.1636, and rebuilt from 1648–55 after a major fire, the sumptuously decorated Double Cube Room, 60-foot long, 30-foot wide and 30-foot high, is often seen as the finest room in England.

Overleaf: The Double Cube Room ceiling, depicting the legend of Perseus, was painted by Emmanuel de Critz; the Pantheon-like dome was perhaps suggested by Inigo Jones. The cove is by Edward Pierce, employed by Jones in masque design.

The first grandiose scheme for Wilton of the early 1630s, but dropped by the end of the decade, is known from a drawing for an engraving which was intended for publication in Isaac de Caus's *Wilton Gardens*. With its 330-foot long elevation, comprising no less than twenty-one bays, this was effectively a royal palace built for the annual visit of the King and Queen. Its central portico of six attached columns was flanked by two ranges, eight bays long, each containing a royal apartment with a Serliana, a Palladian or Venetian window – a form probably invented by Bramante or Raphael but popularized in Serlio's *L'Architettura* (1537–75). Jones had introduced this to England in his still surviving Queen's Chapel at St James's Palace (1623–25).

The design for Wilton is now generally agreed to be that of Inigo Jones because, for example, its central portico, astylar wings and plain

THE BIRTH OF CLASSICISM ON ENGLISH SOIL · 25

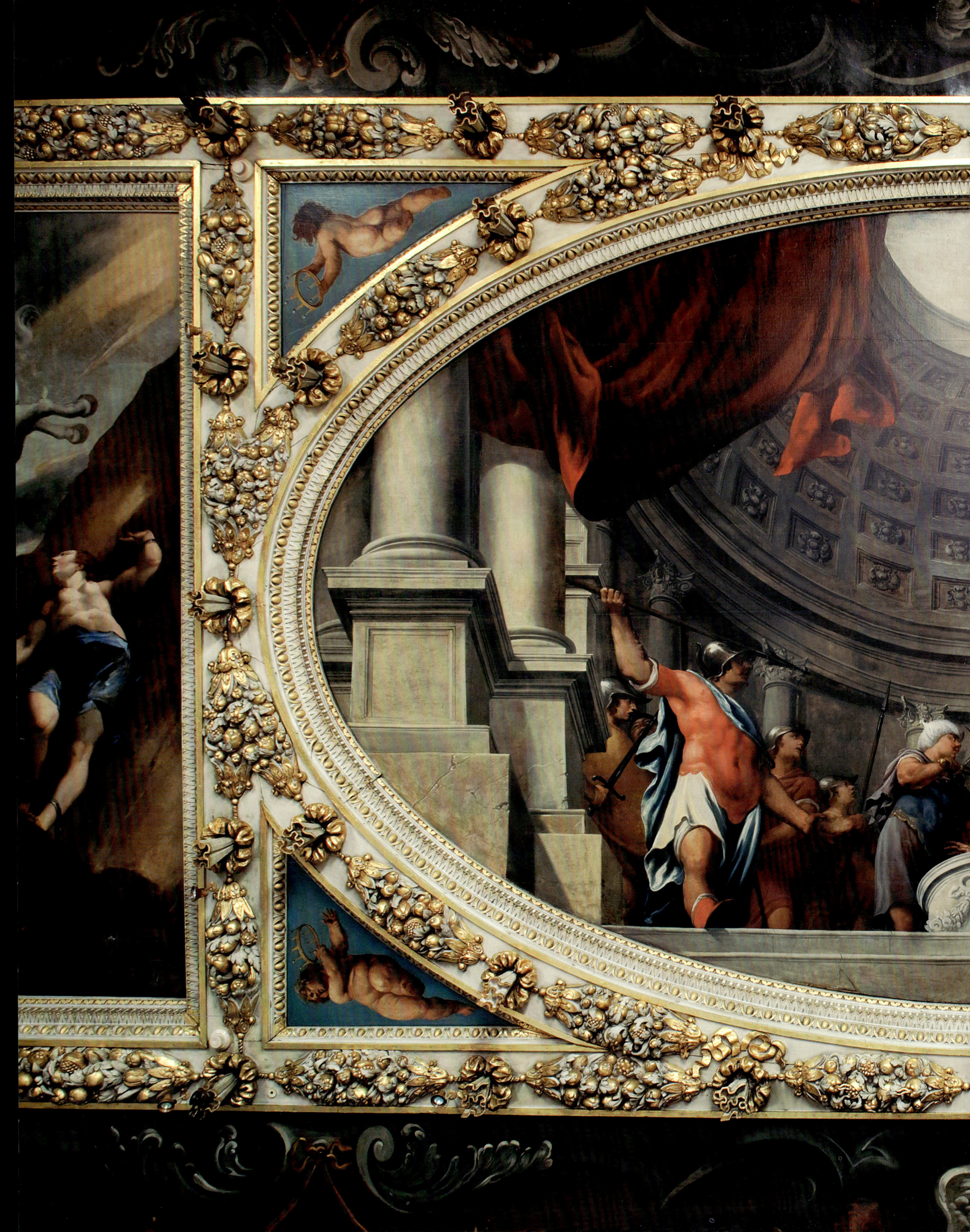

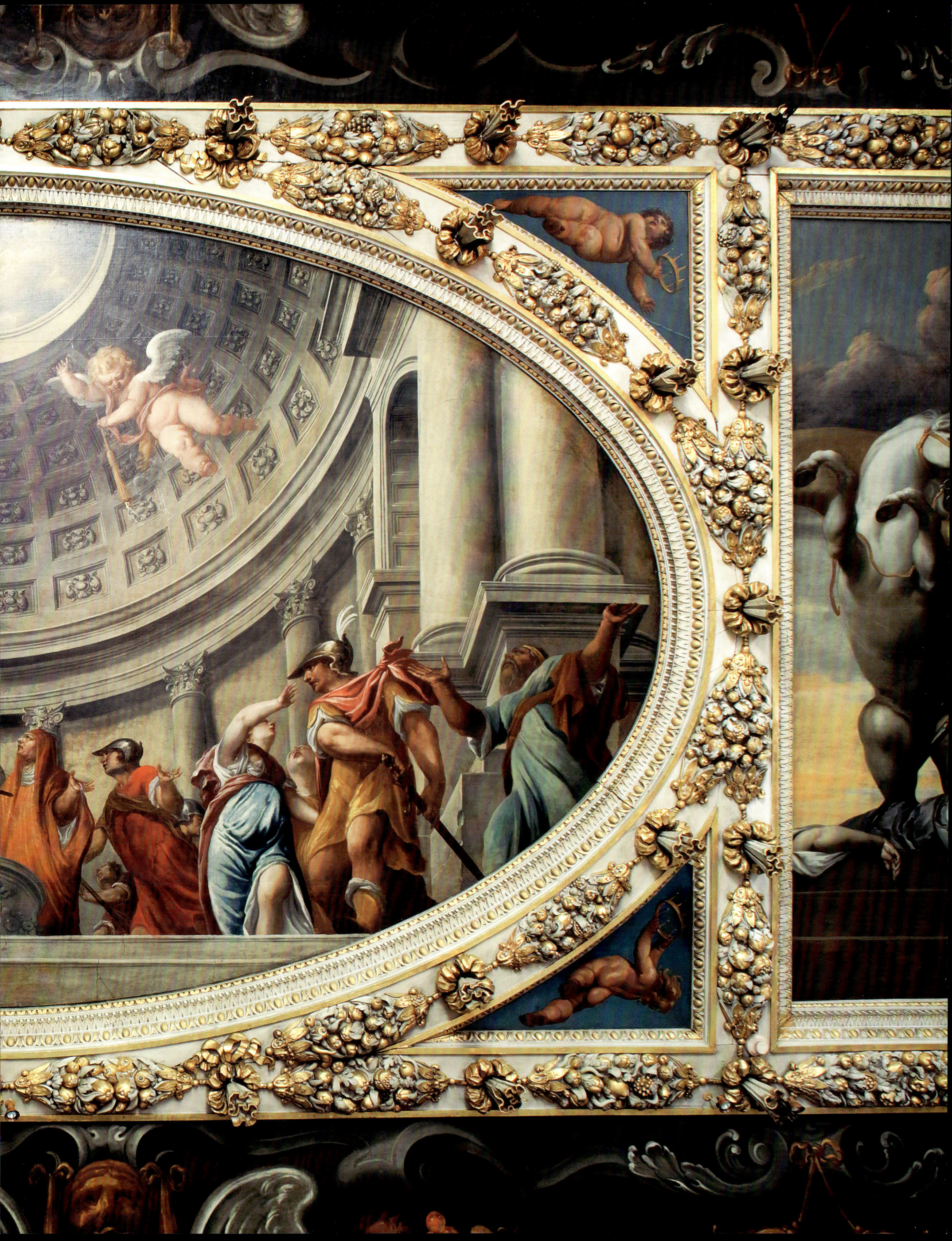

28 · THE SEVENTEENTH CENTURY

ashlar wall surfaces would hardly have been conceived by de Caus, who was accustomed to French channelled and banded masonry. Moreover, it is related to Jones's designs of the 1630s for Somerset House for Queen Henrietta Maria and Whitehall Palace for King Charles I. Jones saw the pediment, portico, and Serliana, as symbols of sovereignty or royal authority. Indeed, Wilton, with its royal associations, was the only aristocratic house for which he designed a portico. Serliana appeared at the Emperor Diocletian's Palace at Split and at Philip II of Spain's Palace of the Escorial, which Charles I saw when Prince of Wales. It also featured in designs by Serlio for a 'Palace of the King' in Book VI of *L'Architettura*, and in Jones's designs for Whitehall Palace, as well as for the chapel at Wilton, which was built on the same site on the west front as its sixteenth-century predecessor.

This vast project for Wilton was dropped, partly because when Lord Pembroke's newly married son died in January 1636, the enormous marriage portion of £25,000 had to be returned to his eighteen-year-old bride's father, the Duke of Buckingham; also Lord Pembroke now separated from his wife, who promptly took her money away from the Wilton estate. The grand design was thus reduced in size after 1636 so that the surviving south front, built in 1636–40, is nine bays long, less than half what was originally proposed. Another and unexpected complication was that after voting against Charles I's ally, Lord Strafford, in 1641, Pembroke joined the Parliamentarian republican cause. It may be thought surprising that Jones should have consented to work at all for Pembroke after this apostasy. Abandoning the grand project for Wilton anticipated Pembroke's breach with Charles I, which led to his dismissal in 1640 from the office of Lord Chamberlain. At the same time, he may have found it embarrassing to build on a palatial scale in view of the King's financial difficulties.

In March 1636, Isaac de Caus had been ordered 'to take downe ... that side of [the Tudor] Wilton house which is towards the Garden & such other parts as shall bee necessary & rebuild it anew with additions according to ye Plott which is agreed.' There has been a long debate about the architect of this new south front of Wilton House and the relative contributions of de Caus and Jones, but, like the first grandiose design, it is now given to Jones, though with de Caus as supervising architect. The desire of the King for something 'all al Italiano', in Aubrey's words, led to the corner towers which feature in Jones's modified design, for though these reflected their Tudor precedents at Wilton, they were also close to those in Scamozzi's grand reconstruction of the *villa rustica* as a seventeen-bay long house on an Ancient Roman country estate, published in his treatise *L'Idea dell' Architettura Universale* (Venice, 1615). The term '*al Italiano*' probably implied a neo-antique design: indeed, Jones did not use Scamozzi as a source because he wanted to imitate an Italian architect, but because he believed that Scamozzi, like his master Palladio, had restored 'the elegant arts of the ancients,' in Edmund Bolton's words. Jones met Scamozzi in Venice in 1614 and bought his *Idea* three years later. The corner towers at Wilton were not really Palladian in origin, but

The Single Cube Room, 30-foot high and 30-foot square, first in the sequence of state rooms, has a high ceiling cove painted with Roman grotteschi, probably the first in England since those for Henry VIII at Nonsuch.

THE BIRTH OF CLASSICISM ON ENGLISH SOIL · 29

the prestige of the house led to their being imitated in many major Palladian houses, such as Houghton, Hagley and Lydiard Tregoze. They were certainly not French in origin, again suggesting that Jones, not de Caus, was the architect.

The elaborate, formal parterre garden had been laid out by Isaac de Caus before it was decided not to build the grandiose, south front of Wilton, twenty-one bays long. The garden was thus aligned on the whole width of that intended front. Though no trace of the garden now survives, it was described by Aubrey as 'a thousand foot long' with parterres, green arbours, fountains, waterworks, marble statues, and, at the southern end, a balustraded terrace featuring a Classical grotto with frostwork, probably by Nicholas Stone, the elder. The garden was doubtless designed to please Queen Henrietta Maria for it was an example of the Franco-Italian type created at Saint-Germain-en-Laye for her father, Henri IV of France.

The next part of this complicated story is the gutting by fire of the interior of Jones's nine-bay south front of Wilton. We know from Aubrey that 'it was burnt ann. 1647 or 1648, by airing of the roomes, in anno 1647', and that after the fire, Lord Pembroke 're-edyfied it, by the advice of Inigo Jones' but Jones 'being then very old, could not be there in person, but left it to Mr Webb.' What is astonishing is that the interiors of this range of Wilton were rebuilt as royal state apartments around the time of the execution of Charles I, following the collapse of the monarchy in 1642. Jones's façade seems to have been left as it was, though the modest, tiled pyramidal roofs of the corner towers were replaced with more Palladian pediments.

Since Aubrey's 'Mr Webb' was Jones's relative and pupil, John Webb (1611–72), the post-fire Wilton that survives today is very Jonesian in feel. The surviving drawings for ceilings and doors in the state rooms were in the hands of Jones or Webb with annotations by both of them. Five rooms on the *piano nobile* survive largely as Jones and Webb left them. The Single Cube Room has a painted ceiling with a cove of arabesques like that in the Queen's Bedchamber at Jones's Queen's House, Greenwich. The overmantel to the chimneypiece is derived from Jean Barbet's *Livre d'architecture, d'autels et de cheminées* (Paris, 1633), the designs in which appealed to Charles I's French wife, Henrietta Maria. The dado panels contain paintings illustrating Philip Sidney's *Arcadia*, said to have been written at Wilton, and were painted by Emmanuel de Critz after sixteenth-century Venetian painting in fashion at the court. The same artist was responsible for the ceiling painting in the adjacent Double Cube Room, with its central oval of Perseus rescuing his mother from Polydectes below a stunning, oval coffered dome, open to the sky like that of the Pantheon.

The Double and Single Cube Rooms have been icons of veneration at least since their publication in *Vitruvius Britannicus* (vol. II, 1717), where Colen Campbell wrote ecstatically of them: ''Tis universally acknowledged that the grand Apartment is one of the noblest Architecture has yet produced.' Perhaps the most famous seventeenth-century interior in England, the Double Cube Room, originally the dining room, gives us the impression of what the interiors of Jones's never executed Whitehall Palace for Charles I would have looked like. Indeed, at 60-foot long, 30-foot wide and 30-foot high, the Double Cube Room has the same dimensions as Jones's Queen's Chapel, St James's Palace. In the centre of the east wall is a giant door-case carved in wood and stone, which can be related to designs for Whitehall Palace, while designs close to its capitals are in John Webb's manuscript 'Book of Capitols' at Chatsworth. Flanked by Corinthian columns, and surmounted by a broken pediment supporting over life-size recumbent figures, it recalls Palladio's similarly grand marble door-cases in the Sala delle Quattro Porte in the Doge's Palace in Venice. The no less sumptuous chimneypiece, owing something to designs by Barbet, has an overmantel flanked by lush, gilded figures of Ceres and Bacchus in front of coupled columns with inventive Corinthian capitals by Webb.

Though the great Van Dyck portraits give the Double Cube Room so much of its character, they were not painted for the room but in the 1630s for the family's London residence, Durham House. They seem not to have been at Wilton before the mid-seventeenth century and Evelyn did not mention them in his account of the house in his diary in 1654, though they were included in an inventory of 1683. Nonetheless, since the largest of them, the portrait of the 4th Earl and his family, 17-foot long and 11-foot high, so neatly fits the space allotted to it on the west wall, it is hard to imagine that the wall was not designed with it in mind. Indeed, as James Lees-Milne observed of Van Dyck's paintings here: 'their character must undoubtedly have influenced the designers of the room, inspiring them to create a setting in harmony with their Flemish, Genoese, and Venetian qualities.'

These state rooms had a very different character in the eighteenth century when they were formal spaces with little furniture. However, great changes were made to the Double Cube Room with the introduction of the luxurious gilt and crimson furnishings in 1824–25, when Catherine Woronzow, second wife of the 11th Earl, re-gilded and refurbished the state rooms, using Italian decorators. She provided the Double Cube Room with the great suite of early-eighteenth-century gilded furniture by William Kent, which she bought at the sale of Wanstead House in 1822. The present doors in both the Cube Rooms were replacements of 1826 by Richard Westmacott, but the character of the rooms is still predominantly that of the mid-seventeenth century. Praising the effect created in the Double Cube Room for its qualities of 'subtle liveliness' and its 'marvellous combination of splendour and spontaneous gaiety that is most rare in palace rooms', Lees-Milne suggested that this 'surely derives from Jones's and Webb's close ties with the theatre.'

Lead amorini *and vases on the South Terrace of the Italian Garden, photographed for* Country Life *in 1904. The gardens were admired as an outdoor museum of Classical sculpture in the seventeenth century.*

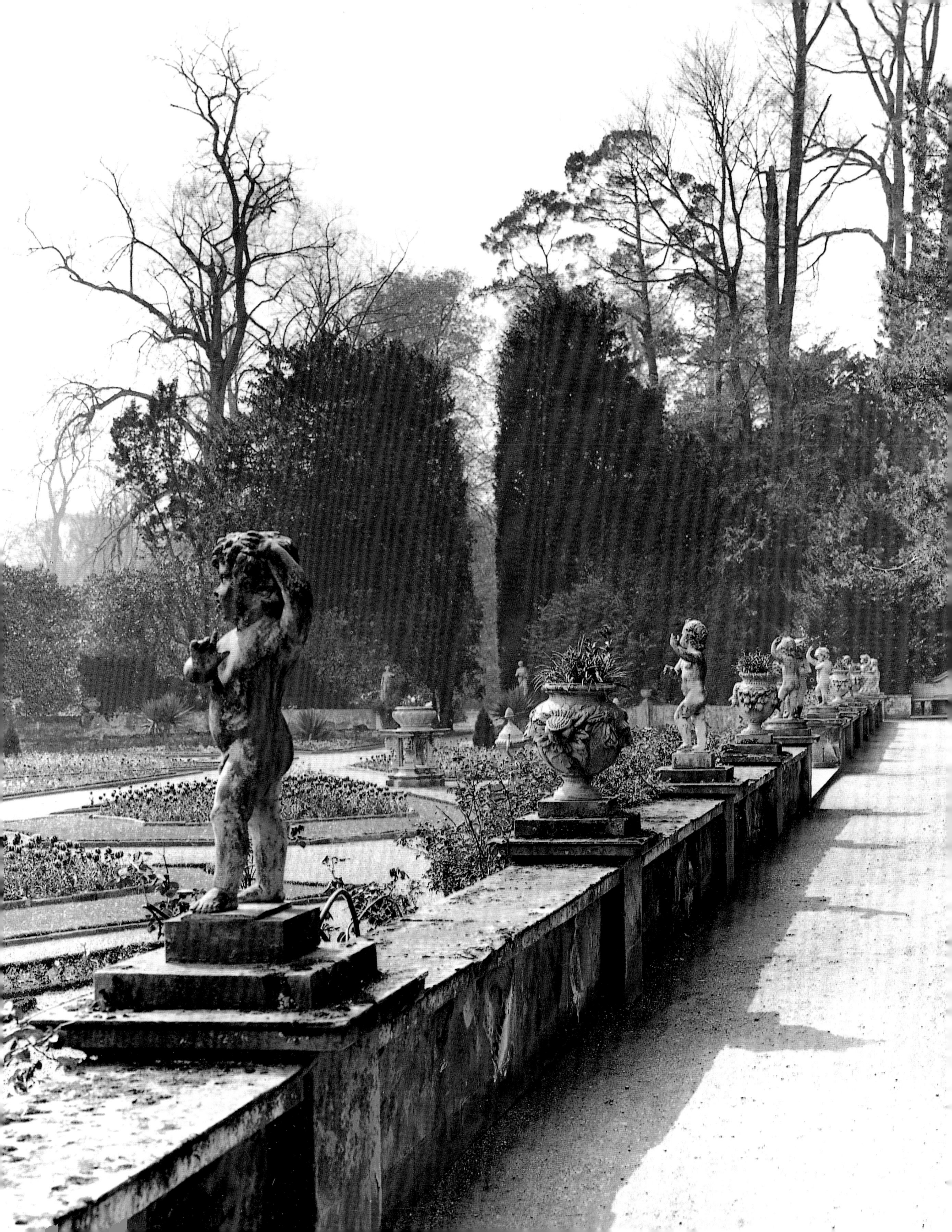

STOKE PARK, NORTHAMPTONSHIRE

Stoke Park is an impressive design with quadrant colonnades leading to pavilions, the first proposal of this kind in England, echoing projects in Palladio's *I Quattro Libri dell'Architettura* (1570), such as his unexecuted Villa Trissino at Meledo. According to Colen Campbell in *Vitruvius Britannicus* (vol. III, 1725), the left-hand, west pavilion was originally a single space occupied entirely by the library, and the east pavilion similarly occupied by the chapel, though some doubt is cast on this by the presence of large windows low in the elevation. But if Campbell were correct about its function, this would have been the first wholly Classical private chapel in a British country house.

The attribution of these pavilions to Inigo Jones has been a matter for debate. Despite Campbell's attribution of Stoke Park to him, the twin pavilions, which are all that survive of it, are in a more Michelangelesque manner than we might expect from Jones. Indeed, Henry Bridges, who died in 1724, stated specifically that Sir Francis Crane, for whom Stoke Park was built, 'brought the design from Italy, and in the execution of it received the assistance of Inigo Jones.' Knighted by James I in 1617, Francis Crane was secretary to his son, Prince Charles, in which capacity he set up the Mortlake tapestry works in 1619, and bought the Raphael cartoons from Genoa in 1623 to be used as models for tapestries. Stoke Park with its 400-acre estate was granted to him in 1629 by Charles I, but work on building a new house *c.*1630 was incomplete when he died of gangrene in Paris after an operation in April 1636.

The design by Jones of the south elevations of these pavilions is a simplified version of his Prince's Lodgings at Newmarket, but their west and east façades, which face each other, are at once both more ambitious and more unexpected. This is because the solid mass of the first floor rests shockingly on the open void of the ground-floor loggia, while the whole composition is pulled together by a Giant and a Lesser

32 · THE SEVENTEENTH CENTURY

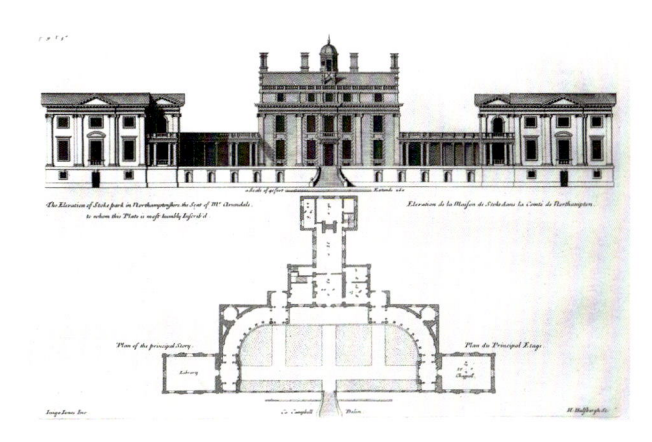

Above: *The imposing mansion planned for Crane c.1630, is shown in* Vitruvius Britannicus *(1725), with quadrant colonnades leading to pavilions, a Palladian pattern here adopted in England for the first time.*

Top: *The twin pavilions, probably by Inigo Jones, were once linked to a central mansion, which has since been demolished, leaving them romantically isolated. The building seen in the centre here is the former estate office.*

Order threaded through it. All this is derived from Michelangelo's powerfully inventive Palazzo dei Conservatori on the Capitoline Hill, Rome (1563–88), imitated in Vicenza by Palladio in the Palazzo Valmarana (1565) and by Scamozzi in the courtyard elevation of his Palazzo Trissino al Corso (1592). In Jones's design of c.1632 for 'Cupid's Palace' for an unknown masque, he adopted Scamozzi's arrangement of this theme at the Palazzo Trissino, a fact that helps confirm his authorship of the Stoke pavilions.

The tall, round-headed window on the first floor of the unusual façades of the Stoke Park pavilions was used by Palladio only at the Villa Barbaro at Maser (1557) for the Barbaro brothers, Daniele and Marc'Antonio, of whom the former published an edition of Vitruvius in 1552, with his own translation and commentary, and illustrations by Palladio. The round-headed window appears frequently in designs by Jones's other hero, Scamozzi, in his *L'Idea dell' Architettura Universale* (1615). Jones introduced a window of this type in his first designs for the Prince's Lodgings at Newmarket. At Stoke Park, as elsewhere, he adopted Scamozzi's version of the Ionic

THE BIRTH OF CLASSICISM ON ENGLISH SOIL · 33

Order with diagonal volutes, rather than the straight ones preferred by Palladio.

One of the revolutions which Jones effected in English architecture was his introduction of the trussed roof, a new kind of roof structure which he had found in Italy, where it was illustrated in the publications of Serlio and Palladio. It enabled the creation of large-scale, flat Classical ceilings, adopted by Jones at the Banqueting House, Whitehall, and at St Paul's, Covent Garden. Such roofs also survive with metal straps at Stoke Park, where they would not have been designed by local carpenters but by Jones, drawing on sources such as the illustrations of them in Barbaro's edition of Vitruvius (of which Jones's annotated copy survives at Chatsworth).

Another striking feature of the pavilions is the strong polychromy created by Jones's use of orangey-red ironstone for the cornice, the giant pilasters, and the rustic or basement, which contrasts with pale brown stone for the Lesser Orders and window surrounds, warm cream limestone for the walls, and greyish-white stone, possibly Portland, for the capitals and bases, and a pulvinated frieze made of timber. This almost overheated effect may surprise us since we are more familiar with seeing such designs in the medium of cold line engravings in *Vitruvius Britannicus*. Also, such colourful exuberance did not appeal to Lord Burlington and his disciples who did not therefore echo it in their work. However, Jones also indulged in this play at the Whitehall Banqueting House, where the basement was originally in brown Oxfordshire stone, contrasting with dun-coloured Northamptonshire stone for the main elevation, and Portland stone for the Orders and balustrade, an effect destroyed when Soane, and later Smirke, refaced the whole elevation in Portland stone. The colourful and painterly character of the Stoke Park pavilions is also reminiscent of Jones's masque designs.

The main house was burnt in 1886 and replaced five years later by an ornate Neo-Jacobean mansion, awkwardly attached to the right-hand pavilion. The quadrants and pavilions fell into grave decay following occupation of the house by the army in the Second World War, but were rescued in 1958 with the help of a grant from the Historic Buildings Council. The Victorian mansion was demolished and the pavilions restored and adapted for habitation, one being divided into small rooms, the other serving as a single large space.

At Inigo Jones's pavilion, the Giant Order threaded with a Lesser Order, and the solid first floor resting daringly on an open ground floor, are inspired by Michelangelo's Palazzo dei Conservatori on the Capitol in Rome.

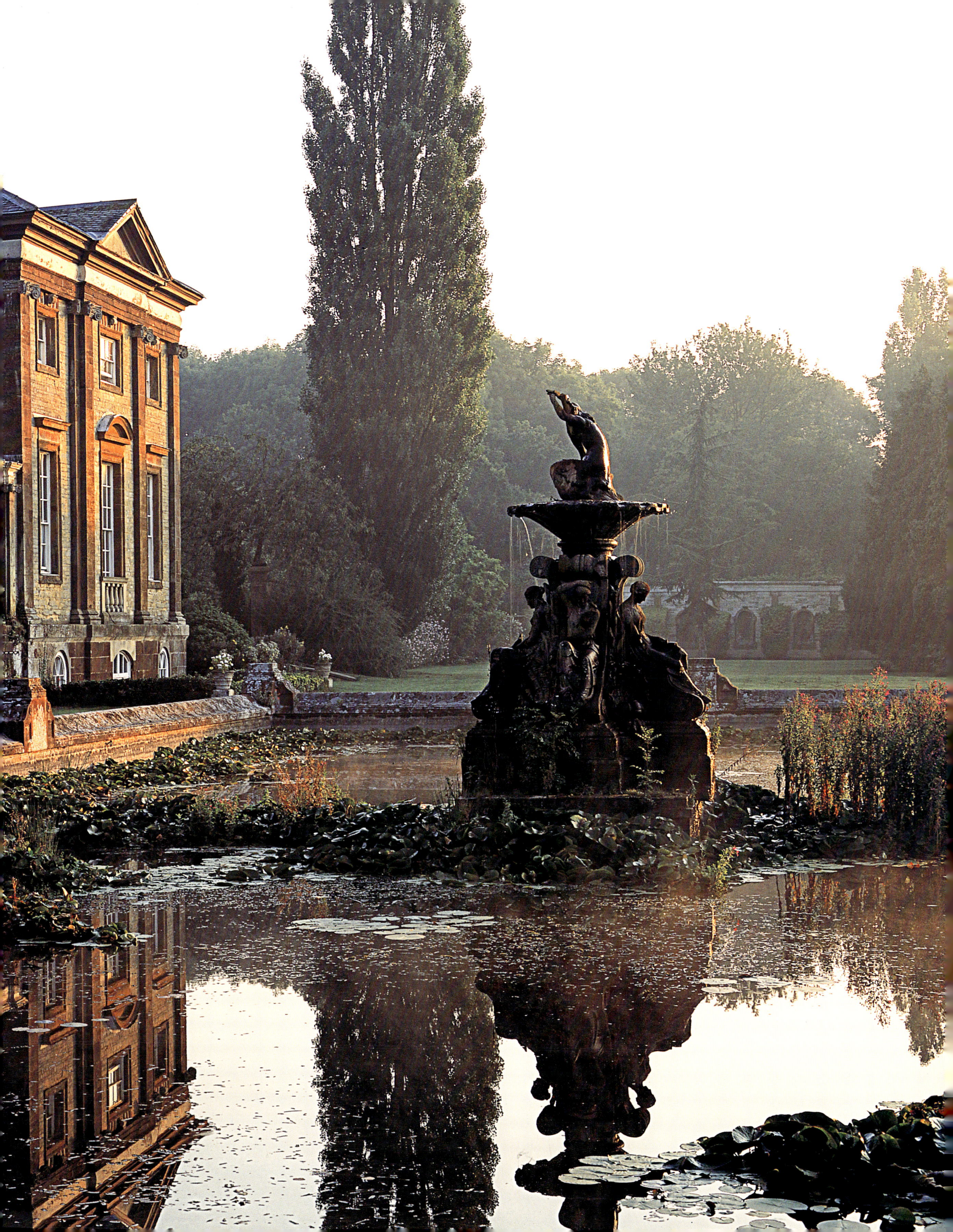

COLESHILL HOUSE, BERKSHIRE

One of the most satisfying Classical houses in England, Coleshill achieved its effect through the masterly creation of mass, symmetry and balance, and not through the possibly easier path of a display of columns, pilasters and pediments. It shares this astylar disposition with designs by Inigo Jones, including one of 1638 for Maltravers House, Lothbury, London, for Lord Maltravers, son of his patron, the Earl of Arundel. According to Woolfe and Gandon in *Vitruvius Britannicus* (vol. v, 1771), Coleshill 'is, perhaps, the most perfect work now remaining of that great architect, Inigo Jones, having undergone no alteration since the year 1650, when it was compleated.' However, as with Wilton, there has been debate about this attribution and it is now generally agreed that the house was designed by the amateur architect, Sir Roger Pratt (1620–85), for his cousin, Sir George Pratt.

Coleshill, the perfect gentry house, was probably built a few years after the creation of the post-fire state rooms at Wilton, the perfect aristocratic house. It was commissioned by Sir George Pratt whose father, Sir Henry Pratt, a city merchant and alderman, bought the old house at Coleshill in 1626, and was made a baronet in 1641. His will of 1645 shows that he was building a house at Coleshill, for he directed his executors to complete it. However, it was burnt *c*.1647 and he died two years later when, instead of completing it, his son George built a house on a different site, probably begun in 1657–58 and definitely finished in 1662.

Sir Mark Pleydell, owner of the house from 1728–68, recorded that according to an aged gardener, 'Pratt and Jones were frequently here, and Jones was also consulted about ye Ceilings.' However, Sir George Pratt, an active republican supporter of the Commonwealth, was unlikely to choose such a royalist architect as Jones who was, moreover, even at the time of the fire at Wilton in 1647–48, already 'then very old, [so] could not be there, but left it to Mr Webb.' It is indeed clear that Sir George Pratt asked John Webb to provide designs for the new house at Coleshill *c*.1649–50, for a few of his drawings survive.

Above: *The entrance front, of this perfectly balanced Classical house of c.1657–62, designed by Sir Roger Pratt for his cousin, Sir George Pratt, draws on designs published by Serlio in 1575.*

Right: *The balustraded lead flat with cupola was widely imitated, as at Ashdown Park, Berkshire, and recently at Merks Hall, Essex, by Quinlan Terry. It possibly echoed the rooftop drama of Jacobean prodigy houses.*

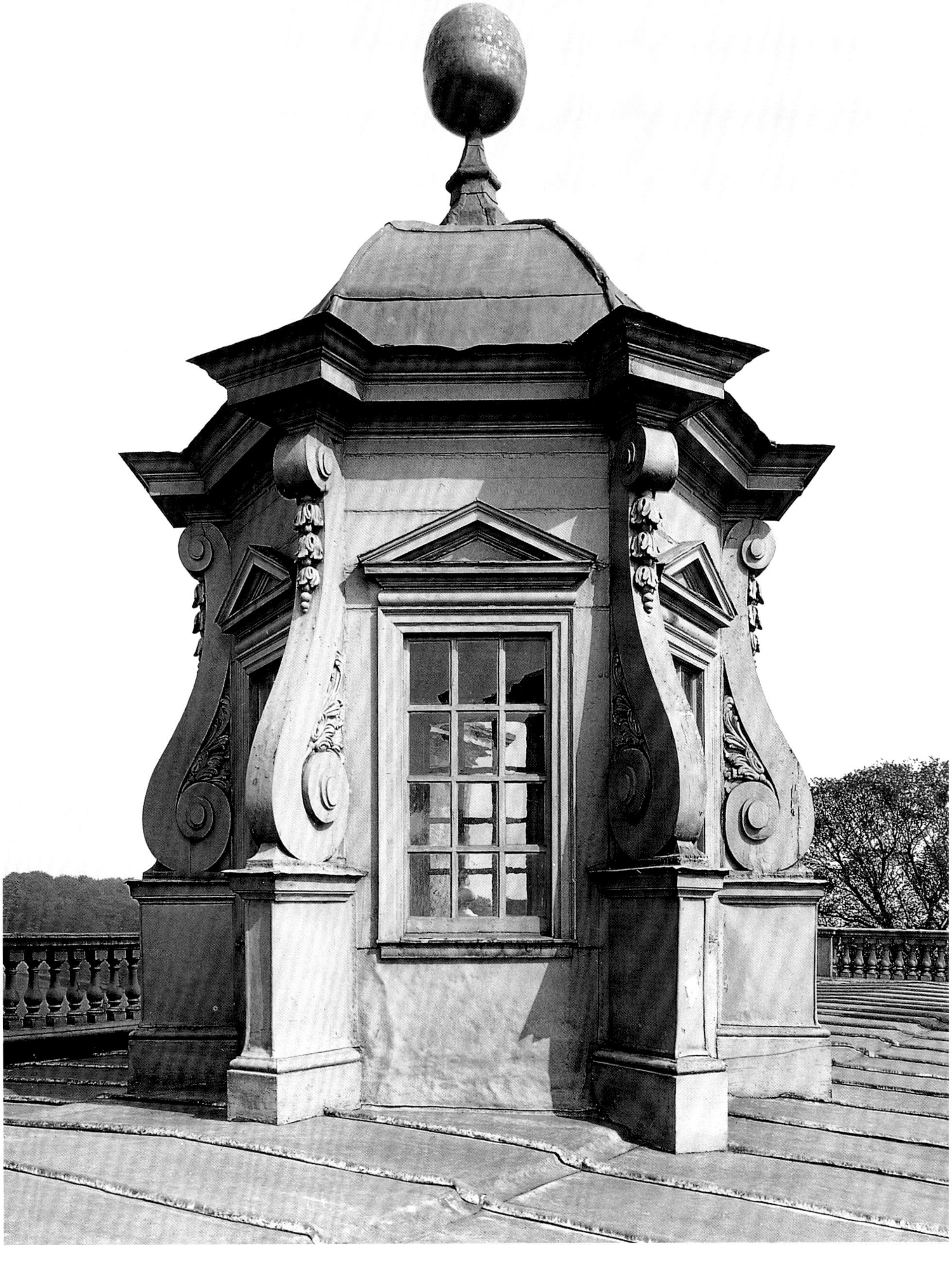

These show that it would have been articulated with the Orders, both internally and externally.

Meanwhile, Sir George's cousin, Sir Roger Pratt, had returned in 1649 from a six-year tour in France, Italy, Flanders and Holland, which he had undertaken to avoid the Civil War and, as he put it, 'to give myself some convenient education.' Architecture was his chief interest, his heroes being Serlio, Palladio and Scamozzi. His three documented works as an architect include Kingston Lacy, Dorset.

The elevation of Coleshill seems inspired by that of the house illustrated by Serlio in Book VII of *L'Archittetura* (1579), for both are astylar, are raised on a sub-basement, have varied window spacing and a high-pitched roof with dormer windows. Like Wilton, Coleshill is nine bays long, though its central three bays are more widely spaced than the three on either side – a subtle touch to avoid overcrowding the composition. The windows would have originally been of the stone mullion and cross type, so the sash windows, which replaced them in the eighteenth century, give the house a somewhat later character. Particularly judicious is the dignified placing of the four massive chimney stacks, with cornices of their own and panels carved with egg and dart mouldings. The balustraded lead flat, surmounted by a richly detailed cupola, was a Classical response to the cupolas and rooftop promenades at prodigy houses like Burghley, Longleat and Hardwick.

This rooftop drama is far from Serlio, unlike the plan with balancing apartments formed by reception rooms and closets. In his architectural notes, Pratt called the Coleshill plan-type 'double pile', that is a block comprising two parallel ranges of rooms divided by a central corridor. With only one window at each end, this corridor must have been very dark in a house the size of Coleshill, a disagreeable arrangement that was nonetheless repeated on all three floors. The dining room was originally on the first floor, a considerable distance from the kitchen at the far end of the basement.

The double-height entrance hall recalls that designed by Jones at Queen's House, Greenwich, which was derived from Scamozzi's Villa Molin, near Padua, where Jones had almost certainly stayed in 1613 with the Earl and Countess of Arundel. However, the entrance hall at Coleshill also contained the staircase, which had paired flights on either side, the first example in England of the 'Imperial' type. Palladio recommended such a disposition 'whereby one may go up and down on the right and left; and are both very convenient and beautiful, and sufficiently light' in *Quattro Libri* (Book II). Lit by as many as five large windows, the entrance hall at Coleshill followed Palladio's prescriptions for maximum light, which he took from Vitruvius. Palladio argued that paired staircases, like that at Coleshill, 'will be commendable if they are clear, ample, and commodious to ascend, inviting, as it were, people to go up.' (*Quattro Libri*, Book I). Pratt may have known Longhena's pioneering staircase at San Giorgio Maggiore, Venice, of the 1640s, which adopted this plan. Pratt partly followed Palladio who explained that: 'The ancients [i.e. Vitruvius] observed to make the steps uneven in number, that beginning to go up with the right foot,

The combined entrance hall and staircase, with a flight on each side as recommended by Palladio, contains fourteen roundels with busts of Roman emperors. The staircase is richly carved with female heads, lion masks and swags.

THE BIRTH OF CLASSICISM ON ENGLISH SOIL · 39

one might end with the same; which they looked upon as a good omen, and of greater devotion when they entered the temple. The number of steps is not to exceed eleven, or thirteen at most ... that the weak and weary may find where to rest themselves.'

The rich carving of the staircase, with its festoons, lion masks and veiled female heads of much beauty, was by Richard Cleave who presented his bill for it in May 1662 and later worked on Wren's City churches. The strongly Classical feel of the whole interior is further emphasized by the presence on all four walls, and on both floors, of fourteen roundels, framed with laurel wreaths and containing busts of Roman emperors. The beamed ceiling was in the manner of Jones who may even have designed it. The interlaced guilloche on the soffit of the ceiling beams in the main rooms is close to that at Palazzo Massimo, Rome (1532–37), an inventive neo-antique masterpiece by Peruzzi.

A fascinating story begins in the early eighteenth century with the arrival at the house of Lord Burlington and his draughtsmen, all anxious to restore it and to claim it for their hero, Inigo Jones. They revered as iconic the harmony, sobriety and lack of ostentation of its façades, a process of veneration which reached a peak when the principal elevation was specially engraved by the antiquary, George Vertue, in 1735 over the improbable caption, 'Built by Inigo Jones in the year 1650.' Sir Mark Pleydell fixed a brass plaque to a staircase in 1748 recording its repair in 1744–45 'by the Direction of the Earls of Burlington and Leicester.' Isaac Ware illustrated two ceilings at Coleshill as the work of Inigo Jones in his *A Complete Body of Architecture* (1756), while the caption to the elevation and plans of the house published in *Vitruvius Britannicus* (vol. v, 1771), praised 'the richness of the ceilings' and noted that 'the late earl of Burlington had, for his own study very correct drawings taken [of them] by Mr. Isaac Ware, which have never been published.'

Coleshill was bought in 1945 by Ernest Cook with the idea of bequeathing it to the National Trust, but during repairs in 1953 a blow lamp left by workmen led to a fire which damaged the interior. Thanks partly to David Eccles, Minister of Public Works from 1951–54, who was shockingly hostile to the preservation of historic buildings, the disastrous decision was made to demolish Coleshill, not restore it. It was one of the greatest losses in the history of English architecture.

Above: *A bedroom of modest size had a lavish ceiling with the beams arranged in a decorative pattern of circles, striking a note of fantasy rather than of structural reality, and further enriched with oak leaves.*

Right: *The house was noted for its plasterwork ceilings with elaborately decorated, beam-like ribs, as here in the Great Dining Room. Inigo Jones, according to an eighteenth-century owner of the house, was 'consulted abt ye Cielings.'*

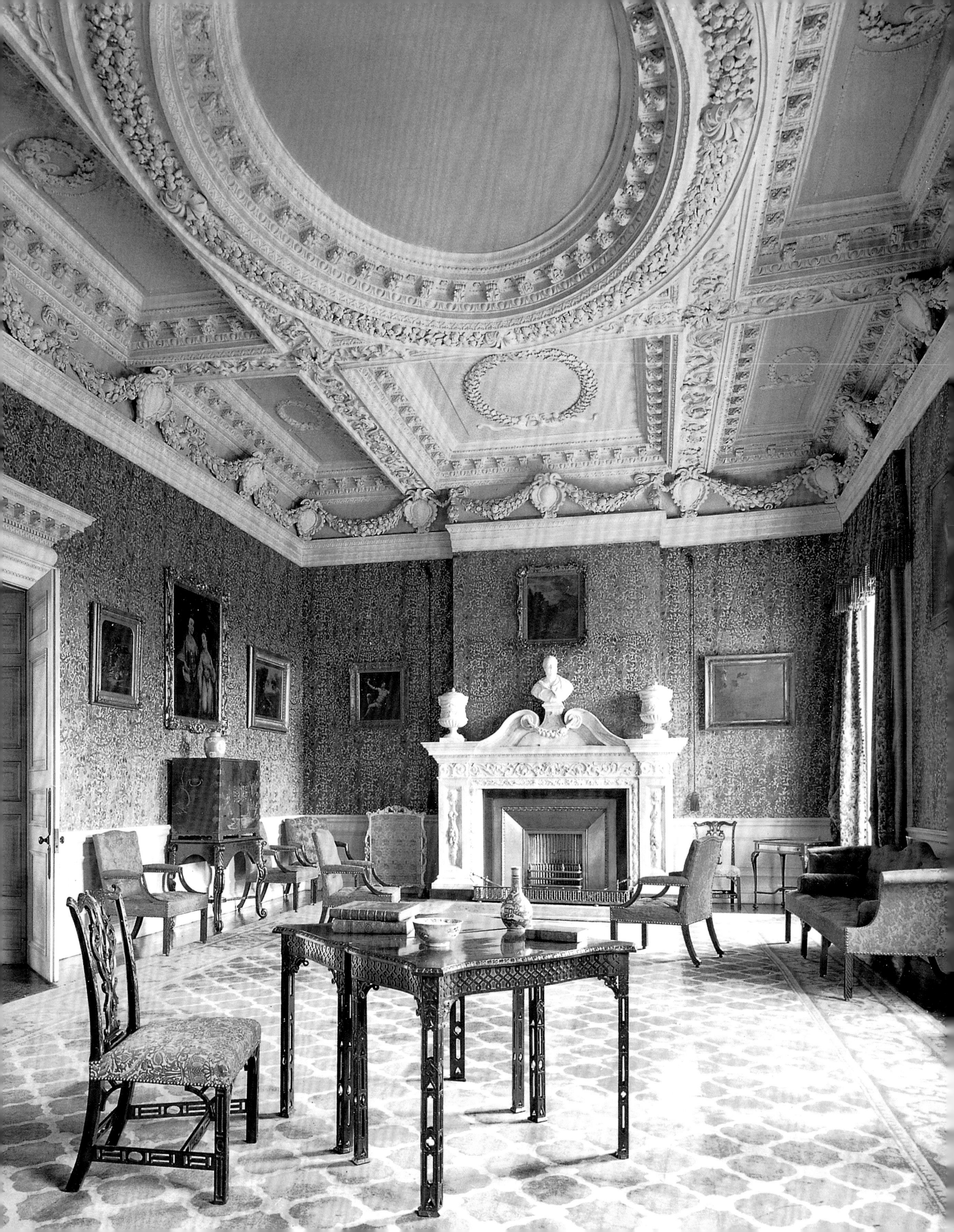

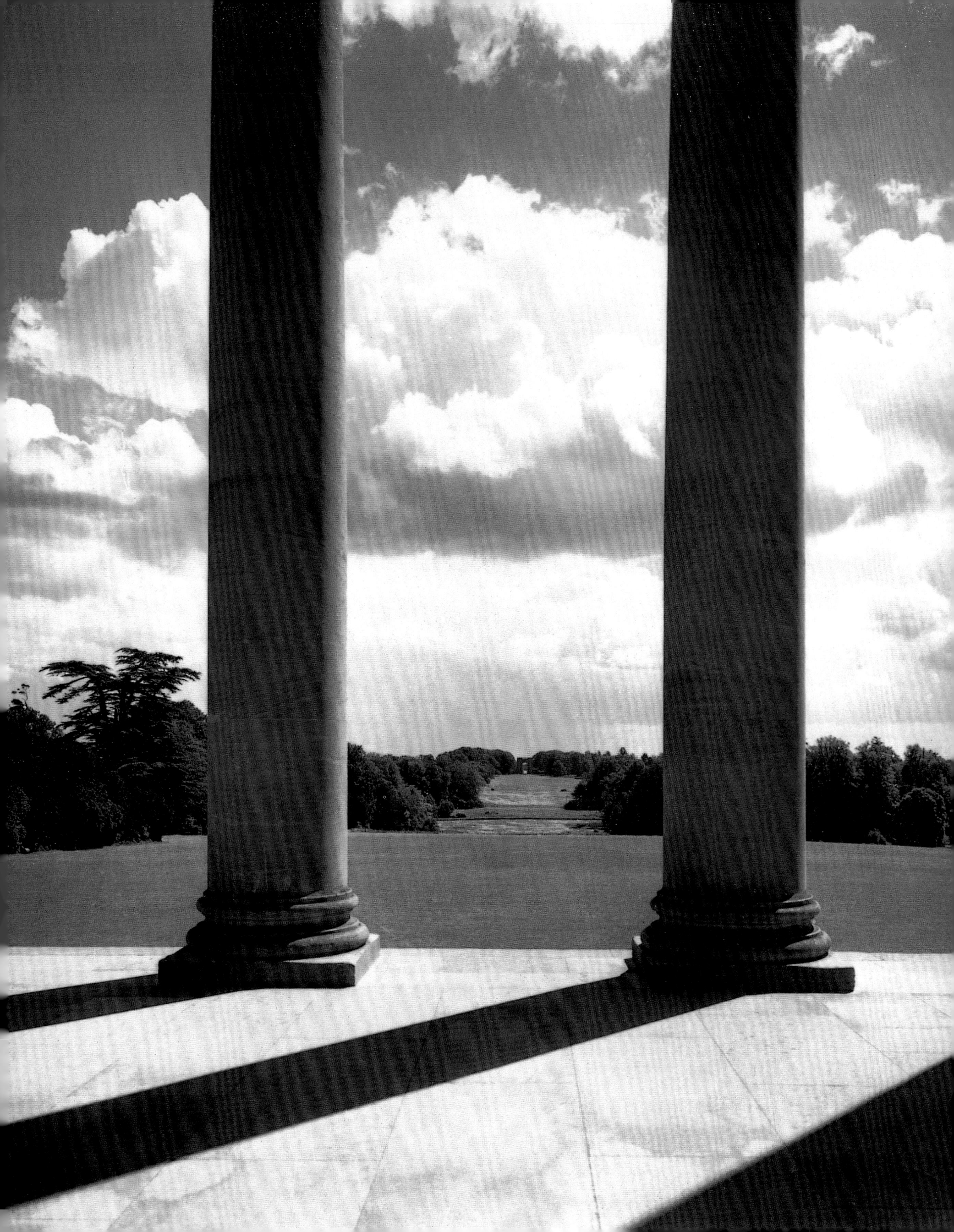

II

THE EIGHTEENTH CENTURY: FROM PALLADIO TO POMPEII

※

The influence of Inigo Jones was rudely interrupted by the Civil War and Commonwealth, or Interregnum, from 1649–60. Yet he cast a long shadow for he was reinvented at the start of the eighteenth century as a national hero by the Earl of Burlington and Colen Campbell. They contrasted his achievement with what they viewed as the licentious foreign language of the Baroque, which had grown up in England since Jones's day. Their aim was to establish a purer Classicism founded in antiquity, particularly that presented by Palladio, who had illustrated ancient buildings together with his own in his *I Quattro Libri dell' Architettura* (1570). Palladio's work suggested a parity between antiquity and modernity that could be recreated even today.

This led British architects to study Classical architecture both ancient and modern, and to catch up with the isolation of Britain from the main stream of Classicism in Italy and France, which had been an unhappy result of the Reformation. This is not how patrons and architects would have expressed their aim but it is in effect what happened. Remarkably, Wren, Vanbrugh and Hawksmoor never visited Italy, but those who investigated architecture in Italy between 1703 and 1780

STOWE HOUSE, BUCKINGHAMSHIRE *The 2nd Earl Temple landscaped the previously formal garden in the 1750s and 1760s, adding the Corinthian Arch at the end of the vista from the great portico on the south front of the house.*

included James Gibbs, William Kent, James Stuart, Nicholas Revett, William Chambers, Robert and James Adam, Robert Mylne, George Dance, James Wyatt and John Soane. So, too, did many of their patrons in what was an astonishing innovation. The six houses discussed in this chapter reflect different outcomes of the search for the perfect Classical house, which involved keeping up with an ever-growing knowledge of antique architecture and decoration, resulting in large part from a new interest in archaeological discovery.

Classicism in the Age of Enlightenment involved a return to nature as well as to the antique. Hence the abolition of the formal gardens of the Baroque Age in favour of the creation of Picturesque parks by 'Capability' Brown and his successor, Humphry Repton. Britain now became the envy of Europe for its technical advances in agricultural production, as well as for its leadership of the emerging Industrial Revolution. This is well conveyed by Arthur Young who, in works such as *A Six Months Tour through North of England* (1770), celebrated 'improvement', whether in agricultural science, picture collecting, architecture, or landscape gardening. New landscaped parks as at Hagley Hall, Worcestershire, Stowe, Buckinghamshire, or Stourhead, Wiltshire, provided ideal settings for garden buildings, which, with their comparatively modest scale, were seen as appropriate vehicles for experimentation with new styles – Greek, Gothic, and even Chinese.

44 · THE EIGHTEENTH CENTURY

◦ CHISWICK HOUSE, MIDDLESEX ◦

Chiswick House, built c.1726–29 from designs by the Earl of Burlington, using Henry Flitcroft as his principal draughtsman, confronts us uncompromisingly as the bold manifesto of an attempt to recreate the Classical house of antiquity. This is how it struck the connoisseur and antiquarian, Sir John Clerk of Penicuik, who, after dining at Chiswick with Lord Burlington in 1727, observed that: 'He is building a new house 70 foot square, all in the ancient manner … [but] rather curious than convenient.' Burlington's aim echoed that of Palladio and Scamozzi, who were his heroes as they had been of Inigo Jones.

One of the richest peers in the kingdom, Burlington undertook his first Grand Tour at the age of twenty from 1714 to 1715 as the typical culmination of a Classical education. His interest in architecture seems to have begun with the publication of two books in 1715: Leoni's translation of Palladio's *Quattro Libri*, the first English edition, and the first volume of Colen Campbell's *Vitruvius Britannicus* in which, inspired by Palladio and Jones, he proposed a new style of architecture by reviving what he called 'the antique simplicity'. This led to Burlington's second visit to Italy in 1719 after which, having spent ten or twelve days in the Veneto studying Palladio, he brought back to London the all important figure of William Kent who had been trained as a history painter in Rome.

In Paris in 1726, Burlington designed an *hôtel particulier*, or town house, along antique lines with the open colonnaded atrium of the Ancient Roman house. This is indebted to Palladio's reconstruction of the Ancient Roman house in Daniele Barbaro's edition of Vitruvius (1556). It was also at about this moment that Burlington began to design a house for himself at Chiswick. This owed much to Palladio's Villa Capra, as had Campbell's Mereworth Castle, Kent (c.1720–25), illustrated in *Vitruvius Britannicus* (vol. III, 1725). More novel than Mereworth, Chiswick differed in many ways from Palladio's villa in elevation and plan. All of the Capra fronts are identical, each with a portico of freestanding columns, but at Chiswick each front was different, conceived and designed in isolation, something of an English trait. Also, only the front elevation has a portico, for Burlington knew that, in England, more than one would have made the interior too dark. For the same reason, he did not follow Palladio's plan, with no less than four narrow corridors leading from the porticoes to the central space. Perhaps the only feature at Chiswick specifically based on Palladio is the rear elevation with three Venetian windows, or Serliana, in relieving arches. This echoes a design by Palladio, perhaps for the Villa Valmarana at Vigardolo.

Burlington was less indebted to Palladio than to Scamozzi, notably his Villa Molin (1597) and Villa Rocca Pisani (1575) of which he owned drawings. Both villas have side façades with a central Venetian window over a doorway, as at Chiswick, while from the Villa Molin Burlington

Lord Burlington designed for himself this iconic Palladian Villa of c.1726–29, taking buildings by Palladio and Scamozzi as his source, though the elaborate double staircase has a Baroque rather than an antique or Renaissance flavour.

FROM PALLADIO TO POMPEII · 45

also took the windows incorporating balusters, the balusters between the portico columns, the string course round the façades at baluster level and the Diocletian windows in the drum, lighting the hall or tribune. From the Villa Rocca Pisani came the columnar under-hall, the first floor twice the height of the ground floor, the omission of the Italian mezzanine, the steps between the octagonal drum and the dome, and even the chimneys in the form of obelisks. These are a feature peculiar to the Veneto and Lombardy, though arriving in the form of finials in Sansovino's St Mark's Library, Venice (1535). Palladio himself never showed chimneys on his villas in the plates in *Quattro Libri*.

The portico is three columns deep, for which the only modern Italian precedent was Palladio's Villa Malcontenta, though there are several examples in England. Burlington noted that the Malcontenta portico was entered by side stairs, an example he followed at Chiswick. The porticoes of the Villas Malcontenta and Capra are Ionic, but that at Chiswick is the more splendid Corinthian taken from Palladio's *Quattro Libri* (Book I). The animated and crisply carved staircase has no antique prototype, but recalls Guarini's Baroque staircase at Racconigi near Turin (1676–83), which Burlington may have seen when visiting the capital of Piedmont on his Grand Tour. By contrast, the Vitruvian scroll and the Greek key motif, derived from the Temple of Mars Ultor in Rome, both feature prominently at Chiswick where they are perhaps the earliest uses of these ornaments in England.

From the entrance door a passage leads to the octagonal lower tribune, which has simple Tuscan columns that were among those recommended by Vitruvius and by Palladio, in *Quattro Libri* (Book II), for the atrium or vestibule on the ground floor. This tribune may have served the purpose described by Palladio as a place where those wishing to see the master of the house on business might conveniently wait. Burlington might thus have had his business room nearby. His extensive library eventually occupied three interlocking rooms approached from the tribune, a space that is lit only from the passages leading to it, an arrangement otherwise unique to the Villa Capra. The location of the four small staircases at Chiswick was also suggested by the Villa Capra. The absence of grand internal staircases at Chiswick provided the house with a certain antique flavour since they were not thought to be characteristic of Ancient Roman houses.

From the portico on the floor above, the visitor who enters the *piano nobile* unexpectedly finds himself in a long, narrow, and rather dark corridor. This seems inspired by a sentence about the planning of the Ancient Greek house in Vitruvius (*De Architectura*, Book VI), but is awkward and not found in other buildings. It leads to the hall or tribune, which, unlike that at Villa Capra, is not circular but,

Above: *The small but rich Blue Velvet Room with a Mannerist ceiling featuring doubled brackets, based on a North Italian drawing of the 1540s in the style of Giulio Romano.*

Left: *Designed as a small picture gallery, the Red Velvet Room has a Palladian window, flanked by chimneypieces, inspired by Inigo Jones, and a beamed ceiling echoing that in his chapel at Somerset House.*

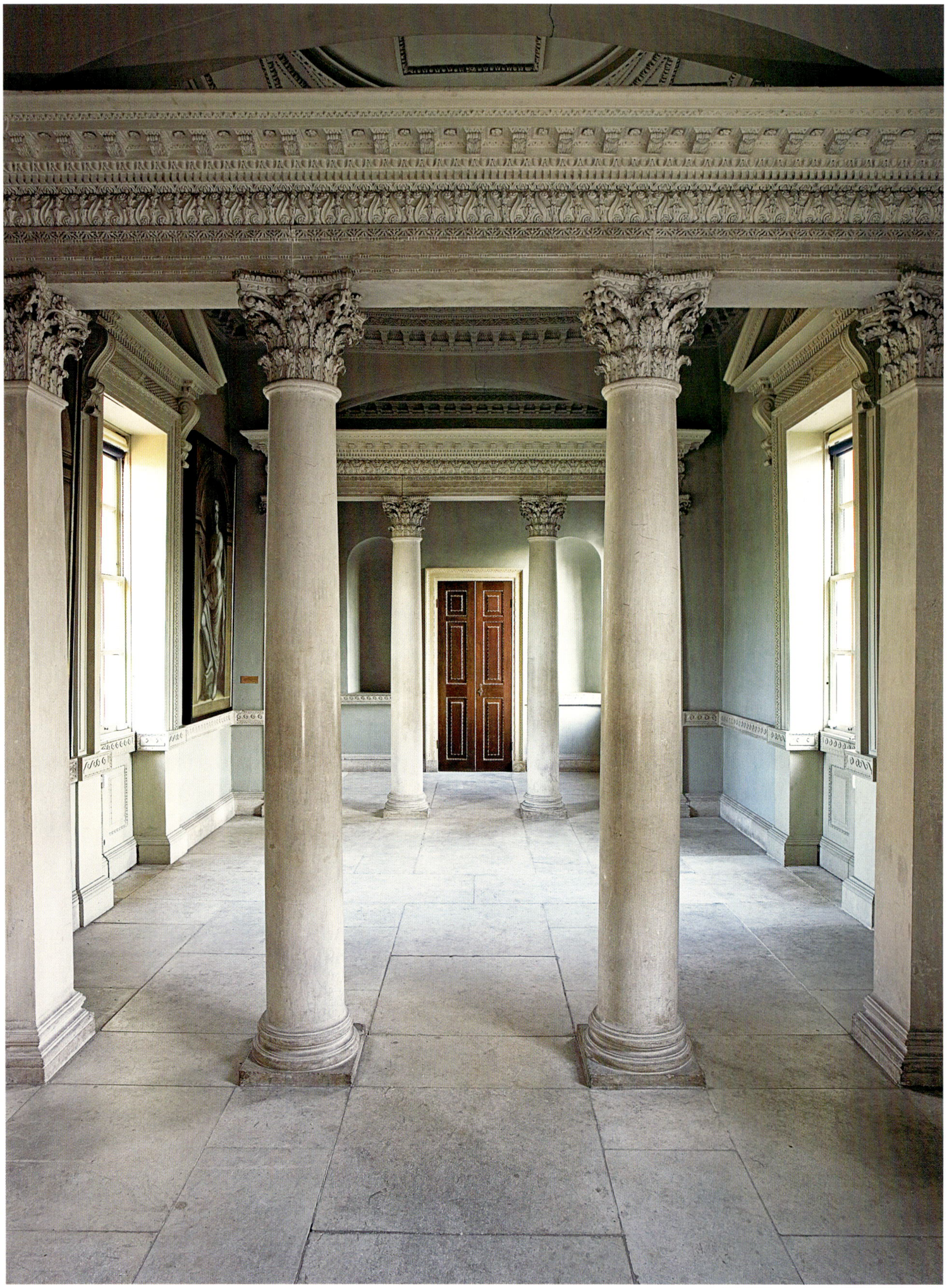

unusually, octagonal, a shape derived from Serlio. Palladio said that the hall is 'for feasts, entertainment and decorations, for comedies, weddings and such like recreations,' but at Chiswick neither it nor the central part of the gallery into which it opens has chimneypieces, so they are unpleasantly cold in winter. Perhaps, like the narrow entrance corridor, this is what Sir John Clerk of Penicuick may have had in mind when he observed that the place was 'rather curious than convenient'. The hall, like the other interiors, follows Vitruvius' prescriptions in having a full Classical cornice but no dado or sculptural decoration, though the dome boasts octagonal coffering derived from the Basilica of Maxentius in Rome. The ceiling was white with gilt enrichments, and the walls stone-coloured.

The centrally-placed hall leads to virtually all the rooms on the *piano nobile* so that the house works smoothly like a piece of clockwork. The whole north front is occupied by a gallery, while an apartment runs down each of the west and east sides: the Red Velvet Room, Blue Velvet Room and Red Closet for Lord Burlington on the west, and the Green Velvet Room, Bedchamber and Closet on the east for Lady Burlington. In planning terms, the apartments have a seventeenth-century royal or court origin, but in decorative treatment are wholly novel. The tripartite gallery, housing a modest amount of sculpture, has a central space resembling the loggias that feature in this situation in houses by Raphael, Giulio Romano, Peruzzi and Vignola. The apses at each end echo those in Palladio's reconstruction of an Ancient Roman house, as well as in his Palazzo Thiene in Vicenza. Their lozenge-shaped coffering derives from the Temple of Venus and Roma on the edge of the Roman Forum, which Burlington would have seen, though he probably took it from Palladio's woodcuts of the temple in *Quattro Libri* (Book IV) or from the vestibule of Peruzzi's Palazzo Massimo in Rome. Apses of antique derivation are rare before Chiswick, which could claim to be the first neo-antique house in England.

The windows in the gallery have an Order of Corinthian columns, while the richly French ceiling beams are inspired by those by Jones in Queen Henrietta Maria's bedroom at Queen's House, Greenwich. The room follows the recommendation in *Quattro Libri* (Book II) that Corinthian rooms should have convex friezes with garland and crossed ribbons. In the end rooms of the gallery are charming plaster

Above: In the centre room of the tripartite gallery, one of the earliest in England, the gilded coffering in the apse is inspired by the Temple of Venus and Roma in the Roman Forum, as illustrated in Palladio's Quattro Libri.

Left: The link building between the new villa and the (demolished) Jacobean manor house has the most antique interior at Chiswick, its columnar screens deriving from the Baths and the ceiling from an Ancient Roman one at Pozzuoli.

FROM PALLADIO TO POMPEII · 49

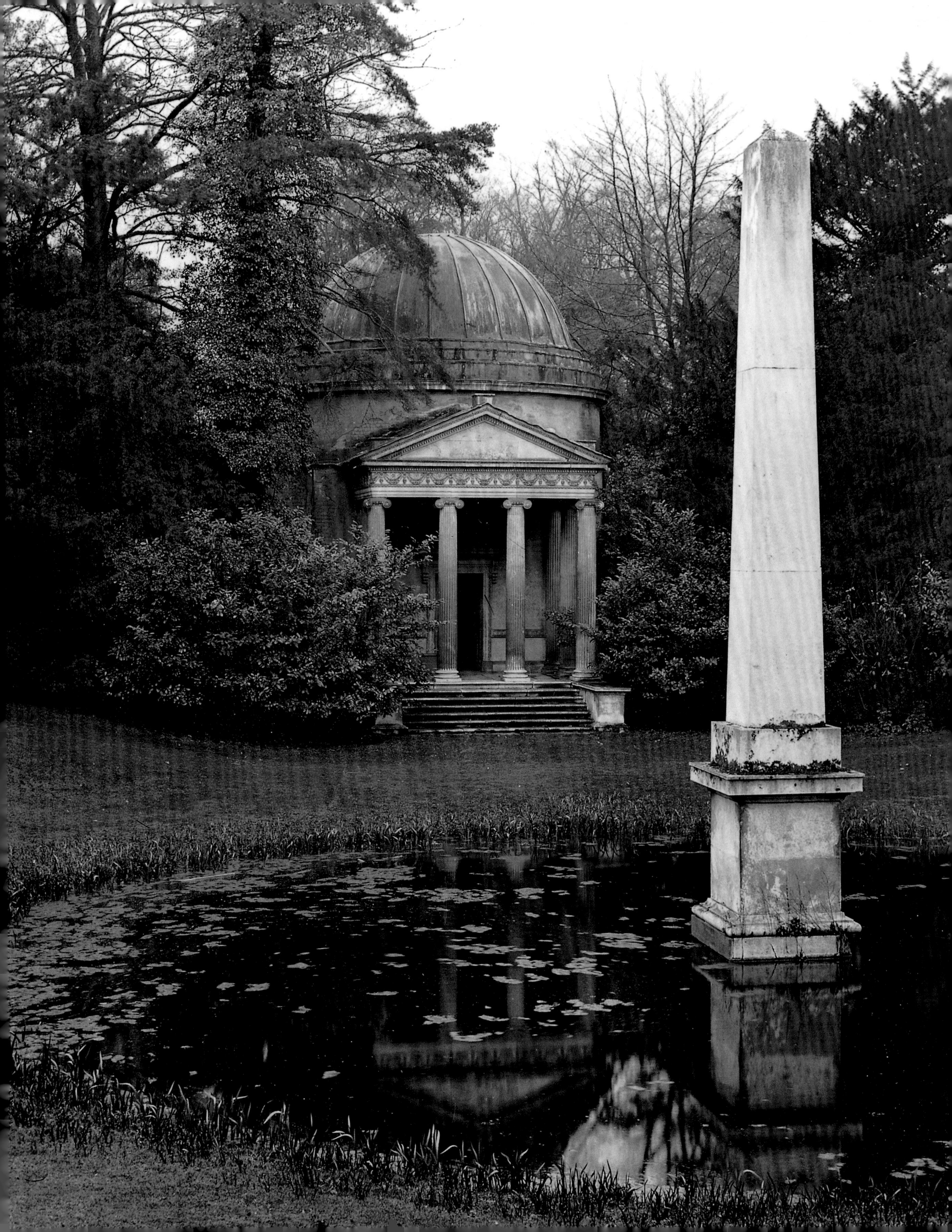

decorations showing the Vitruvian origin of the Corinthian Order, with tall leaves growing up like basket-work. These echo those in Giulio Romano's ribbed half domes in the loggia of the Villa Madama, Rome. It should be noted that there are just five chimneypiece types at Chiswick, all from Inigo Jones. Palladio chose not to illustrate any, though his buildings do contain them.

Beginning with the Red Velvet Room, the rich colours in the two apartments are in striking contrast to the gallery and hall. Burlington hung twenty-eight of his finest pictures in the Red Velvet Room, half of them on religious subjects. The beamed ceiling pattern derives from Jones's Catholic chapel for Henrietta Maria at Somerset House, while in the centre is William Kent's painting of *Mercury and the Arts*. The Blue Velvet Room ceiling with its curious projecting consoles echoes one by Giulio Romano in the *studiolo* in the Ducal Palace at Mantua. Though Kent, not Burlington had seen this, it is probable that Burlington gave him as a model a drawing, now at Chatsworth, which he had acquired from John Talman. In the centre of Kent's ceiling a female figure representing 'Architecture' wears a Corinthian capital as a crown and is surrounded by boys with drawing instruments.

Despite his closeness to Kent, Burlington made the designs for the house himself, leaving only the ceiling paintings to Kent. He was unusual in the extent to which, as a nobleman, he acted as a professional architect, deploying his skills in the exercise of civic virtue. Frederick the Great of Prussia, an important Neo-Classical and Neo-Palladian patron, asked his agent, Count Algarotti, to obtain drawings for him of Burlington's work. Thus in 1751 Algarotti wrote a letter to Burlington containing the words, 'Now it rests with you, my Lord, to show his Majesty that you are in this century the restorer of true architecture.'

No personal statement by Burlington survives on his architecture or his garden design. Since no antique gardens survive and neither Palladio nor Jones had designed a garden, the latter leaving it to a professional, Isaac de Caus, Burlington was faced with a problem, which it cannot be said he fully solved. He developed the garden in about three stages, which, before he had designed the house, began with a *patte d'oie* with three radiating avenues terminated by buildings. This disposition was possibly inspired by the stage-set he had seen in 1715 at Palladio's Teatro Olimpico in Vicenza on his first visit to Italy. The central vista was closed by a small, domed Baroque building of 1716 by James Gibbs, while the left or west vista was terminated by the Casina, designed in 1717 by Burlington to incorporate themes from Jones's and Webb's designs for Whitehall Palace.

When he later began to design the house, he decided to create a more antique atmosphere, as though populating an Ancient Roman estate with statues and garden buildings. He designed a grass amphitheatre with a circular pool surrounded by orange trees in tubs and containing an obelisk, overlooked by a small Ionic temple, which he modelled on the Pantheon. In a later phase, beginning in 1733, William Kent created the exedra or hippodrome in the form of a semi-circle of yew with niches cut for Roman statues and urns. This was part of the mood that led to a book subsidized by Burlington, Robert Castell's *The Villas of the Ancients Illustrated* (1728). This was a recreation of the villas of the younger Pliny as described in his letters, of which Castell provided a translation. Pliny's stress on nature and the views of scenery from his villas was an important precedent for Kent and Burlington. Of course Castell read back into antiquity the kind of garden he knew Burlington wanted to create and thus gave it a partly spurious antique justification. In this spirit, Kent attempted to break down the formal divisions of the garden so as to open up views in the spirit of Pliny's *imitatio ruris*, the imitation of nature of the ancients.

Above: On the north front, the three centre bays are based directly on a drawing by Palladio, but the flanking wings, demolished in 1952, were a clever addition of 1788 for the 5th Duke of Devonshire.

Left: The Orange Tree Garden of c.1718 forms a neo-antique composition, with a pool, originally surrounded by a grass amphitheatre, an obelisk and a domed temple, perhaps inspired by the 'Temple of Romulus' in the Roman Forum.

FROM PALLADIO TO POMPEII · 51

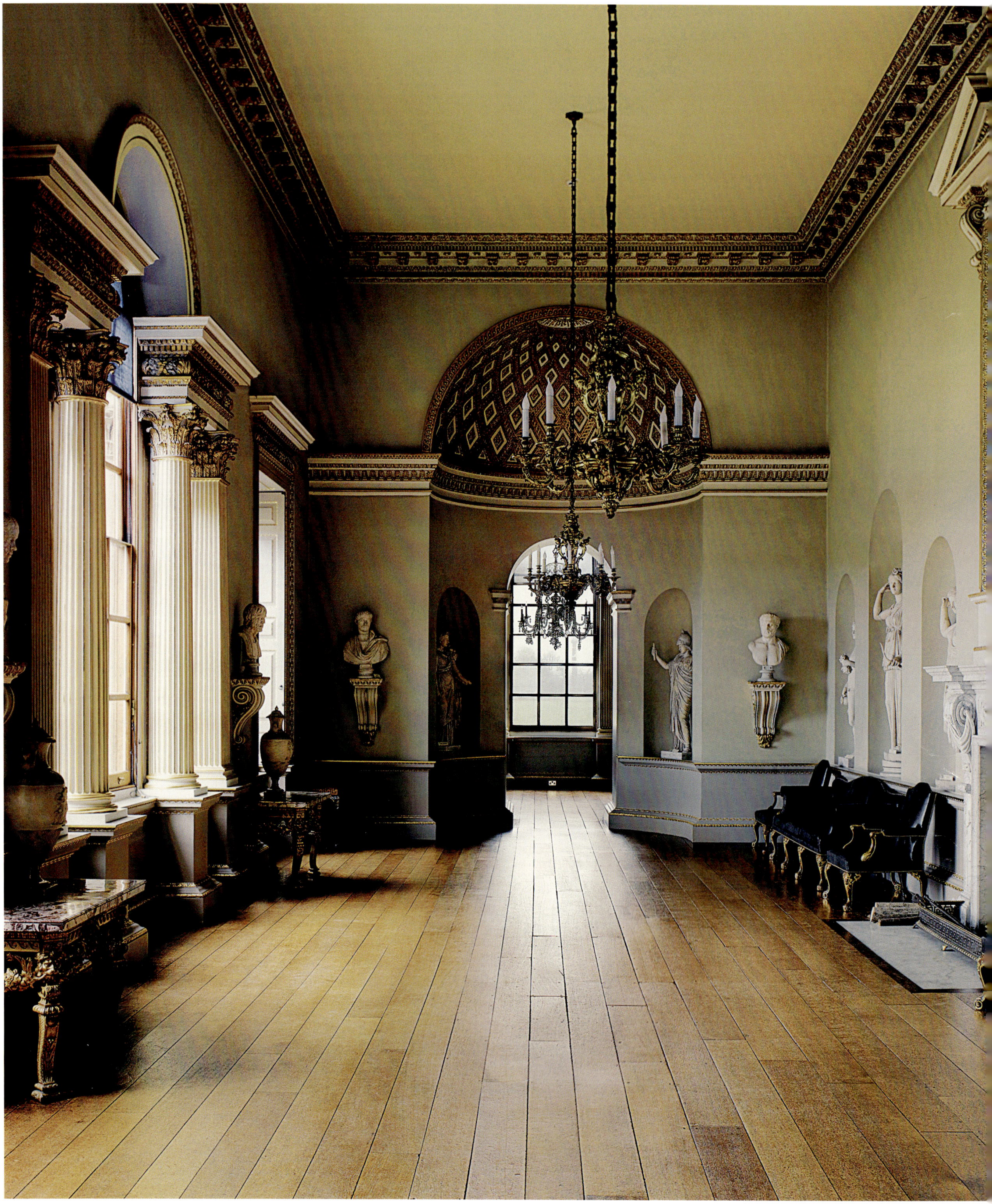

HOLKHAM HALL, NORFOLK

Holkham Hall was created as a purpose-built palace in a remote spot near the north-east coast of Norfolk in 1734–65 to form an appropriately designed Classical setting for a collection of antique and modern works of art, mostly from Italy. This unique product of the Grand Tour was conceived by Thomas Coke (1697–1754), a keen Whig who was created Lord Lovell by George II in 1728 and, at Sir Robert Walpole's instigation, Viscount Coke and Earl of Leicester in 1744. A synthesis of antique, Palladian, Baroque and modern Classicism, this tribute to the cultural impact of Italy from Ancient Rome to the mid-eighteenth century was carried out by Coke, and subsequently his widow, with advice from the Earl of Burlington and with the help of the architect, Matthew Brettingham, and of William Kent. Coke was a patron and collector for forty-five years, but on his death in 1759 the body of the house was still only a partially decorated shell, though he had been living in the family wing for some years and had also seen the sculpture gallery completed. The slow progress on the house was partly due to the enormous financial loss he sustained in the South Sea Bubble in 1720.

Coke had been sent on his Grand Tour in 1712 aged fifteen with a Cambridge don as tutor, returning six years later in 1718, in which year he married. With an annual disposable income of £10,000, he began collecting as a boy and was passionate about architecture from the start. He travelled in France, Switzerland and Germany as well as Italy, unusually for that period seeing Greek temples at Paestum and in Sicily. In Rome in 1714, he met William Kent whom he employed as his agent in buying works of art, and was taught architecture by Kent's friend, the Roman architect, Giacomo Mariari. He was also advised by

Above: *The entrance front is low like an Ancient Roman villa and built of the brick recommended by Vitruvius, but the grandeur of the estate is clear from William Kent's 80-foot high obelisk on the horizon.*

Left: *Conceived for a major collection of antique sculpture, still in situ today, the Statue Gallery, a larger version of Lord Burlington's at Chiswick, was possibly inspired by the planning of Scamozzi's 'House of the Ancients'.*

FROM PALLADIO TO POMPEII · 53

an antiquarian, probably Francesco de' Ficorini, on his first acquisitions of antique sculpture of which he eventually formed what is still the finest private collection in England. It was during his Grand Tour that Coke conceived the idea of replacing his ancestral seat at Holkham, where the grounds were prepared from 1722. He began to plant the park in 1726, building an 80-foot high obelisk by William Kent in 1730–32 as a focal point in a grove of ilexes, the Classical oak tree. A drawing by Kent, perhaps from a window in the house, shows the relation across the landscape of the 'seat on the mount', which he built south west of the house, and one of the pavilions at the end of the lawn by the south pool. He opened out the vista, providing scattered trees, which suggest nature taking over from a more formal garden.

Undated drawings by Matthew Brettingham for the house, now in the British Library, have recently been attributed to 1726, which would predate the arrival of Burlington and Kent. They include the corner towers, going back to Scamozzi's *villa rustica* of 1616 and to Wilton, which are close to what was built, but they also show a mezzanine storey, which was not executed. More significantly, they do not include the four wings with which Coke had decided to enlarge the house by the time building began in 1734. These final designs for the house were doubtless made *c*.1731–34, following discussions with Burlington and Kent. On the model of the wings at Palladio's never completed Villa Mocenigo, the four wings at Holkham were intended respectively for the family, chapel, guests and kitchen. Their construction showed a novel if costly concern for convenience. In *The Plan, Elevations and Sections, of Holkham in Norfolk* (1761), Brettingham made few references to Kent, though his characteristic, free-hand designs for the house and park buildings survive in the archives at Holkham, where he was responsible for the interior decoration of the family wing, contributions to the design of the Marble Hall, designs for the furniture, and the layout of the gardens.

Kent's surviving drawings show that he wanted to rusticate the main block of the house right up to the cornice and add a frieze of swags, though such overall rustication is technically incorrect since, according to the rules, it should be only on the ground floor to suggest the strength needed to carry the weight of the upper storeys. Coke rejected this fancy decoration as not fitting his conception of a Roman house, so Kent used it instead at his Treasury Buildings of 1733–37 in Horse Guards Parade. The grave austerity of the exteriors of Holkham was further emphasized by the substitution of locally made, yellow stock bricks for the Bath stone of which Coke had originally intended to build it. These were thought to resemble Roman bricks, Vitruvius having recommended brick for villas as economical. Palladio's villas, of course, were of stuccoed brick.

The composition of Holkham is anti-Baroque in its rejection of flowing masses building up to a central climax. Instead, it consists of separate, equal parts, a concatenation of forms creating a staccato effect which we might consider Neo-Classical, though it was criticized as un-Classical by William Chambers in his *Treatise on Civil*

The Drawing Room, always hung with red silk velvet, contrasts strikingly with the chaste Statue Gallery adjacent. The sumptuous frieze with gilded griffins is from the Temple of Antoninus and Faustina in the Roman Forum.

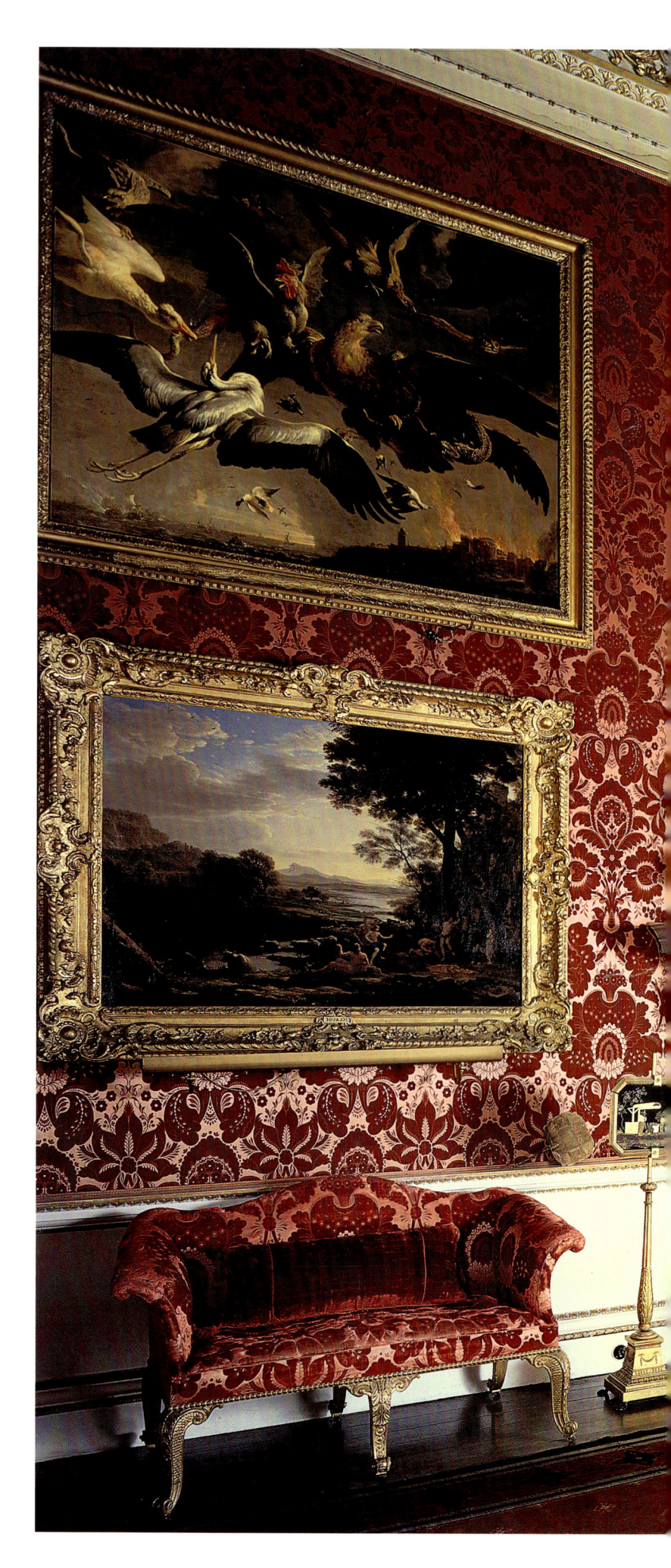

FROM PALLADIO TO POMPEII · 55

56 · THE EIGHTEENTH CENTURY

Architecture (1759). He complained of the number of Venetian windows on the entrance front: 'no less than seven of them, which added to the quantity of trifling breaks, and ups, and downs, in the elevation, keep the spectator's eye in a particular dance to discover the outlines.'

Building began in 1734 on the south-west family wing, where Coke chose to make his beloved library the principal interior. Its coved ceiling echoes that in Longhena's library of 1641–53 at the monastery of San Giorgio Maggiore, Venice, which he had seen on a visit with Kent in 1714. The only room completed at Holkham to Kent's designs in his lifetime, he had wanted to adorn it with Roman arabesques, nudes and shells, but instead it was decorated in white and gold, probably representing Coke's chaste Classical taste. Over the chimney-piece is a Roman mosaic of a lion and shepherd, supposedly from Hadrian's Villa at Tivoli, while busts over the bookcases recall the elder Pliny's reference to 'likenesses set up in libraries in honour of those whose immortal spirits speak to us in the same places.' Here, Coke's old tutor, Domenico Ferrari, presided as curator of a major collection of books and manuscripts, including the Leicester Codex, a note book of Leonardo da Vinci, which was sold in 1980.

The main house containing the state apartments owes much to the Ancient Roman house as described by Vitruvius and reconstructed by Palladio to illustrate Daniele Barbaro's edition of Vitruvius. Indeed, it is entered through the Marble Hall for which, according to Brettingham, 'The idea ... was suggested by the Earl himself, from the judicious and learned Palladio's example of a Basilica, or tribunal of justice, exhibited in his Designs for Monsignor Barbaro's translation of Vitruvius.' It may have been Kent's imaginative genius that translated Coke's ideas into an exciting three-dimensional space, though in 1757 when building was under way Coke dropped the original proposal for a double, semi-circular staircase in favour of one consisting of a single straight flight. This would have been dominated half way up by the colossal statue of Jupiter, which he had acquired in Rome in 1717, thus making the Marble Hall resemble a Roman temple with its cult statue.

Six of the eighteen, fluted Ionic columns of variegated Derbyshire alabaster, coloured purple, light brown and ivory, form a semi-circular apse round the top of the staircase. This is indebted to the similar theatrical arrangement before the choir of Palladio's church of the Redentore in Venice. The Order of the columns is that of the Temple of Fortuna Virilis in Rome, and Coke instructed that it should be based on the plates in Desgodetz's *Les édifices antiques de Rome* (1682).

The modern visitor normally moves from the Marble Hall to the State Dining Room, a dining room being an unusual designation in a house plan of this date. A plain white cube broken only by the apsed and coffered service niche, it was unexpectedly designed to display four, superb antique busts of the goddess Juno, the Emperors Marcus Aurelius and Lucius Verus, and Geta, brother of Caracalla, by whom he was assassinated. The adjacent Statue Gallery, virtually all white with apses containing coffering inspired by the Temple of Venus and Roma, is an enlarged version of Burlington's gallery at Chiswick, as

Thomas Coke's important collection of books and manuscripts was housed in William Kent's library-cum-living room in the family wing. Kent wanted to adorn its coved ceiling with Classical arabesques.

Brettingham acknowledged in his book on Holkham. After the Earl of Arundel's gallery by Inigo Jones *c.*1618 at Arundel House in the Strand, this was the first gallery in England designed specifically for sculpture, and not intermingled with paintings.

Coke, who was one of the very few Englishmen to take a serious and extended interest in Classical works of art in the first half of the eighteenth century, displayed Ancient Roman masterpieces in the long central section of this gallery: eleven statues in niches and eight busts on brackets, mainly bought by him in 1716–17 on his Grand Tour, or in 1749–52 with the younger Brettingham as his agent in Rome. These included the gem of the collection, a bust of Thucydides, after an important Greek original; an Aphrodite after an original of the fifth century BC, attributed to Callimachus or, recently, to the school of Polycleitus; a statue of Marsyas from the collection of Cardinal Albani; and a Diana, a statue supposedly described by Cicero.

The other state rooms are highly coloured as a background for paintings, beginning with the drawing room, hung with crimson flowered silk velvet (now an Edwardian cut velvet). It has a ceiling based on a design by Inigo Jones but with a griffin frieze, added at Coke's suggestion in 1757, inspired by Desgodetz's engraving of that at the Temple of Antoninus and Faustina in the Roman Forum.

The saloon, the main reception room of the house in the centre of the garden front, was planned to contain eight paintings on historical and mythological subjects, hung on still surviving cut wool velvet, a Genoa caffoy ordered in 1754. These included Pietro da Cortona's *Coriolanus* and Giuseppe Chiari's *Continence of Scipio*, both commissioned in Rome and framed for Holkham in 1758. They are in a style we might consider Baroque, but their Classical themes made them suitable for Coke with his great knowledge of ancient literature. Antique features elsewhere in the room include the coffered ceiling with diminishing octagonal panels containing rosettes, inspired by those in Desgodetz's plates of the Basilica of Maxentius. The room contains two superb pier tables with tops made from sections of Ancient Roman mosaic pavements found at Hadrian's Villa at Tivoli.

The Landscape Room, an ante-room in Lord Leicester's state apartment, is devoted principally to paintings by Claude, some bought from Cardinal Albani, hung on crimson Genoa damask as a more delicate and subdued background for the Classical landscapes. The adjacent Green State Bedroom has walls hung with tapestry, old fashioned but chosen for warmth. The enormous chapel was completed in 1761 by Coke's widow, who dismissed Brettingham and appointed in his place James Miller, a fine woodcarver, to work on the interiors. The interior of the chapel is his design, with its walls lined half way up with light-brown Staffordshire alabaster below a Greek key frieze. The massive grandeur of the room is emphasized by an ambitious coffered ceiling, doubtless indebted to illustrations of Ancient Roman temples in a book published five years after Kent's death: Robert Wood's *The Ruins of Palmyra, Otherwise Tedmor, In the Desart* (1753).

The magnificent Marble Hall draws inventively on the Temple of Venus and Roma, Basilica of Maxentius, Temple of Fortuna Virilis and Pantheon in Rome. The apse, with its columnar screen, is unique in English country houses.

FROM PALLADIO TO POMPEII · 59

WEST WYCOMBE PARK, BUCKINGHAMSHIRE

As an architectural composition, West Wycombe Park lacks the clarity of aim for which most of the houses in this book have been selected, but its west portico and interiors represent an ambitious attempt to create the perfect Classical house. It was given its present form between 1748 and 1771 as a key product of Grand Tour mentality by Sir Francis Dashwood, 2nd Baronet, (1708–81). He undertook three Grand Tours, travelling first in Italy in 1729–31, staying in Venice and Padua, and then visiting St Petersburg on a diplomatic mission in 1733. He made a more significant tour of Italy in 1739–41, taking in Florence, Modena, Siena, Rome and Herculaneum, where he saw the beginning of the excavations. He met antiquarians and writers such as Montesquieu, and sent back from Livorno crates of marble, paintings and sculpture. He also travelled in Greece and Asia Minor and may even have visited Egypt.

If not the actual founder of the Society of Dilettanti in 1732, Dashwood played a central role in it throughout his life, establishing as an offshoot of it *c.*1745 the wonderfully wicked Hellfire Club, variously known as the Monks of Medmenham and the Society of Saint Francis of Wycombe. An exceptionally cultivated man, he was a Fellow of the Royal Society and of the Society of Antiquaries and, somewhat improbably, Chancellor of the Exchequer in Lord Bute's administration until Bute fell in 1763, in which year he succeeded as 11th Baron Le Despencer.

Dashwood inherited West Wycombe in 1724, a substantial if somewhat dull, three-storeyed house built by his father *c.*1709. He made extensive alterations to this from 1748, creating a new Jonesian north

Above: The entrance front by Nicholas Revett of 1770–71 was known at the time as the 'Temple of Bacchus', its Greek Ionic portico being modelled on the temple to that god at Teos in modern Turkey.

Right: The hall formed in the 1750s is an early recreation of an Ancient Roman atrium with its screen of Tuscan columns at each end, a ceiling after one at Palmyra, and even a hypocaust.

FROM PALLADIO TO POMPEII · 61

front and porticoes at the east and west ends, as well as adding a colonnaded south front. His architectural tastes were probably influenced by his uncle, the Hon. John Fane, who became his guardian after his father's death in 1724, when Dashwood was just sixteen. At this moment, Fane was building Mereworth Castle, Kent, from Palladian designs by Colen Campbell. Closer in spirit to what Dashwood was to create at West Wycombe was the church at Mereworth, built by Fane in 1744–46 as an archaeological recreation of a Roman basilica. Dashwood began at West Wycombe by remodelling the north and east ranges of the house in 1748–50, where his eastern portico seems inspired by those on the pavilions at Mereworth Castle.

In a second phase of building in 1755, he turned to the more important south front, using John Donowell as draughtsman and clerk of the works, rather than as an architect. He may have sketched out the initial drawings himself, for he had made a design for remodelling the old house as early as 1739. His long south front with its two-storeyed colonnade, or loggia, possibly more appropriate for a hotter climate, seems inspired by the two-storeyed peristyle in Palladio's reconstruction of a Roman house in Daniele Barbaro's edition of Vitruvius (1556), though there are similar features in Palladio's Villa Cornaro and in his first designs for the Palazzo Chiericati. The neo-antique flavour at West Wycombe is underlined by the unusual use of a baseless Doric Order for the ground-floor colonnade, though this is irregularly combined with a Roman Corinthian Order on the first floor.

The ceiling of the ground-floor colonnade has three Bacchanalian frescoes by Borgnis showing Bacchus crowning Ariadne, flanked by panels of young bacchanals at play. Bacchus/Dionysus, the ancient god of wine and intoxication, and of ecstasy and ritual madness, was seen as a subversive figure, both man and animal, male and effeminate, young and old. He was a natural choice for Dashwood as an antiquarian with a reputation for debauchery. These Bacchic frescoes in the manner of Annibale Carracci or Veronese were regarded in 1776 by the Duchess of Northumberland, a perceptive sightseer and architectural patron, as 'in the stile of the antique'. Their artist, Giuseppe Borgnis, born at Craveggia near Domodossola in 1701, was trained in Bologna and Venice and called to England by Dashwood *c.*1751. He worked at West Wycombe until his death in 1761. He and his two

Right: *The walls of the imposing staircase hall were painted in* grisaille *by the Piedmontese artist, Giuseppe Borgnis, c.1755–60, following the recommendations of Vitruvius, though taking Raphael and Annibale Carracci as his models.*

Below: *The sunlit, open, entrance portico leads surprisingly into this shadowy vestibule, an ante-room evoking the atmosphere of an Ancient Roman tomb with its segmental vault and marbled walls.*

62 · THE EIGHTEENTH CENTURY

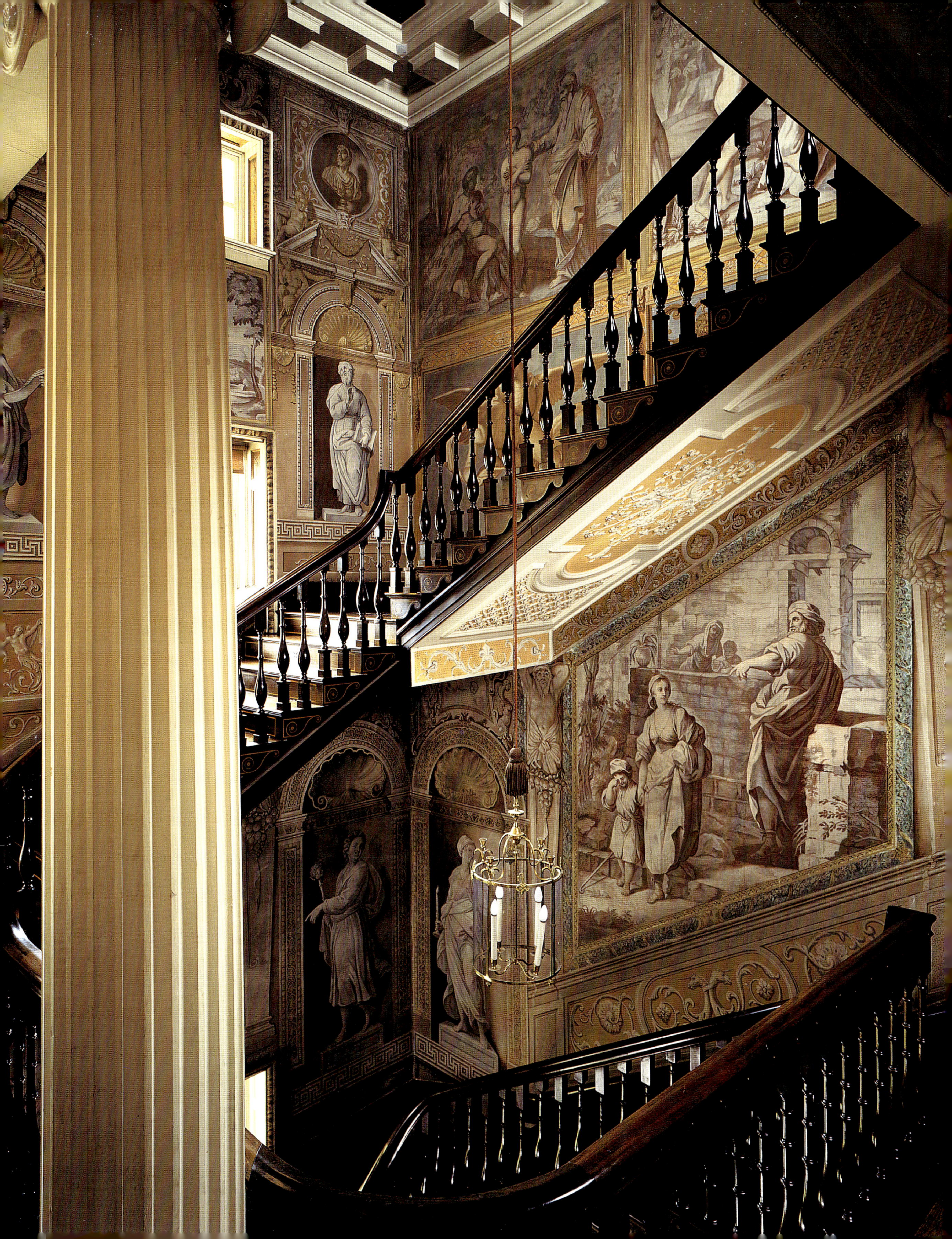

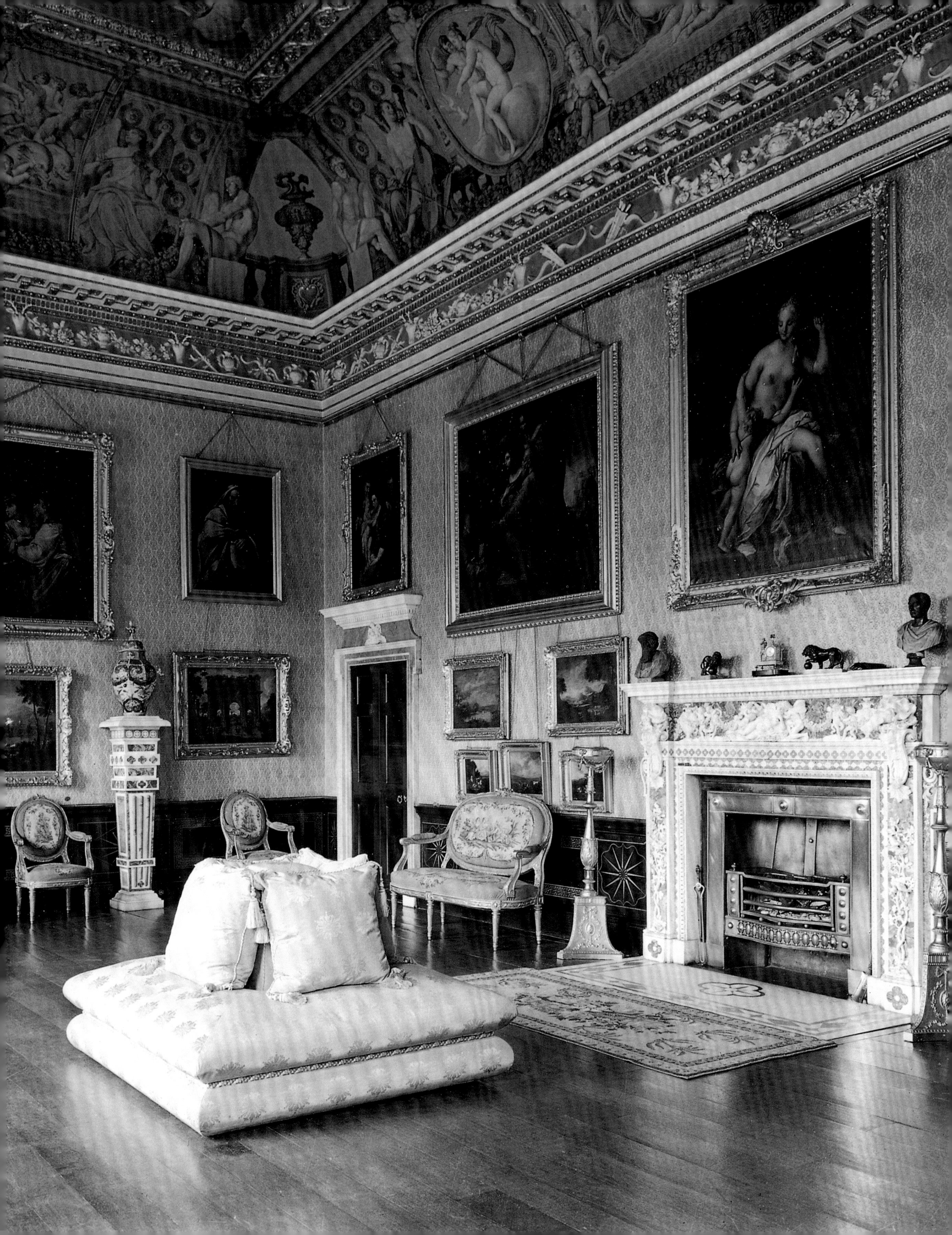

sons were the ideal decorative painters for Augustan England, playing to the increasingly antiquarian taste of the mid-eighteenth century.

Dashwood remodelled the entrance hall as a Classical atrium, giving it a *trompe l'œil* ceiling by Borgnis modelled on one in the southern adyton (unlit chamber) at the Temple of Bel (the Levantine god Ba'al) at Palmyra, Syria. Featuring a central rosette surrounded by octagonal coffering, its source was, of course, the plates in Robert Wood's *Ruins of Palmyra* (1753) to which Dashwood was a subscriber. The room was also given a hypocaust, with brick hot-air flues, based on one recently excavated near Lincoln. The decoration of other interiors has a richer flavour with mythological frescoes by Borgnis of *c.*1760, as in Roman Renaissance and Baroque palaces. These include the music room with a ceiling from Raphael's *Banquet of the Gods* in the garden loggia of Peruzzi's Villa Farnesina, and figures in the high cove from Annibale Carracci's ceiling in the gallery of the Palazzo Farnese. Borgnis had probably based these on engravings.

All this work can be seen as neo-antique, for Vitruvius had said that the ancients decorated their rooms with life-sized paintings of the gods and other mythological heroes, though he lamented the decadent style of fresco painting in his own day. Since there were no surviving large-scale Ancient Roman paintings of gods for Dashwood and Borgnis to follow, they echoed the fresco paintings of Renaissance Italy. The staircase was also decorated with full-length figures of gods as recommended by Vitruvius, though following models by Raphael in the Vatican Loggie and by Carracci at the Palazzo Farnese. Two further interiors, the Red Drawing Room and the tapestry room of the later 1760s, represent a closer attempt to revive antiquity with painted ceilings inspired by stuccoed work at Hadrian's Villa at Tivoli. That in the tapestry room by the Scottish decorator, William Hannan, is based on a drawing by Francesco Santi Bartoli in the library at Eton College, where Dashwood had been educated.

In 1763, Dashwood was chairman of the committee of the Society of Dilettanti, which drew up the instructions for the first archaeological expedition to be financed by an institution. This was to conduct

Above: *In the Blue Drawing Room, originally the dining room, the ceiling by Borgnis is based on one by Carracci in the Palazzo Farnese; the frieze derives from the Tomb of Bacchus, then in Santa Costanza, Rome.*

Left: *Borgnis's music room ceiling echoes Raphael and Carracci, while the sumptuous chimneypiece in white marble and Sicilian jasper is by Henry Cheere, who probably also designed the marble pedestal, one of four in the room.*

archaeological fieldwork on sites in Ionia, western Asia Minor, in 1764–66, the results of which were presented at a meeting of the Society of Dilettanti in 1767 and published as *Ionian Antiquities* (2 vols, 1769–97), a copy of which Dashwood presented in person to King George III. This included the Temple of Dionysus (Bacchus) at Teos, about twenty-five miles south of Smyrna (Izmir), of which Nicholas Revett made drawings. In 1770, Dashwood commissioned Revett to build a monumental new entrance portico on the west front of West Wycombe, based on this temple. An archaeological continuation of the Bacchic theme of the decorations of the south colonnade, it was completed in 1771 when it was known as the 'Temple of Bacchus'. It fulfilled the ambition of the Society of Dilettanti, which, according to a review of the *Ionian Antiquities* in 1770, was to give support 'to the revival of Greek architecture in its purest stile.'

It is not always recognized today that this is the earliest and most convincing large-scale recreation of a Greek temple in Europe in the eighteenth century. Its model, the hexastyle, peripteral Temple of Dionysus was built in the Ionic Order *c.*220–205 BC from designs by the Hellenistic architect and theorist, Hermogenes of Priene. According to Vitruvius, who mentioned it twice, Hermogenes wrote a book on it. It was the largest temple dedicated to Dionysus in the ancient world, though all that survives of it today are the platform and two re-erected columns. In the Ionic columns of the recreation of its portico at West Wycombe, Revett omitted the fluting of the antique original, but it still has a strongly Greek flavour with its shallow pediment of a lower pitch than that preferred by the Romans. Hermogenes, significantly, was himself an architect who harked back to an earlier phase of Greek architecture than that of his own day.

The ceiling of the portico was painted with simulated coffering of Palmyrene inspiration and with frescoes by William Hannan in October 1770. These depicted in the centre *Night in her Chariot*, flanked by *Bacchus and Ariadne* after Guido Reni, and *A Bacchic Procession*. The right hand of the two doors in the portico leads into the vestibule or ante-room by Revett, with a segmental coffered vault, perhaps inspired by the underground tomb chambers of Ancient Rome. Considered as a garden temple rather than part of the house, the portico or 'Temple of Bacchus' was dedicated in 1771 with an amazing reconstruction of an ancient religious ceremony. A contemporary described how:

a procession was formed of Bacchanals, Priests, Priestesses, Pan, Fauns, Satyrs, Silenus etc, all in proper habits & skins, wreathed in vine leaves, ivy, oak etc. On the arrival of the procession in the portico the High Priest addressed the statue [of Bacchus] in an invocation which was succeeded by several hymns and other pieces of music suitable to the occasion, & having finished the sacrifice proceeded through the groves to a Tent pitched at the head of the lake where the Paeans and libations were repeated – then ferrying to a vessel adorned with colours & streamers, again performed various ceremonies with discharges of cannon & bursts of acclamation from the populace.

The state rooms of 1748–50, with frescoes of mythological scenes reflecting those which Dashwood had seen in Rome in the 1730s, may be regarded as in a different mode from the sequence of marmoreal rooms at West Wycombe, probably inspired more by Revett than by Borgnis. Beginning with the 'Temple of Bacchus' itself, these are followed by the vestibule, loggia or south colonnade, the grand entrance hall and the first hall or Palmyra Room. With their inlaid marble pavements, marbled walls and ceilings with illusionistic coffering, these form a sculpture gallery with statues, casts, busts on brackets and sculpture on marble-topped tables. They constitute an imaginative and unusual attempt to recreate the atria or courtyards of Ancient Roman houses.

No less remarkable is the huge mausoleum, described by Howard Colvin as 'probably the largest built in Europe since Antiquity', which Dashwood built in 1764–65 on a hill outside the park, probably with Donowell as architect. A roofless, hexagonal enclosure with walls pierced by tall open arches and columbaria, it is inspired by the Tomb of the Household of Augustus on the Via Appia, Rome, and by the Mausoleum of Augustus near the Tiber in Rome of which, by the eighteenth century, only the outer walls survived with the interior used as a garden. These monuments would have been known to Dashwood from sources such as the engravings by Piranesi in *Antichità Romane* (vol. III, 1756), and by Francesco Bianchini in *Camera ed inscrizioni sepulchri de' liberti, servi … della casa di Augusto …* (1727). In his astonishing, neo-antique mausoleum, Dashwood placed the remains of his family and monuments of his ancestors.

The eclectic assembly at West Wycombe of ancient and Renaissance Italianate echoes was continued in the park with features such as a milestone copied from that in the Roman Forum, a version of the Tower of the Winds in Athens in 1759, and Nicholas Revett's elegant Music Temple of 1778–80, which survives on one of the three islands in the lake. The deliciously watery landscaped park was developed in several phases: first, in the formal manner in 1739; next in 1752 by Maurice-Louis Jolivet, a pupil of Servandoni, in a more Rococo manner; and then by Revett and Thomas Cook, a pupil of 'Capability' Brown, in the 'natural' Brownian style in 1770–81, after which it was recorded in eight views painted by Thomas Daniell in 1781. Humphry Repton who made modest changes in 1794–95 complained of 'the profusion of buildings and ornament which the false taste of the last age lavished upon this spot.' However, the antique passion of the eighteenth century was revived in further striking additions made in the 1980s and 1990s for Sir Francis Dashwood, 11th Baronet, by Quinlan Terry: the Ionic Temple of Venus, a reconstruction of a building by Donowell of 1745–48, Edward's Bridge, and the Cricket Pavilion, designed as the Vitruvian 'primitive hut.'

The approach to the 'Temple of Bacchus', with the central niche housing a lead statue of Bacchus, is protected by magnificent sphinxes, appropriate here as they were seen as guardian spirits in Greek art.

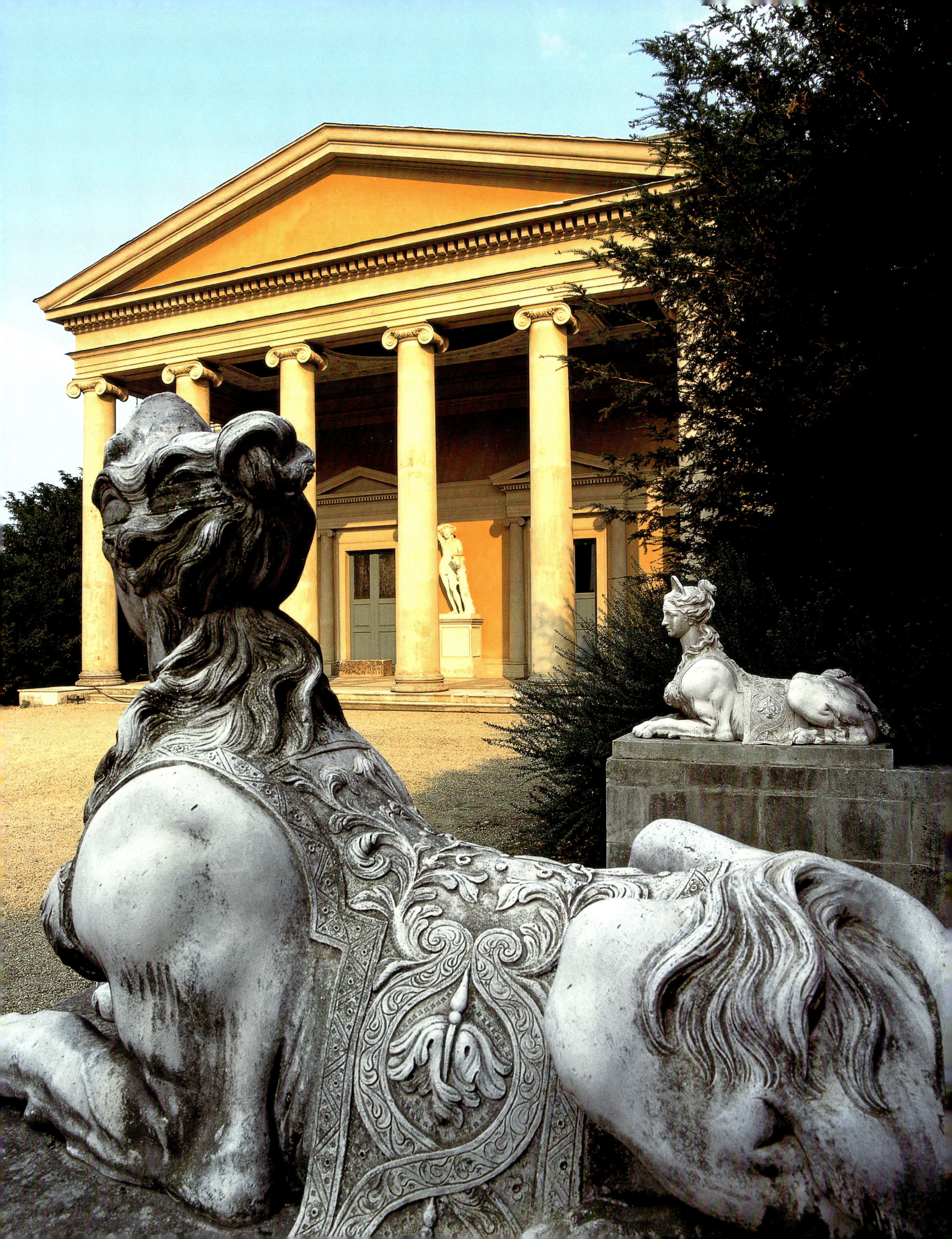

KEDLESTON HALL, DERBYSHIRE

With its breathtaking axial sequence from columnar hall to domed saloon, both lined with casts of antique sculpture, and its garden front inspired by the Arch of Constantine, Kedleston is probably the grandest response to the architecture of Imperial Rome in any English country house. The property had been in the possession of the Curzon family since the twelfth century when a red-brick mansion was built c.1700 by William and Francis Smith of Warwick for Sir Nathaniel Curzon, 2nd Baronet. This seemed insufficiently sophisticated in 1757–58 when his grandson, Nathaniel Curzon (who became the 5th Baronet in 1758), invited three architects, including James 'Athenian' Stuart and Matthew Brettingham, to design interiors in the house in order to display his collection of paintings and plaster casts.

Though he never undertook the Grand Tour to Italy, Curzon was a poet and connoisseur who inherited at least a hundred pictures from his predecessors and began his own collection when in France, Belgium and Holland in 1749. He bought over fifty paintings at London sales between 1753 and 1759, and also acquired casts, comprising twenty-one statues and twenty-six busts, in 1756–58 with the help of dealers in Italy, including Matthew Brettingham, junior.

Curzon had succeeded his father as MP for Derbyshire and taken over Kedleston at the age of twenty-eight in 1754. Following his father's death in November 1758, he began to demolish the house and to replace it with a new one on the same site from ambitious designs, which he commissioned from Matthew Brettingham, senior. In December 1758, a new figure appeared on the scene in the form of the canny Robert Adam to whom Curzon showed the designs of his rival, 'Athenian' Stuart. Adam ridiculed these in a letter to his brother as crowded

with belts of Stone and great Pannels & Roses and festoon & figures all Ramm'd in wherever there was a hole to be got for them. & he wanted to fitt frames for Sir Nat's Pictures but not having, or rather I suppose, not being willing to confine his Genius to the sizes of the pictures, he Cutts 3 foot off the length of the best pictures ... to make them answer, and Draws all the Pictures & Colour them in his Drawings But they are So ill done that they move pity rather than contempt.

This shows how terrified Adam was that Stuart, with his unique, first-hand knowledge of Ancient Greek architecture and ornament –

68 · THE EIGHTEENTH CENTURY

Above: *Adam's remarkable south front, designed in 1768, echoes the Arch of Constantine in Rome. John Soane, normally an admirer of Adam, questioned the propriety of applying a triumphal arch to a private house.*

Left: *The entrance front, with hexastyle portico and quadrant corridors leading to substantial wings, was inspired by Palladio's uncompleted Villa Mocenigo. Begun by Brettingham in 1758, it was continued by Paine, and completed by Adam from 1761.*

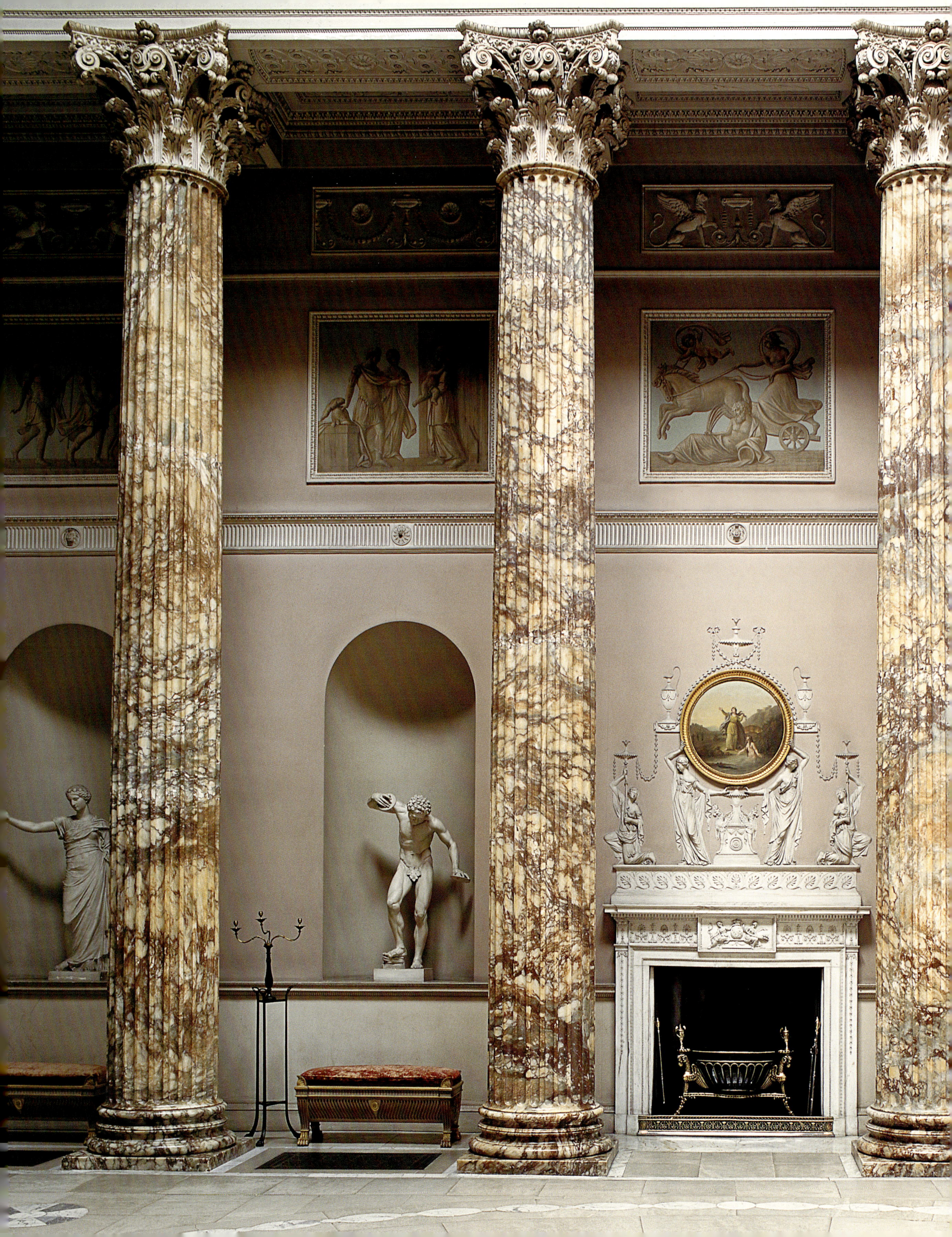

shortly to be published in the first volume of *The Antiquities of Athens* (1762) – would steal all his best clients as the most fashionable designer going. Adam therefore took advantage of the occasion by showing some of his own drawings to Curzon who, as he wrote to his brother James on 11 December, was 'struck all of a heap with wonder and amaze' by them, and 'made him grieve at his previous engagement with Brettingham.' When Curzon showed Brettingham's designs to Adam, he proposed a few changes, cleverly suggesting that Curzon 'might call them his own fancies.' Had Adam been on the scene a month earlier, it seems clear that he rather than Brettingham would have gained the commission for the new house. However, his time was soon to come.

The house which was begun from Brettingham's designs in 1759 consisted of a central block with four wings linked by quadrant corridors, as at Palladio's Villa Mocenigo and its English echoes, Holkham Hall, Norfolk (1734–65) and Nostell Priory, Yorkshire (*c*.1737–*c*.1750), the latter with interiors by Robert Adam of 1766–75. Brettingham was the executant architect of Holkham which, together with Houghton, was the model for Kedleston as a seat with rooms of state to receive major guests who would promote the patron's political career, and in which Old Master paintings and Classical sculpture would be displayed to please and impress visitors. Work began with the north-east pavilion, the family wing, but by the end of 1759 Brettingham left the project to make designs for Lord Lowther at Lowther Castle, Westmorland. Curzon employed in his place James Paine, who had been the executant architect, though not the designer, of Nostell Priory and was at the time working at Chatsworth in Derbyshire.

In building the north-west pavilion, the kitchen wing, at Kedleston in 1759, Paine followed Brettingham's designs, but for the body of the house he dramatically transformed Brettingham's plans. His principal innovation here was to create a Pantheon-like rotunda, projecting on

Above: The saloon, approached axially from the hall, is 62-foot high and 42-foot in diameter, with an octagonally coffered dome and four apsed and coffered niches. It serves no purpose other than that of display.

Left: Approached directly from the entrance portico, the top-lit hall is an imposing, neo-antique space, shown in Paine's plan but executed with some alterations by Adam, who introduced the chimneypieces with their elegant stuccowork decoration.

FROM PALLADIO TO POMPEII · 71

the south garden front as a domed, semi-circular temple, ringed with giant, free-standing columns like the Temple of Vesta at Tivoli. Such a feature was unprecedented in country-house design, but Eileen Harris has suggested that Paine's model could have been the reconstruction of Pliny's Laurentine Villa in Robert Castell's *The Villas of the Ancients Illustrated* (1728), a copy of which was in Curzon's library.

Such a monumental scheme must have seemed prohibitively expensive, even to someone like Curzon with a vast fortune derived from land and coal-mines, but Robert Adam who, as we have seen, first met Curzon in December 1758, intervened again by proposing as early as May 1760 a more economical but still imposing arrangement. Paine's projecting templar structure was to be replaced by an echo of the Arch of Constantine in Rome, applied more or less flat to a projection on the garden front, rather as in one of Adam's models, the much admired Trevi Fountain (1732–37) in Rome by Nicola Salvi.

By 1760, Adam was already designing ceilings, wall decorations and furnishings for the family pavilion and the state rooms on the east front, while Paine continued work on the west front. However, Paine left suddenly in 1761 when Adam took complete charge, though keeping Paine's plan, with the exception of the templar projection of the saloon on the garden front and of the domed staircase hall between the saloon and the hall. Ice-cold, since it is approached directly from the north portico with no intervening entrance vestibule, the vast hall is 67-foot by 37-foot in plan and 40-foot high, and is lined with twenty columns of pink, veined Nottinghamshire alabaster, 25-foot high, with capitals of white marble. In between the columns are panels, which Adam filled with *grisailles* in imitation of antique bas-reliefs and, below these, niches containing statues. Adam retained Paine's articulation of the room, which had been inspired by Palladio's probably over imaginative reconstruction in *Quattro Libri* of the interior of what he called the Temple of Mars, in fact the Temple of Deified Hadrian (AD 145), now part of the Rome Stock Exchange.

With the aim of displaying the place as an historic site like those visited on the Grand Tour, Curzon printed a *Catalogue of the pictures, statues etc., with some account of the architecture at Kedleston* (1769, reprinted in 1770, 1778 and 1796). Here he explained that: 'The Hall and Salloon were after the Greek Hall and Dome of the Ancients, proportioned chiefly from the Pantheon at Rome and from Spalatra [i.e. Spalatro]. The columns were proportioned from the three Columns in the Campo Vaccino at Rome, supposed to have belonged to the Temple of Jupiter Stator [i.e. Castor and Pollux]'.

In keeping with this solemn atmosphere the only furnishings in the hall are a set of twelve benches designed by Adam after the red porphyry bath known as the Sarcophagus of Marcus Agrippa, which had been in the portico of the Pantheon from the twelfth century, where it was illustrated in Antoine Desgdotez's *Les édifices antiques de Rome* (1684). It was taken to St John Lateran, Rome, in 1734 to serve as the tomb of Pope Clement XII in the Corsini Chapel, where it would also have been well known to Adam.

Adam designed the 'Ceiling in the Antique Stile' in the drawing room, the chimneypiece flanked by massive caryatids, and possibly also the sofas with dolphins, sea nymphs and tritons, supplied by John Linnell in 1763.

FROM PALLADIO TO POMPEII · 73

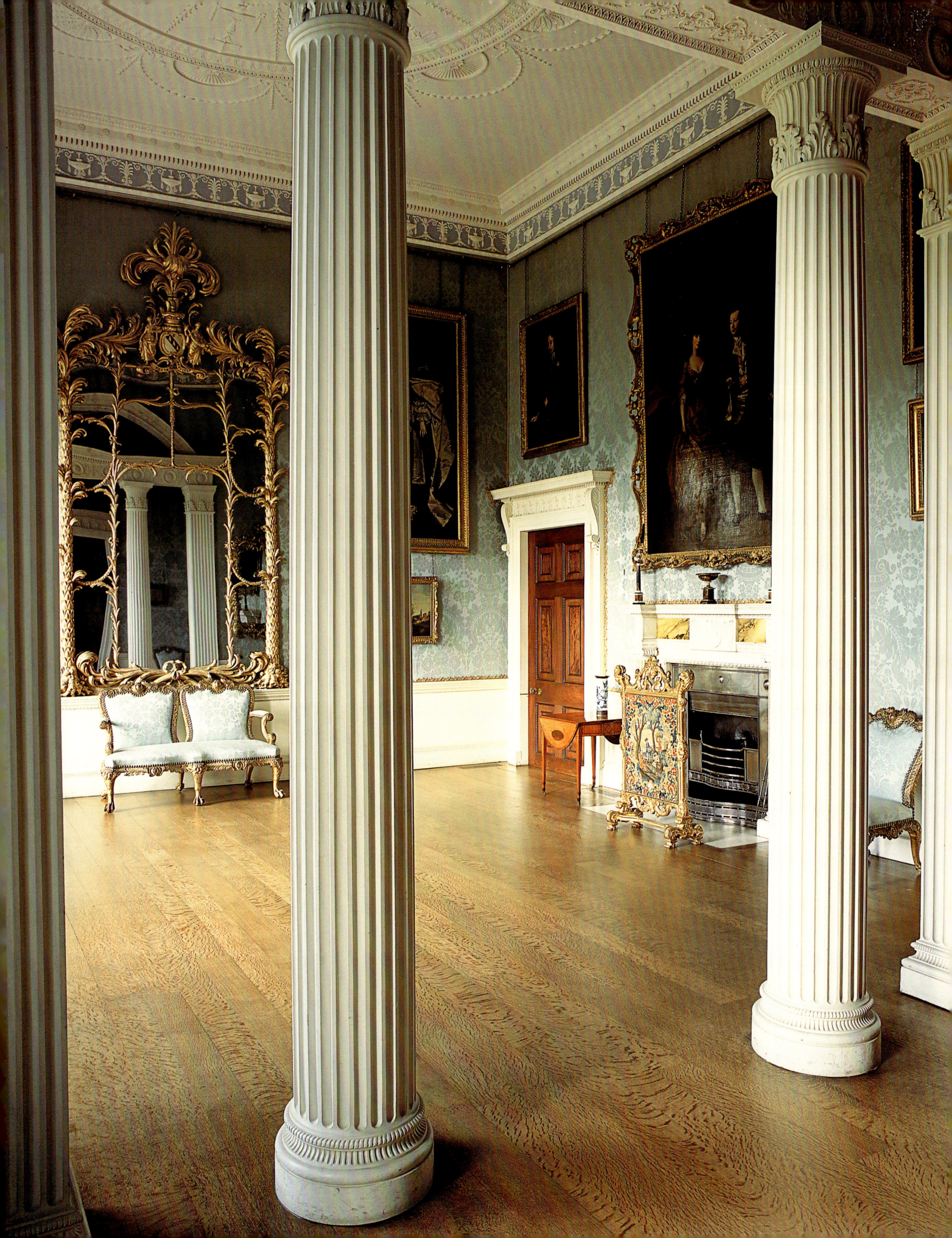

The hall leads directly into the circular saloon or rotunda, an arrangement echoing the relationship between 'atrium' and 'vestibulum' in Roman domestic planning, as described by Adam in *Ruins of the Palace of the Emperor Diocletian at Spalatro* (1764) in which he claimed that the atrium was consecrated to ancestors and hung with military trophies, while the vestibulum was sacred to the gods. There are, indeed, stucco panels of military trophies, including shields and helmets over the doors in the hall, while the form of the saloon, 62-foot high, echoes the Pantheon, a temple, dedicated to all the gods. Its coffering is derived from the Temple of Venus and Roma and the Basilica of Maxentius, doubtless based on the illustrations of them in Palladio's *Quattro Libri*. The spatial contrast between the long, rectangular hall and the circular saloon, 20-foot higher, reflects Adam's claim in his book on Spalatro that Roman interiors provide models of 'diversity of form, as well as of dimensions', in contrast to modern architects who often produce merely 'a dull succession of similar apartments.'

Curzon had planned the house with a suite of three state rooms along the east front, devoted respectively to the arts of music, painting and literature, each with an appropriate architectural Order: Corinthian for the largest and most splendid, the withdrawing room, Ionic for the music room, and Doric for the more austere and masculine library. These contained his principal pictures, including works by Luca Giordano and Benedetto Luti, many set into the walls as part of the fixed architectural scheme.

The west side of the house was conceived as an old-fashioned state apartment consisting of ante-room, bedchamber and dressing room. The last of these leads into the dining room at the north-west angle of the house, where the great, semi-circular apsed niche appears in Paine's design. The radiating plasterwork of its semi-dome and the curved sideboard are by Adam, who placed at the centre of the display a neo-antique, tripod perfume burner made c.1760 from designs by 'Athenian' Stuart. It is an elegant, archaeological reconstruction of the tripod that once stood on the Choragic Monument of Lysicrates in Athens. Its incorporation by Adam is ironical in view of his recent condemnation of Stuart's ability as a designer. However, the tripod, vases and knife cases placed on the sideboard by Adam, and still present today, created an effect described by George Montagu in a letter to his friend, Horace Walpole, following his visit in September 1766, as resembling an ancient altar 'set out for a sacrifice with numberless vases of crystal, lamps, *et cetera*, which has been fetched up from Herculaneum.'

The house may be seen as something of an architectural game of pass-the-parcel with its contributions from Stuart, Brettingham, Paine, Adam, and doubtless Curzon himself, but it has a unity through the superb quality of its craftsmanship and materials, and above all through the guiding hand of Adam in everything from the design of lock furniture and carpets to architecture and complete schemes of interior decoration.

Adam was also a key player in the development of the English eighteenth-century aesthetic of the Picturesque in which he believed that movement was a vital part. He and his brother James explained in their *Works in Architecture* (vol. I, 1773) that: '*Movement* is meant to express, the rise and fall, advance and recess, with other diversity of form, in the different parts of a building, so as to add greatly to the picturesque of the composition. For the rising and falling ... have the same effect in architecture, that hill and dale ... have in landscape.' As an example, they boasted that 'we really do not recollect any example of so much movement and contrast, as in the south front of Kedleston house.' Numerous drawings survive in Adam's hand for the landscaped park and its ornamental buildings at Kedleston, showing that the park was carefully contrived as part of a scene including the house itself. The effect can be seen in two paintings attributed to George Cuitt of c.1780 at the house. Adam's buildings include the Doric north entrance lodge, thatched hermitage and the three-arched bridge, which plays a vital scenic as well as functional role since it commands a fine view of the house from which it also serves as an eye-catcher among the lakes and trees.

No less important is the unique fishing room-cum-boathouse-cum cold bath, a complex structure, which Adam built with great ingenuity c.1770 on two levels on the slope down to the edge of the upper lake. At the centre is the fishing room, lit by a large Venetian window and decorated with neo-antique stuccowork and wall paintings. From this a double stair leads down to the semi-circular cold bath, lit by a window on the edge of the water. No Ancient Roman or Renaissance follower, such as Raphael or Pirro Ligorio, could have designed anything more convincingly Classical or more inventive than this miniature masterpiece.

Above: The austere library, in deliberate contrast to the richness elsewhere in the house, is dominated by the Doric door-case, perhaps suggested by Lord Scarsdale. It boasts the full complement of fluted columns, triglyph frieze and pediment.

Left: The unusual capitals of the columns screening the ante-room from the dressing room were derived from those Adam had discovered in the peristyle at Diocletian's Palace at Spalatro. He also designed the exotic mirror with palm-tree columns.

PACKINGTON HALL, WARWICKSHIRE

The 4th Earl of Aylesford (1751–1812) was the ideal Grand Tour client for an architect: he was an architect *manqué*, a talented painter, a friend of the Picturesque theorist, Uvedale Price, and of the collector, Sir George Beaumont. As Lord Guernsey, he had been well educated at Westminster School and Christ Church, Oxford, laying the foundation that enabled him to become a Fellow of the Royal Society in 1773 and of the Society of Dilettanti in 1776, a Trustee of the British Museum from 1787 to 1812, and the holder of appointments at court. He had travelled in Italy before 1776, probably in 1771–73.

On the death of his father, the 3rd Earl of Aylesford, in 1777, Guernsey inherited the Aylesford earldom at the age of twenty-six, as well as Packington Hall, Warwickshire. This was a large and very old-fashioned Palladian mansion, which was the result of a complete remodelling and encasing in stone for his father in 1766–72 by the elder Matthew Brettingham of a house built in 1693. Few of the interiors were finished in the 3rd Earl's lifetime and, following his marriage in 1781, his son decorated the rooms successively over a number of years. The 4th Earl employed the Italian architect, Joseph Bonomi (1739–1808), who was born in Rome into a successful professional family and became a pupil of the architects Antonio Asprucci and Marchese Teodili. Bonomi came under the influence of the painter, Charles-Louis Clérisseau, by whom, in common with Robert Adam and William Chambers, he was taught draughtsmanship, and doubtless also met the French architectural students at the French Academy in Rome. In 1757, Bonomi probably accompanied Adam on his tour to measure and publish Diocletian's palace at Spalatro and may also have joined Adam's brother James on his expedition in November 1763 to record the Greek temples at Paestum. In 1767, the Adam brothers called Bonomi and Antonio Zucchi to work for them in England, where Bonomi remained for most of the rest of his life.

Above: Bookplate designed for himself in the manner of Piranesi by the 4th Earl of Aylesford, a talented artist.

Right: The Palladian mansion was formed by Brettingham in 1766–72 for the 3rd Earl of Aylesford, who died in 1777 when the interiors were unfinished. In completing them, his son, the 4th Earl, created the Pompeiian Gallery.

76 · THE EIGHTEENTH CENTURY

FROM PALLADIO TO POMPEII · 77

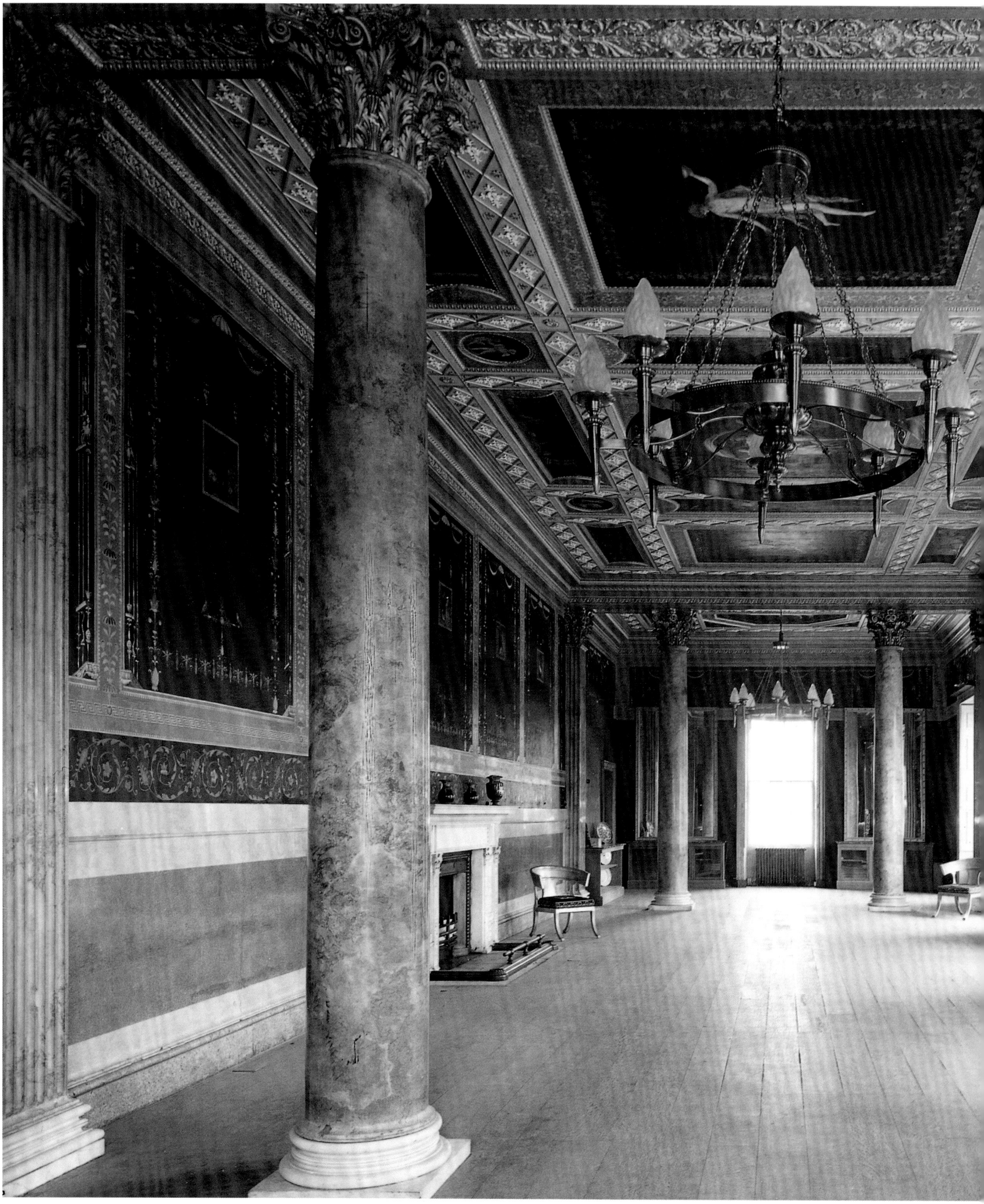

At Packington Hall, the whole of the five-bay, south front on the *piano nobile* had been intended by Brettingham to have been taken up by a gallery, 74-foot long by 22-foot wide. His drawings show its walls lined with semi-circular headed niches containing statues, a development from the sculpture gallery on which he had been involved at Holkham. This was not executed and in August 1782, Bonomi made a design for dividing the space into two rooms, but the decision was soon made to turn it into a single, sparkling, neo-antique gallery. As executed in 1785–88, and variously known as the Pompeiian Gallery or Library, this was one of the most remarkable Neo-Classical interiors in Europe.

Bonomi employed a large team to create it, including the French painter Jean-François Rigaud (1742–1810), the Italian Giovanni Borgnis, son of Giuseppe Borgnis who had worked at West Wycombe, and three craftsmen from the Adam brothers' team: Joseph Rose, junior, responsible for the stuccowork, and two Italians, Benedetto Pastorini, painter and engraver, who had made some of the plates for *The Works in Architecture of Robert and James Adam* (2 vols, 1773–79), and Domenico Bartoli, *scagliola* manufacturer. Rigaud, the most distinguished artist of these, was born in Turin where he studied, as well as in Florence and Bologna. He lived in Rome in 1768–70 and moved to London in 1771 where he became known as John Francis Rigaud. A popular painter of historical subjects, portraits and decorative compositions, he became a Royal Academician in 1784 and died at Packington in 1810.

The lower part of the walls by Pastorini are of *scagliola* imitating panels of porphyry surrounded by borders of Siena marble, a disposition discovered at Pompeii, which Bonomi had visited in May 1784, perhaps with the aim of designing the gallery. The upper parts of the walls and the ceiling panels by Rigaud are powerfully coloured in black and terracotta red, the strength and richness of which were heightened by the application of melted wax blended in with hot irons in an attempt to revive the encaustic technique of the ancients. Described by the elder Pliny and Vitruvius, this process had been the subject of a book of 1755 by the antiquarian, Comte de Caylus, which had been taken up by J. H. Müntz in *Encaustic: or, Count Caylus's Method of Painting in the Manner of the Ancients* (1760). In notes by Rigaud preserved in a memoir by his son, we read of the ceiling: 'painted on the spot in water and size colours, and in the style of Titus' baths, upon a black ground. There are flying figures, alluding to the mysteries of Bacchus; according to the Mythology explained by D'Ankerville [D'Hancarville] ... The whole is painted in the most lively colours of flesh and draperies.'

Pierre-François Hugues, self-styled 'baron d'Hancarville', was the author of *Recherches sur l'origine, l'esprit et les progrès des arts de la Grèce; sur leur connexion avec les arts et de la religion des plus anciens peuples connus* ... (3 vols, 1785), a work widely consulted by collectors and architects, such as Charles Townley and John Soane. While the iconography was drawn from the speculations of d'Hancarville, the exact

The gallery, inspired by the Domus Aurea and Pompeiian decoration, was designed by Bonomi, and executed in 1785–88 by Italian, French and English craftsmen as one of the most innovative interiors of its date in Europe.

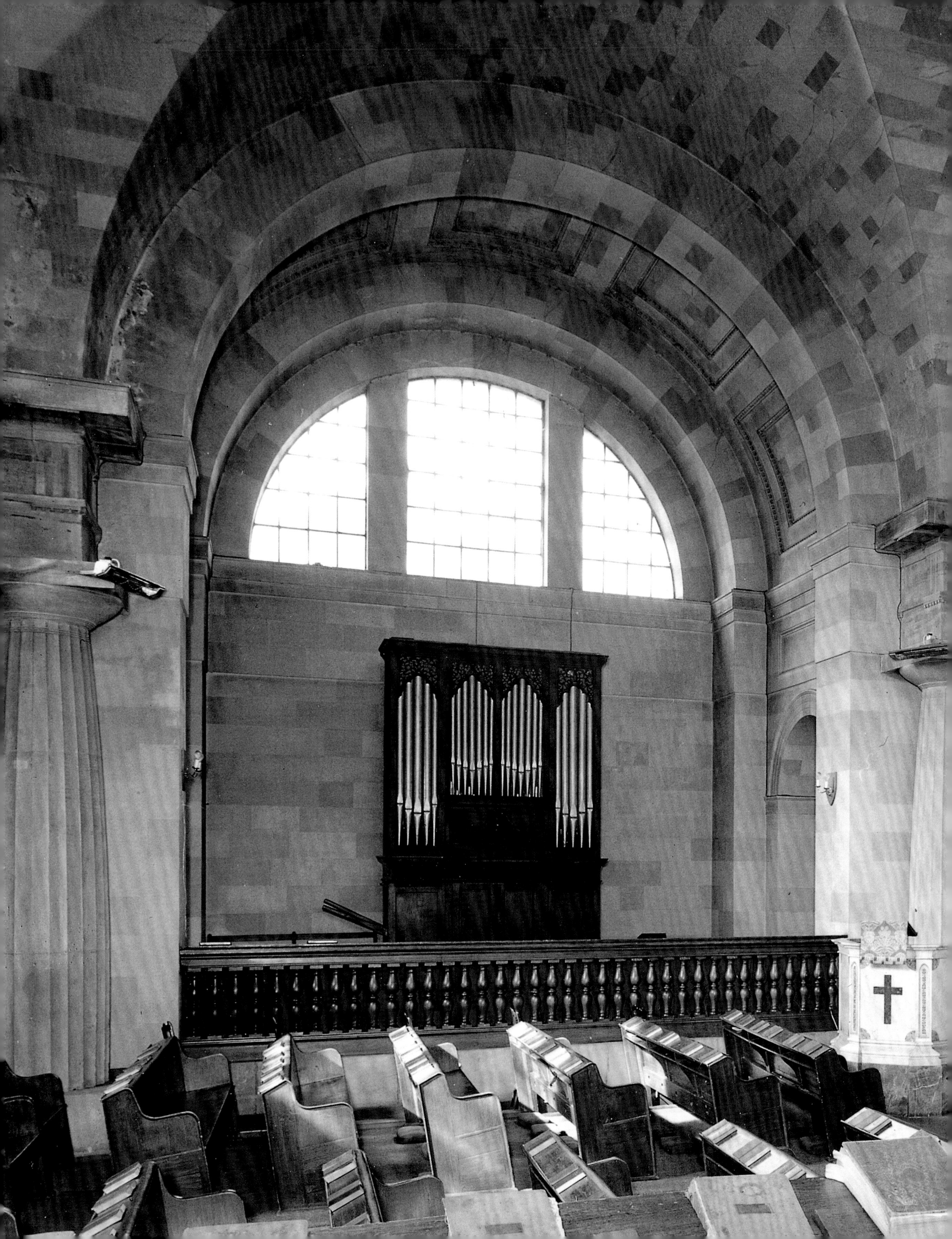

source for the decorative work was the plates in Nicolas Ponce's *Description des bains de Titus ou collection des peintures trouvées dans les ruines des Thermes de cet Empereur* (1786). The building known in the eighteenth century to Rigaud and others as the Baths of Titus is now known to have been the Domus Aurea, the famous Golden House of Nero. Bonomi divided his gallery into three compartments separated by two screens of columns of golden Siena marble *scagliola* with the complex Corinthian capitals of the Temple of Castor and Pollux in the Forum.

The gallery was in harmony with the ideas of contemporaries such as John Moore in *View of Society and Manners in Italy* (1781), who advocated roofing one of the excavated houses in Pompeii and reinstating the contents. Indeed, Bonomi seems to have designed for the gallery at Packington a set of Greek chairs of the *klismos* form with sabre legs, a type later popularized by Thomas Hope in *Household Furniture and Interior Decoration* (1807). One of these surviving at the house has a decorative panel on the squab seat repeating that of the painted panel beneath, on which it must originally have been placed. Possibly the first Greek Revival chair in Europe, it is inspired by those depicted on Greek vases of which Lord Aylesford was a collector – one of which, still at Packington, shows such a *klismos* chair. The black and red colouring in the gallery also recalled that of Greek painted vases. So is the gallery Pompeiian, Roman or Greek? This is not a very meaningful question in terms of eighteenth-century taste when the distinction between Etruscan, Greek and Roman art was not always clear. Indeed, Piranesi had urged that these styles should be imaginatively combined with Egyptian details so as to form a new decorative language.

The same combination of Greek and later elements is found in the parish church of St James at Packington, designed by Bonomi and Lord Aylesford and built in 1789–92. The evolution of its design can be seen in a series of drawings and sketches of 1788–89 by Bonomi as well as by Aylesford, who we know had earlier made copies of drawings by Piranesi. It stands in the park that had been laid out in 1751 as an early work by 'Capability' Brown for Lord Aylesford's father, who had also commissioned designs for replacing the original church, which had fallen into disrepair.

The new church is a startling cube of red brick with the upper parts and the interior columns of reddish sandstone. The four corner towers, unrelated to the plan or structure and serving no real purpose, recall those at Houghton Hall. The Diocletian windows come from the Roman Baths but the semi-circular niches derive from columbaria, antique funerary recesses. The absence of pilasters, quoins, string courses, and full entablature, makes this gaunt, Neo-Classical monument echo the massive geometry of the near contemporary Barrières by Claude-Nicolas Ledoux in Paris.

The powerfully inventive interior has Roman groin vaults resting on unfluted, baseless, Greek Doric columns, based on those at Paestum, which Bonomi had recently visited. They have the entasis, which was not included in the plates depicting them in *The Ruins of Paestum* (1768) by Thomas Major, who had not visited Paestum but obtained information from those who had, including Antonio Jolli and Robert Mylne. Lord Aylesford had also drawn Greek ruins, which were published as etchings in Henry Swinburne's *Travels in the Two Sicilies* (vol. 4, 1790).

There was no more inventive Greek Revival monument than Packington church in Gloucestershire anywhere in eighteenth-century Europe. It anticipated Soane's similar but much smaller Greek Doric vestibules at Bentley Priory, Middlesex, and Tyringham Hall, Buckinghamshire, both built in the 1790s, as well as his unexecuted Royal Gallery at the House of Lords of 1794, and James Wyatt's chapel of *c.*1805 at Dodington Hall, Gloucestershire.

Above: *The church in the park at Packington, built in 1789–92 from designs by Bonomi, resembles no other church. Its stark unornamented mass somehow recalls a mighty tomb on the Appian Way outside Rome.*

Left: *With accurately detailed Greek Doric columns based on the temples at Paestum, the church is one of the earliest monuments of the Greek Revival in Europe. However, the vaults and Diocletian windows are Roman.*

PITZHANGER MANOR, MIDDLESEX

More than any other architect in this book, John Soane was obsessed by the memory of his Grand Tour, which filled his imagination for the rest of his life with images of ancient and modern buildings. Every year, he and his pupils observed in his office the anniversary of the day in March 1778 when he had set out for Rome with a three-year travelling scholarship from the Royal Academy, where he was then a pupil. Pitzhanger Manor, built in 1801–03, was one of the many fruits of what he had learned in Italy. In a strange manuscript of 1813, he considered showing a view of the façade of the house to his students at the Royal Academy Schools and inviting them to guess its purpose:

in the fronts of Italian villas we see an immense quantity of ancient remains of sculpture and architectural fragments ... in the building before you, if we suppose the person about to build possessed a number of detached pieces of ornament, such as eagles and wreaths, demiboys and foliage, columns and statues, pedestals and acroters &c., and that from a desire to preserve them from ruin, or to form a building to give a faint idea of an Italian villa, this building may thus be considered as a picture, a sort of portrait.

This picture was the story of his life, one might say, and of his deep attachment to Italy.

Soane had known Pitzhanger from the age of fifteen when, as a pupil in the office of George Dance in 1768, he had worked on Dance's drawings for adding a two-storeyed wing to the existing red-brick, five-bay villa. Thirty-two years later, in August 1800, as Architect to the Bank of England and at the height of his career, Soane was in a position to buy the house and its 28-acre estate, nine miles from the City of London. Though retaining the wing by Dance out of respect for his old master and for the quality of its Neo-Classical, plasterwork ceilings, he demolished the villa itself, replacing it with a unique building, which only he could have designed.

The narrative told by his new house includes identifying him as Architect to the Bank of England, for the imposing façade of Pitzhanger, echoing the Arch of Constantine in Rome, recalls his Lothbury Arch of 1801 at the Bank. Like the Villa Medici, the front is

Above: Gandy's watercolour of 1802 shows the breakfast room with wall decoration inspired by the Ancient Roman house discovered in 1777 at the Villa Negroni in Rome. In the library beyond, Mrs Soane reads a letter.

Right: Soane's country house of 1800–03 distantly echoes the Arch of Constantine, thus proclaiming it as the home of the Architect to the Bank of England, where his contemporary Lothbury Arch derived from the same antique source.

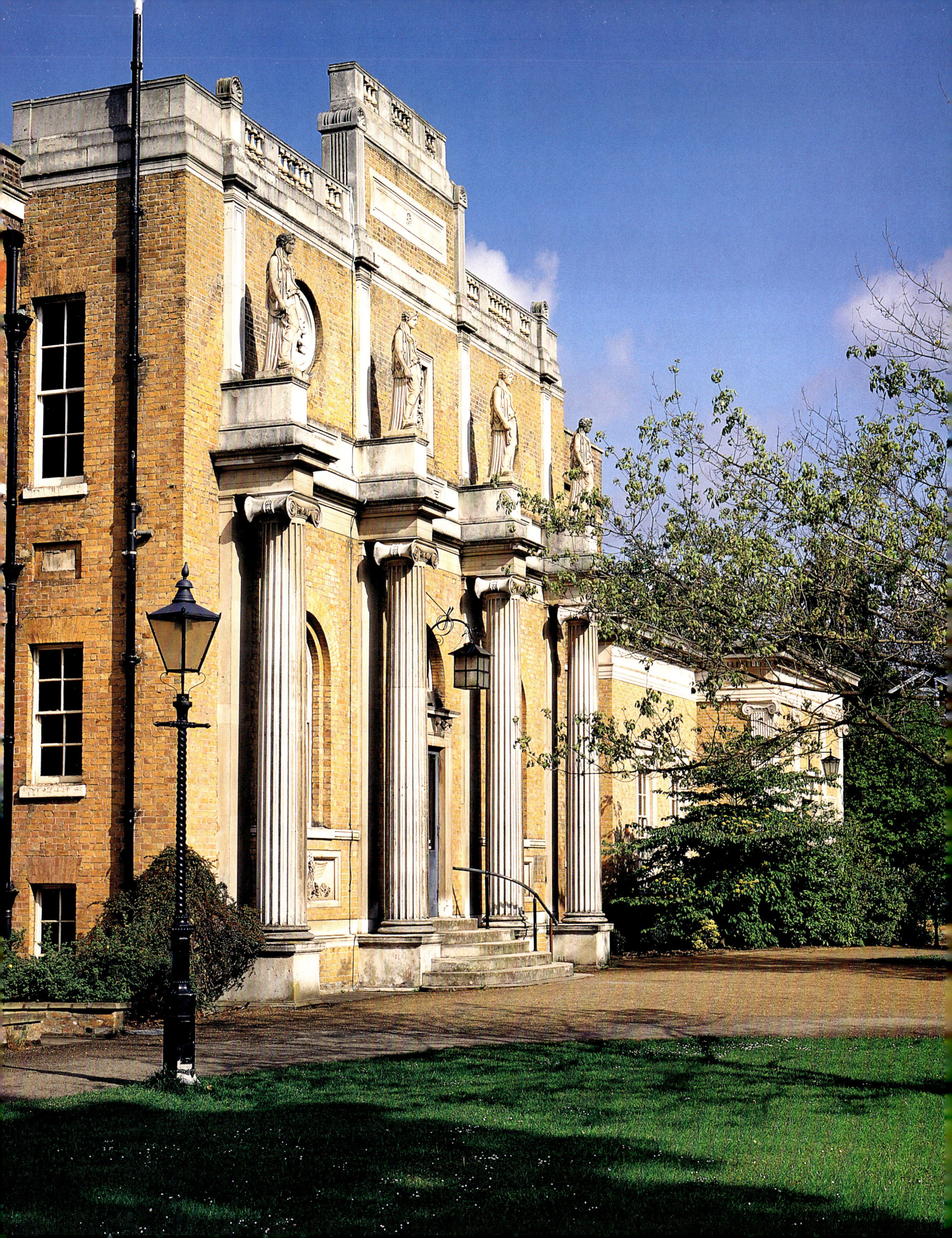

encrusted with antique fragments, though here casts, in conformity with Italian practice, as Soane noted in 1813. These include, below the windows, panels of eagles within wreaths derived from the Ancient Roman bas-relief, originally in the Forum of Trajan, and moved long ago to the church of SS Apostoli, Rome, which appears prominently in the frontispieces to two of Piranesi's books in Soane's collection: *Della Magnificenza ed Architettura de'Romani* (1761) and *Vasi, Candelabri, Cippi, Sarcofagi* (1778). The four, free-standing Ionic columns of Portland stone on this façade are proudly surmounted by Coade stone figures based on the caryatids on the Erechtheion in Athens, bought in 1801. Between the statues are roundels with reliefs of the Medici lion, and in the centre a square panel with an ambitious relief with acanthus scrolls, based on one supposedly from the Temple of Venus Genetrix in the Forum of Caesar in Rome, and now in the Canopus of the Villa Albani (now the Villa Torlonia), where Soane would have seen it in Rome in 1779–80. Built from 1751–1764 to house Cardinal Albani's superb collection of antique sculpture, the Villa Albani was a profound influence on Soane, who studied it carefully as an example of a house-cum-museum. Work on its terraces and garden buildings continued until 1767, the later phases influenced by Cardinal Albani's librarian, Johann Winckelmann. The disposition of the entrance front of Pitzhanger echoes the caryatid portico on the western Tempietto at the Villa Albani, where three of the four caryatids were antique figures discovered in 1766 in Rome. Set in the raised central attic at Pitzhanger is a panel based on a Roman sarcophagus with a Vitruvian wave scroll.

In 1802, Joseph Michael Gandy prepared two watercolours for Soane with proposals for the principal interiors: the west-facing library at the back, opening through double doors into the small breakfast room at the front. The walls of the library were grained to resemble satinwood, while the vault of the ceiling was of the starfish pattern found in an Ancient Roman tomb in the grounds of the Villa Corsini in Rome. Soane would have seen Dance's more elaborate version of this form at Cranbury Park, Hampshire (c.1780), and had already adopted it himself for the ceiling of his breakfast room at 13, Lincoln's Inn Fields, in 1792. His ceilings here and at Pitzhanger were painted with *trompe l'œil* trelliswork and flowers. Both the Pitzhanger interiors incorporated niches inspired by Roman columbaria for cinerary urns, of which Soane was buying examples at London sales at this time. On top of square cineraria he placed circular vases, an arrangement shown in plates by Piranesi.

In May 1802, Soane visited Thomas Hope at the splendid house in Duchess Street, London, which he had remodelled and enlarged from 1799–1802 as a colourful museum for his collection of ancient and modern sculpture, paintings and furniture. Hope displayed his collection of Greek vases in columbaria, since they had mostly been discovered in tombs. The designs which Soane made in June 1802 for the columbaria in the breakfast room at Pitzhanger Manor show that he was also influenced by Hope's example. One of Hope's four Vase

Gandy's dramatically lit view of the library shows the cinerary urns and starfish ceiling echoing one in an ancient tomb in Rome. We look east into the smaller breakfast room, where Soane's wife stands by the window.

84 · THE EIGHTEENTH CENTURY

FROM PALLADIO TO POMPEII · 85

Rooms also contained, according to Hope, 'a bronze lamp, bronze candelabra, and a few other utensils, of a quiet hue and of a sepulchral cast, analogous to the chief contents of this room.' It would have been characteristic of Soane to have enjoyed this sombre atmosphere, which he echoed at Pitzhanger, though not in the interiors he designed for his clients.

Soane's first design for the breakfast room, as shown in Gandy's watercolour of 1802, features wall panels in blue, based on wall paintings in three rooms of an antique Roman town house of the Hadrianic period, which had been discovered in 1777 buried in the grounds of the Villa Negroni (formerly Montalto) in Rome. Their excavation is recorded in a remarkable painting by Thomas Jones of c.1779 (now in Tate Britain, London), produced in the atmosphere of excitement that the event inspired. Soane doubtless visited it because his friend Thomas Hardwick had drawn the frescoes in 1777, while Soane acquired the hand-coloured engravings of them by Camillo Buti and Angelo Campanella. He displayed eight of these in the breakfast room at 13, Lincoln's Fields, and probably also used them as an inspiration for the design and colouring of the adjacent dining room and library.

The Villa Negroni scheme would have given Pitzhanger a little of the flavour of the Pompeiian Gallery at Packington, but before the house was ready for occupation in the spring of 1804, Soane had dropped it in October 1802 for walls richly marbled in slate blue-green and porphyry around niches containing ancient sculpture. He retained from the first scheme the shallow segmental dome and the caryatids at the four corners of the room, painted to imitate bronze, and bought from the Coade Manufactory in 1802.

Another parallel at Pitzhanger with the Villa Albani is Soane's extraordinary creation in 1801–02 of elaborate Roman ruins in the garden, designed so as to appear half-buried. These are similar in conception and even in detail to the artificial ruin he had seen at the Villa Albani, which incorporated antique architectural remains and was modelled on the small Temple at Clitumnus, near Spoleto. This had itself been remade from earlier antique fragments in the fourth or fifth century AD. Soane had visited Clitumnus in August 1779, where he made a beautiful drawing of the celebrated temple, a copy of which he sent, shortly after, to Lady Miller in the hope of persuading her to erect a replica of it in England. She had praised the temple in her *Letters from Italy* (2 vols, 1771), which he had used as a guide while in Italy. In the relation of portico to courtyard, Soane's ruins also recalled the Temple of Isis at Pompeii, which he had visited, and the Forum of Nerva in Rome, as recorded by Palladio in *Quattro Libri* where the Clitumnus temple had also been illustrated.

In 1800, Soane employed John Haverfield, who had succeeded his father as chief gardener at the Royal Gardens at Richmond and Kew, to landscape the ornamental gardens at Pitzhanger. Soane had acquired the first of as many as four copies of Robert Castell's accounts of the villas of Pliny in his *The Villas of the Ancients Illustrated* (1728), in 1780, studying it from c.1808 in preparation for his Royal Academy lectures, particularly noting the information about the relation of a villa to its setting. An ornamental bridge by the serpentine lake was now built at Pitzhanger from Soane's designs, incorporating carved heads of a medieval type to give an impression of antiquity. This survives, as does his entrance gateway with primitivist flint pilasters strangely capped by Classical features in stone, including an eagle in a wreath, preparing the visitor for those on the façade of the house itself.

Soane's aims at Pitzhanger had included establishing it as a place of social and professional advancement for himself, as well as one in which he could educate his two sons in architecture so that the elder, John, could succeed him in his practice and thus establish a dynasty like that of the Adam or Dance families. But Soane was an impossibly demanding father and it was his son's refusal to work on the rather absurd task he was set of making detailed hypothetical restorations of the ruins, which began the process of disenchantment with Pitzhanger that led Soane to sell it in 1810. He transferred his interests from the training of his sons to that of his pupils at the Royal Academy, where he had been Professor of Architecture since 1806. He moved the contents of Pitzhanger to 13, Lincoln's Inn Fields, which became a museum on an even larger scale.

The ruins at Pitzhanger Manor had disappeared by 1832 and the house became a local library in 1901 for which purpose unfortunate additions were made to it. However, a well-informed programme of careful restoration was carried out in 1985–87 by Ealing Borough Council and it has been open to the public ever since.

Above: Detail of the breakfast room ceiling as executed, simpler than as shown by Gandy, but with plasterwork incorporating Soane's characteristic, sharply incised lines.

Right: Soane designed the entrance front to give 'a faint idea of an Italian villa' displaying 'ancient remains of sculpture and architectural fragments', though the Coade stone Erechtheion caryatids crowning the columns are Greek not Roman.

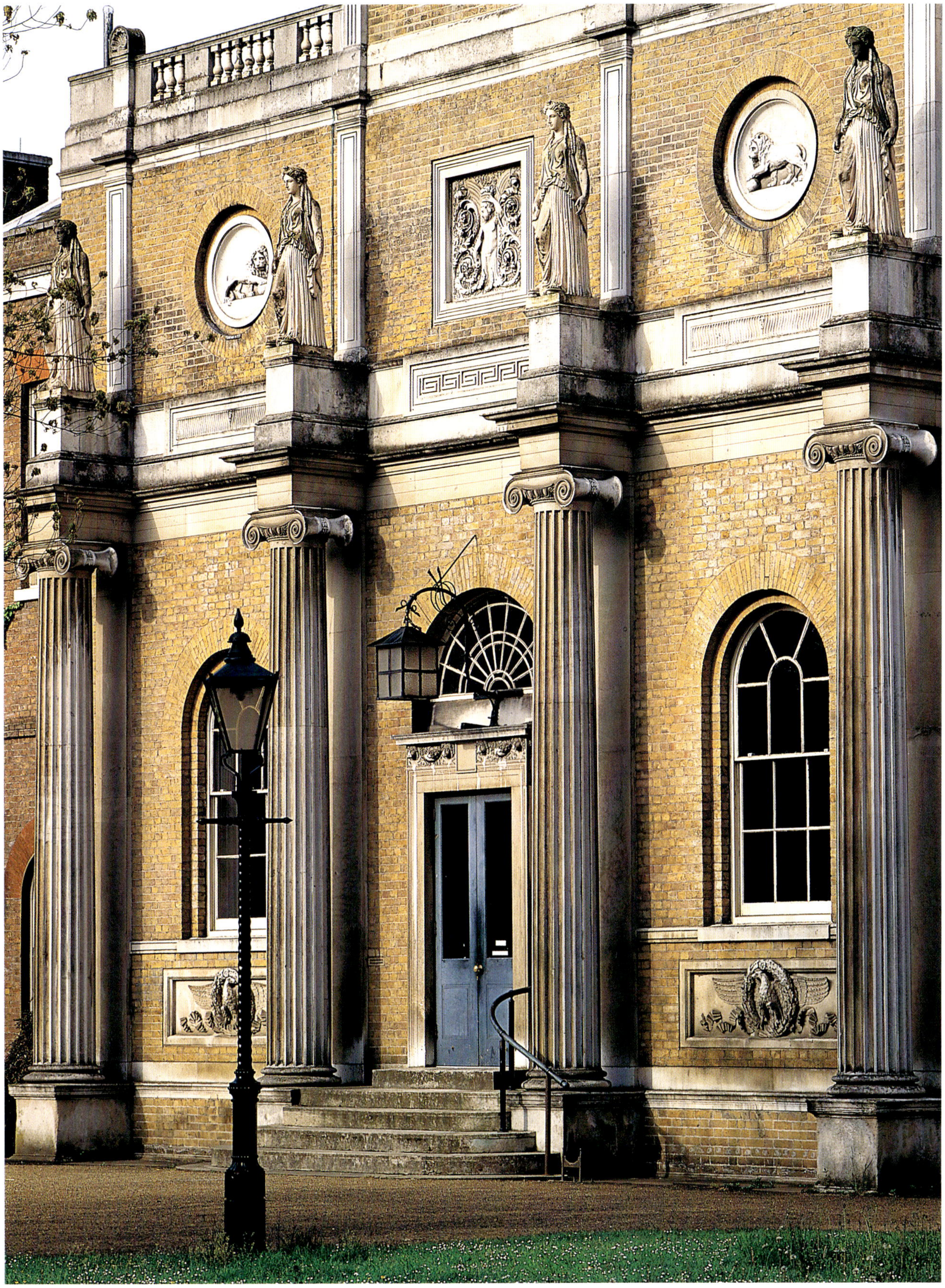

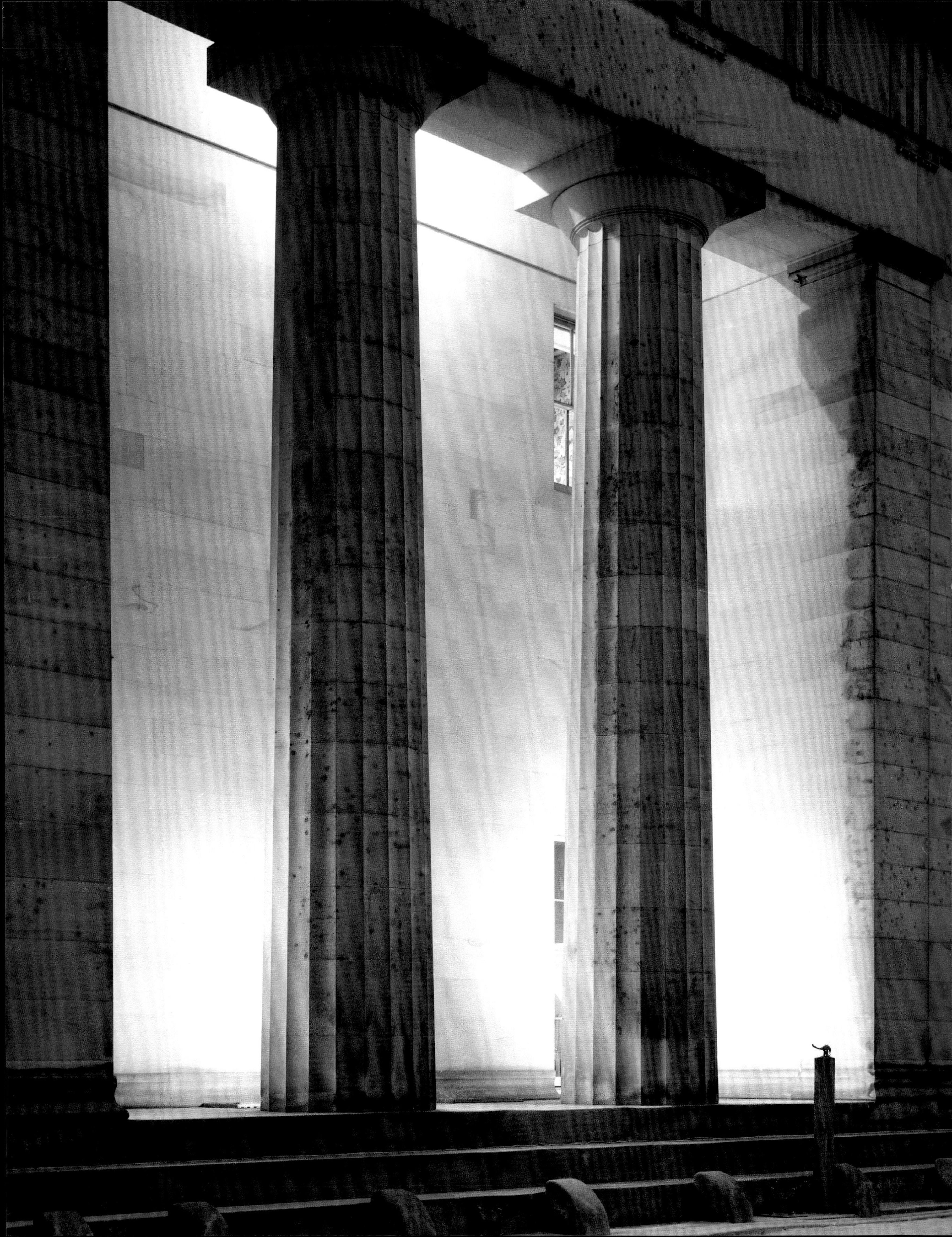

III

THE NINETEENTH CENTURY: BACK TO GREECE AND FORWARD TO ROME

The ideals of the Grand Tour had an increasing appeal in the eighteenth century since the Age of Enlightenment envisaged an international community, rooted in scholarship, archaeology, connoisseurship and fraternal sociability. As the century wore on, the Classical ideal shifted in focus, as the search for antique perfection led architects to look beyond Rome to Greece. The way back was paved by Stuart and Revett's pioneering work, *The Antiquities of Athens* (5 vols, 1762–1830), but despite Stuart's garden building with a Greek Doric portico at Hagley Hall, Worcestershire (1758), his aim was not to promote a full-scale Greek Revival, but rather to widen the range of Classical ornament to include Grecian sources. A new mood was already evident in the influential *Reflections Concerning the Imitation of the Grecian Artists in Painting and Sculpture* (1755) by Winckelmann who argued that: 'There is but one way for the moderns to become great, and perhaps unequalled; I mean, by imitating ... the ancient, especially the Greek arts. But then we must be as familiar with them as with a friend.'

Architects demonstrating this familiarity included Benjamin Latrobe at Hammerwood Lodge, Sussex (1792), better known for his later work at the Capitol, Washington, and John Soane, notably at Tyringham Hall, Buckinghamshire (1793). Belsay Hall, Northumberland (1807–17), was designed for himself by Sir Charles Monck, Baronet, as a starkly uncompromising Greek Revival monument. But little was known of Ancient Greek domestic architecture and the temple provided an inhospitable model for a private house, as shown at Grange Park, Hampshire (1809), by William Wilkins.

The resultant call for something warmer and richer led back to the Renaissance, on which path Winckelmann was again a guide, for he praised Raphael for having 'sent young artists to Greece, to copy there, for his use, the remains of antiquity.' Sir Charles Barry took Raphael's Palazzo Pandolfini, Florence (1516), as a source for his Travellers' Club, Pall Mall (1830–32), founded in 1819 for members to entertain foreigners who had aided them on their Grand Tour. Barry led the Italianate revival in country-house and garden design, as at Trentham Hall, Staffordshire (1834–49), with its loggia-topped towers, and Shrubland Park, Suffolk (1848–54), where spectacular hillside gardens recall the Villa d'Este at Tivoli. Both The Deepdene, Surrey, home of the connoisseur, Thomas Hope, as remodelled in 1836–41 in imitation of the Villa Medici, Rome, and Osborne House, Isle of Wight (1845–48), built by Thomas Cubitt (whom Prince Albert directed to create a Mediterranean flavour), continued the tradition of country houses as the joint product of architects and cultivated patrons committed to the search for Classical perfection.

BELSAY HALL, NORTHUMBERLAND *The daunting entrance to the most consistently Greek Revival house in Britain, designed by its owner, Sir Charles Monck, Baronet, in 1807, following his honeymoon, appropriately spent in Greece.*

⦿ GRANGE PARK, HAMPSHIRE ⦿

Intellectual and archaeological exploration of Greece grew from the middle years of the eighteenth century, as recorded in works such as Winckelmann's *Reflections Concerning the Imitation of the Grecian Artists in Painting and Sculpture* (1755) and Stuart and Revett's *Antiquities of Athens* (1762–1830). England was the first country since the ancient world to revive the language of Greek architecture, a process in which William Wilkins (1778–1839), architect of Grange Park, played a key role. While studying at Cambridge he won a grant in 1801 enabling him to travel for three years in Greece, Asia Minor and Italy, where he gathered material for many of his future archaeological publications. The first of these was *Antiquities of Magna Graecia* (1807), a pioneering study of Greek architecture in Sicily and Italy, by which time he was already building Downing College, Cambridge, an early programmatic statement of Greek Revival ideals.

More sensational was Grange Park, an ambitious seventeenth-century country house, which he transformed into a Grecian temple from 1809. The house was then attributed to Inigo Jones but is now known to be by William Samwell (1628–1767), an influential gentleman architect like Roger Pratt and Hugh May, who had built it c.1670 for Sir Robert Henley, a Middle Temple lawyer. Wilkins's patron was the young Henry Drummond (1786–1860) who, with a banking fortune, had travelled to Russia in 1807. He was described by Thomas Carlyle as 'a singular mixture of all things – of the saint, the wit, the philosopher – swimming, if I mistake not, in an element of dandyism,' and by a more recent author as a 'scholar and mystic, banker and politician ... chiefly memorable as a co-founder of the Catholic Apostolic Church.'

Wilkins unusually wrapped a skin of Roman cement round the red-brick house, reducing its five storeys to two by forming a terrace round the raised basement on the south and east sides, hiding the attic behind

On the right are two columns of Wilkins's Greek Doric portico; in the centre, his portico modelled on the Choragic Monument of Thrasyllus in Athens; and at the end, the Ionic portico of Cockerell's conservatory.

a giant Doric entablature and removing the high roof with its garrets. Along the entire south front, he added a huge Greek Doric portico modelled on that of the Hephaesteion, the Temple of Hephaestus, then thought to be of Theseus, which still overlooks the Agora in Athens. In the centre of the longer east and west façades, he placed novel porticoes with massive square piers inspired by the Choragic Monument of Thrasyllus, which survived on the side of the Acropolis in Athens until its destruction in 1826 during the Greek War of Independence. The whole composition of the house seems influenced by a design for a Grecian house published by Robert Mitchell in *An Essay to elucidate the Grecian, Roman and Gothic Architecture*, appended to his folio volume *Plans and Views in Perspective with Descriptions of Buildings erected in England and Scotland* (1801). The design, which Wilkins cribbed, was the most advanced of its kind at that date in Europe, Mitchell stressing his European outlook by publishing his book in English and French.

A drawing for the portico by Wilkins at the RIBA shows it set about with no less than six neo-antique sarcophagi, which were not executed but would have emphasized its solemn character as though Grange Park were a public or sacred building rather than a private house. Its giant columns, of which there were to have been a double row, were of red brick covered with stucco though with stone capitals. But if the effect outside was dramatic, the inside was almost unworkable, for the three porticoes darkened all the principal rooms on both floors; the entire basement was cold and dark; Samwell's twelve bedrooms were reduced to seven; and the servants' rooms in the attic were lit only by indirect light through the central well because their windows were blocked by the Doric frieze.

Drummond is supposed to have commissioned this templar house to rival nearby Stratton Park which Sir Francis Baring, Baronet, a fellow banker, had remodelled in 1803–06 with a Greek Doric portico by George Dance. A contemporary recorded how this 'aroused the ire and contempt of Mr Henry Drummond [who] determined to show the country a real portico.' Though Wilkins undoubtedly enabled him to achieve that ambition, Drummond sold the house and estate in 1817 and travelled with his wife to Palestine. The purchaser was the second son of Sir Francis, Alexander Baring (later 1st Lord Ashburton, 1774–1848), who explained to the architect, C. R. Cockerell, in 1823, that 'Drummond spent £30,000 in this work, turned religious, thought he had spent too much idly, sold it, quarrelled with Wilkins before it was finished.'

In about 1818, Baring invited George Dance to make improvements to Grange Park but he handed the commission over to his former pupil, Robert Smirke. What Smirke built is uncertain but in 1823 Baring asked Samuel Pepys Cockerell to continue the work. Now aged seventy, Cockerell in turn passed on the commission to his son, Charles Robert, a Classical architect of genius, who had made important discoveries about Greek architecture and sculpture when excavating at the Temple of Apollo Epicurius at Bassae in 1811. Cockerell humanized the house in 1823–25 with an L-shaped wing containing bedrooms, an elegant dining room, and one of the most sophisticated and advanced conservatories in the country, for Baring was a member of the Royal Horticultural Society.

Cockerell wrote in his diary in January 1823: 'walked over grounds with him and his son Mr Bingham Baring. Viewed it from the ground opposite to river, nothing can be finer, more classical or like the finest Poussin, it realises the most fanciful representations of the painter's pencil or the poet's description.' He summed it up on a visit four months later with the words, 'there is nothing like it on this side of Arcadia.' The landscaped park, with the serpentine lake and ruined folly which still survive, had been laid out in 1764 by Lord Chancellor Henley, later 1st Earl of Northington. Though Cockerell was enchanted by the role of Grange Park in this landscape, recalling paintings such as Poussin's *Gathering of the Ashes of Phocion* (1648) or Claude's *Pastoral Landscape* (1651), he found the details of the columns and entablature of the portico technically 'incorrect in many instances', and even felt that, 'as to the propriety of making a Grecian Temple a domestic habitation, that is a question admitting of much doubt.'

However, he admired the Greek 'squareness' of the Thrasyllan piers, 'the boldness of the conception', and the fact that

its elevation on terraces gives it that which is essential to the effect of Grecian architecture and which no modern imitations possess. It also has dimensions so seldom obtained and has thereby that imposing aspect which awes and seems to have a proportionate scale without surrounding objects of nature. The portico, a parallelogram, fills and satisfies the eye and the beauty and stability of the proportion of the order vindicate the claim of Grecian architecture to preference over most others.

Visiting it again in warmer weather in May 1823, he wrote: 'a steady sunshine upon the building, as clear a sky, the lights and shades and

---

Above: *Shortly before creating this monumental work, Wilkins had gained experience by designing three Greek Revival public buildings: Downing College, Cambridge, Haileybury College, Hertfordshire, and the Lower Assembly Rooms, Bath.*

Right: *The portico of the Temple of Hephaestus in Athens recreated in the Hampshire countryside.*

reflections as in Greece, the rooks and jackdaws in the lime tree avenue sailing and cawing in the air brought home the recollections of the Acropolis, the buzzing of the blue flies and the flowers something of the aromatic scent of thyme ... tufted trees finer and more luxuriant than ever grew on the banks of the Ilissus [in Athens]'. He stressed again that the portico has 'strength yet lightness, though robust yet fine, colossal like the Hercules and yet with traits delicate and elevated shewing a mind within elegant and refined'.

He also gave consideration to the character he should adopt for his own work at Grange Park, noting that: 'The variety of ground about affords points of view which remind one of the Villa d'Este and the ornamental character of that villa should be had in view in decorating this. Doubt whether portico is quite suited to our climate ... in England porticos should be loggia porticos.' In August 1823, when he began designing his new dining room at Grange Park, he spent three days staying with Thomas Hope, an early promoter of Wilkins, at his country house, The Deepdene, Surrey. Here he sketched its Tuscan tower with its belvedere and its Pompeiian loggia portico, all of 1818, and admired its just completed new wing in which sculpture galleries and a conservatory were mingled. Cockerell observed of it enthusiastically, 'Novelty has a vast effect in architecture. We are sick to see the same thing repeated & over again what has been seen any time these 100 yrs. The Deepdene attracts in this respect exceeding but if the Pompeiian style can be so cultivated as to practise well it may supercede the Templar style in which we have so long worked.'

He considered that 'The view of the Tower in the approach is fanciful & delightful. The front of the house is altogether novel & reminds me of the ancient villas at Pompeii.'

After his return to London, he recorded that 'Mr Hope in answer to a letter of mine respecting the excellent adaptation of Pompeiian style at the Deepdene, says if that style & that of Alhambra were united an effect of enchantment might be produced & at half [the] expense of those gloomy stately mansions.' Cockerell now considered using a Pompeiian Ionic Order for the columns of his library at Grange Park, though in the end chose his favourite Ionic from the Temple of Apollo at Bassae.

It is significant that his visit to The Deepdene convinced him that, despite his admiration for Greek Doric architecture, it was not suitable for new country houses in England. Instead, he now believed that Italian villas and gardens, both Ancient Roman as well as Renaissance – like the Villa d'Este at Tivoli – provided a more appropriate model. This marked a turning point in the design of the English country house and garden, for in 1825–26 Cockerell laid out formal Italianate gardens at Grange Park, complete with terraces, balustrades and urns, on the south and west sides of his conservatory. He thus anticipated the full-scale revival of such gardens from the late 1840s under William Andrews Nesfield and Charles Barry. A charming indication of his devotion to Grange Park was that he took his bride to see it on their honeymoon in 1828. He must have regarded it, with its setting, as the perfect Classical country house of the period just before his own.

PRESTWOLD HALL, LEICESTERSHIRE

The interiors of Prestwold created in 1842–44 represent a new conception of the ideal Classical house as a return to the inspiration of the High Renaissance and the work of Raphael. The names of the artists who painted and decorated these handsome Italianate interiors are unknown, but the architect was William Burn (1789–1870), son of Robert Burn, a builder and architect of Edinburgh. He was sent to London in 1808 to enter the office of Robert Smirke, whose pupil he remained for about four years before returning to Scotland. By 1842, when he received the commission for Prestwold, he had already designed or altered as many as forty-six country houses, a number which had mounted by his death to the almost unbelievable number of one hundred and eighty-nine, in addition to numerous churches and public buildings. His patrons were drawn mainly from the aristocracy in Scotland and England who doubtless appreciated his reticence in not publicizing his work in exhibitions at the Royal Academy or in contemporary architectural journals.

His patron at Prestwold was Charles William Packe (1792–1867) whose family had acquired the property about two centuries earlier. The house he inherited in 1837 was a large if rather dull building of c.1760 erected by his grandfather, Charles Packe (1730–1816), possibly incorporating Jacobean elements. Minor alterations were made to this in 1805 for which a plan bearing the name of William Wilkins survives, but it is unclear whether this is the elder Wilkins (1751–1815), working in Gothic on Donington Hall, Leicestershire, in 1802, or his son William, future architect of Grange Park. The entrance was now wisely moved from the south to the west side of the house and a new entrance

Above: *The restrained Italianate entrance front of 1842–44 by William Burn, who remodelled and enlarged the Georgian house, adding the Doric porte-cochère seen here and the emphatic balustrade on the skyline.*

Right: *Burn extended the south garden front and brought it forward with two, shallow projecting wings of three bays on each side, providing a satisfying pattern of rectangular masses, advancing and receding.*

94 · THE NINETEENTH CENTURY

BACK TO GREECE AND FORWARD TO ROME · 95

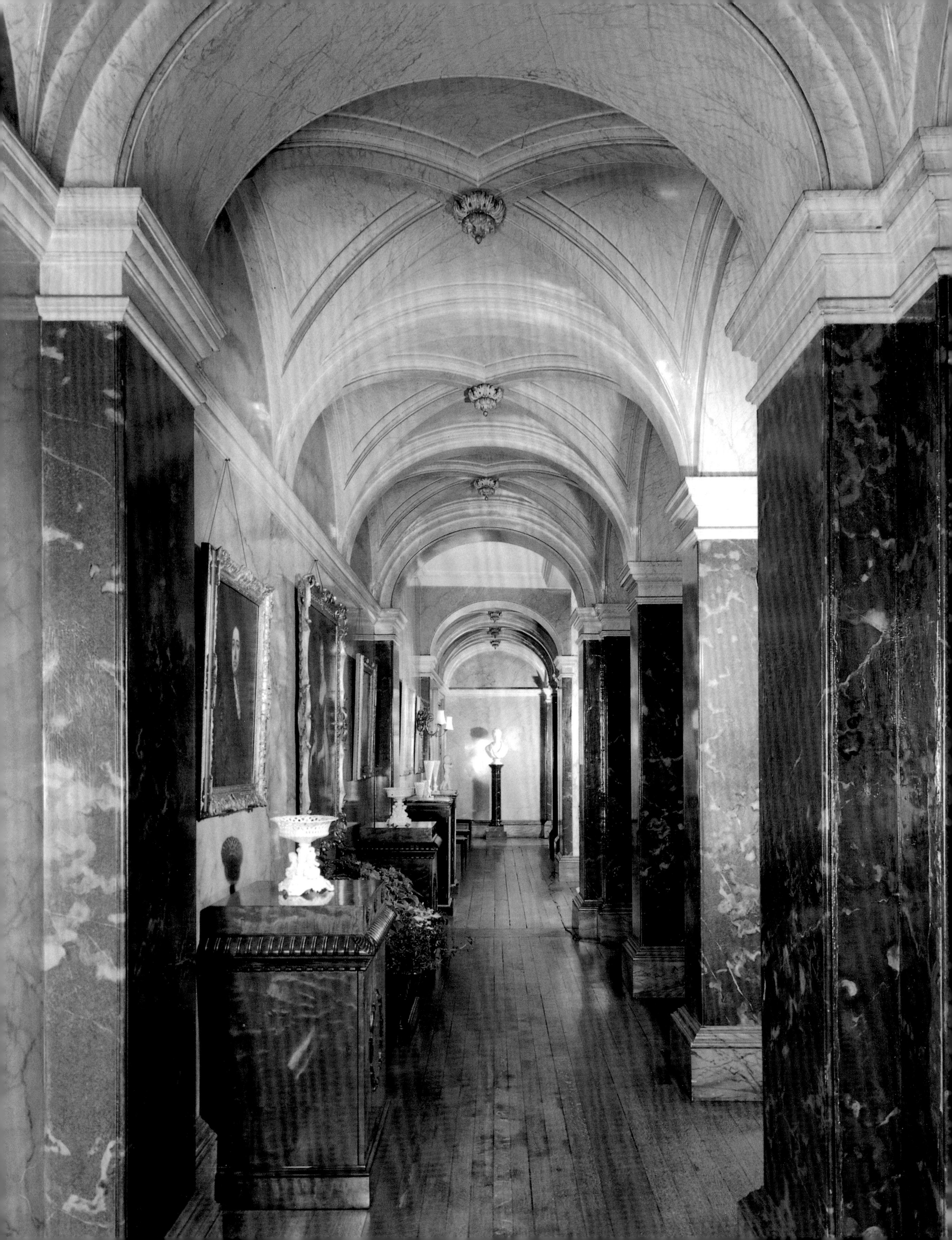

hall was formed, as well as a long corridor leading past the staircase to a domed vestibule next to the dining room.

In 1821, an elegant pair of entrance lodges was added, perhaps from designs by the younger Wilkins, sporting porticoes of Greek Doric columns inspired by those of the Hellenistic Temple of Apollo on Delos. In this rare Delian Doric Order, illustrated in Stuart and Revett's *The Antiquities of Athens* (vol. III, 1794), only the tops and bottoms of the columns are fluted. Another unusual refinement is that the lodges are placed at a slightly skewed angle to the drive, like welcoming outstretched human arms.

When Charles William Packe called on William Burn to enlarge and remodel the house in 1842 it was probably on the strength of his recent work at two vast houses in Lincolnshire, about twenty miles from Prestwold: Harlaxton Manor (1838 onwards), and Stoke Rochford House (1841–43). The former had been begun by Anthony Salvin in 1832 in the Elizabethan style but Baroque elements were introduced into it from 1838, either by him or by William Burn and his assistant, David Bryce. At Prestwold, Burn and Packe wisely kept to the Classical style of the existing Georgian house, though in keeping with the more opulent tastes of the day, Burn enriched the façades in Ancaster stone, adding a crowning balustrade, angle quoins and

Above (left): *The entry from the corridor to the library;* (right): *A lively note at the end of the corridor, where a lobby with a top-lit dome on pendentives marks the entry to the dining room.*

Left: *The groin-vaulted, L-shaped corridor from which all the principal ground-floor interiors are entered. Its picturesque chiaroscuro is further enlivened by two screens of open round-headed arches opening into the hall and former billiard room.*

mouldings to the windows, as well as making those on the south front round-headed. Though this made the composition more plastic, an architect such as Charles Barry would probably have added a tower and made the grouping more asymmetrical.

Burn's sense of architectural form was expressed in the geometrical massing of the house into a satisfying series of cubic blocks, while a drawing by him in 1842 shows his creation of the long balustraded parapet, or low wall, with a ha-ha before the whole garden front, where flower borders featured the formal bedding then coming into fashion. The unbroken horizontal line of the parapet provides a kind of basement for his Italian villa, marked by a reticent calm very different from the way Grange Park is seen pictorially as part of an idealized Poussinesque landscape.

Burn extended the south front of the old house by four bays, bringing it forwards at both ends with shallow, three-bay wings between which he ran an elegant columnar conservatory. He created a dining room and drawing room in a new eastern extension, and linked his conservatory to a suite of three rooms in the south front to be used as a library and forming a spatially interesting and comfortable setting for civilized life. In this process, he made extensive use of iron beams so as to bridge the wide spans of the rooms and open them into each other. Mark Girouard in *The Victorian Country House* (1979) described the brilliance of Burn's planning in opening up 'the whole spine of the house into a series of linked spaces, each space being treated individually as a formal and symmetrical design, but all the spaces adding up to an irregular and asymmetrical whole ... It is a synthesis of classical and picturesque principles of planning.'

Burn was a contemporary of Charles Barry, C. R. Cockerell, and Lewis Vulliamy, all born in the 1780s and 1790s and who all moved from late Georgian Classicism to something richer and more Italianate. At Prestwold there is an early Renaissance feel in the hall and corridor, where the arches are not supported on columns or pilasters but on square piers and half piers with roundels between the spandrels, an arrangement probably based on Alberti's San Francesco, Rimini (Tempio Malatestiano), begun c.1450. The corridor, a lively and varied space with ribbed vaults on pendentives creating a rich pattern of light and shade, turns left by the entrance to the dining room in a pretty, top-lit domed lobby, perhaps incorporating work by Wilkins.

The painted walls in the hall, corridor and former billiard room, are marbleised in oil paint, green, brown, and red in the hall, where the semi-circular lunettes over the doors contain cameos of Classical figures in white on a porphyry ground. Between the spandrels of the arches are *paterae* bearing busts of British poets from Chaucer to Walter Scott. The most remarkable feature of the room is the polychromatic ceiling with Raphaelesque grotesques inspired by those at the Vatican Loggie and elsewhere. Amid the painted rinceaux and scrollwork in the pendentives of the coves below are eight small landscapes in the manner of Claude, of which four show Prestwold before its remodelling by Burn, and four after.

Though we do not know who painted this sophisticated work, it is close to the exactly contemporary encaustic painting by the German firm of Fredrick Sang and Naundorff in the two-storeyed main hall or saloon and adjacent staircase at the Conservative Club, St James's Street, designed by George Basevi and Sydney Smirke. The form of the saloon, with its round arches on square piers surmounted by lunettes and coves, also repeats that of the hall at Prestwold. Fragments survive of Sang's work of 1843 at the Travellers' Club, Pall Mall, which had been founded in 1819 as a late product of eighteenth-century Grand Tour mentality, for its members were encouraged to entertain in it foreigners who had helped them while travelling on the Continent. C. R. Cockerell was a founder member and the clubhouse was built in 1830–32 by Charles Barry, who took as his model the Palazzo Pandolfini in Florence of c.1518 by Raphael.

Above: *In the top-lit former billiard room an arched screen of an early Renaissance flavour opens to the corridor; its walls are richly marbleised in oil paint.*

Right: *In the hall, the coved ceiling is elegantly painted with Raphaelesque grotesques after the Vatican Loggie, perhaps by the German artists, Frederick Sang and Naundorff.*

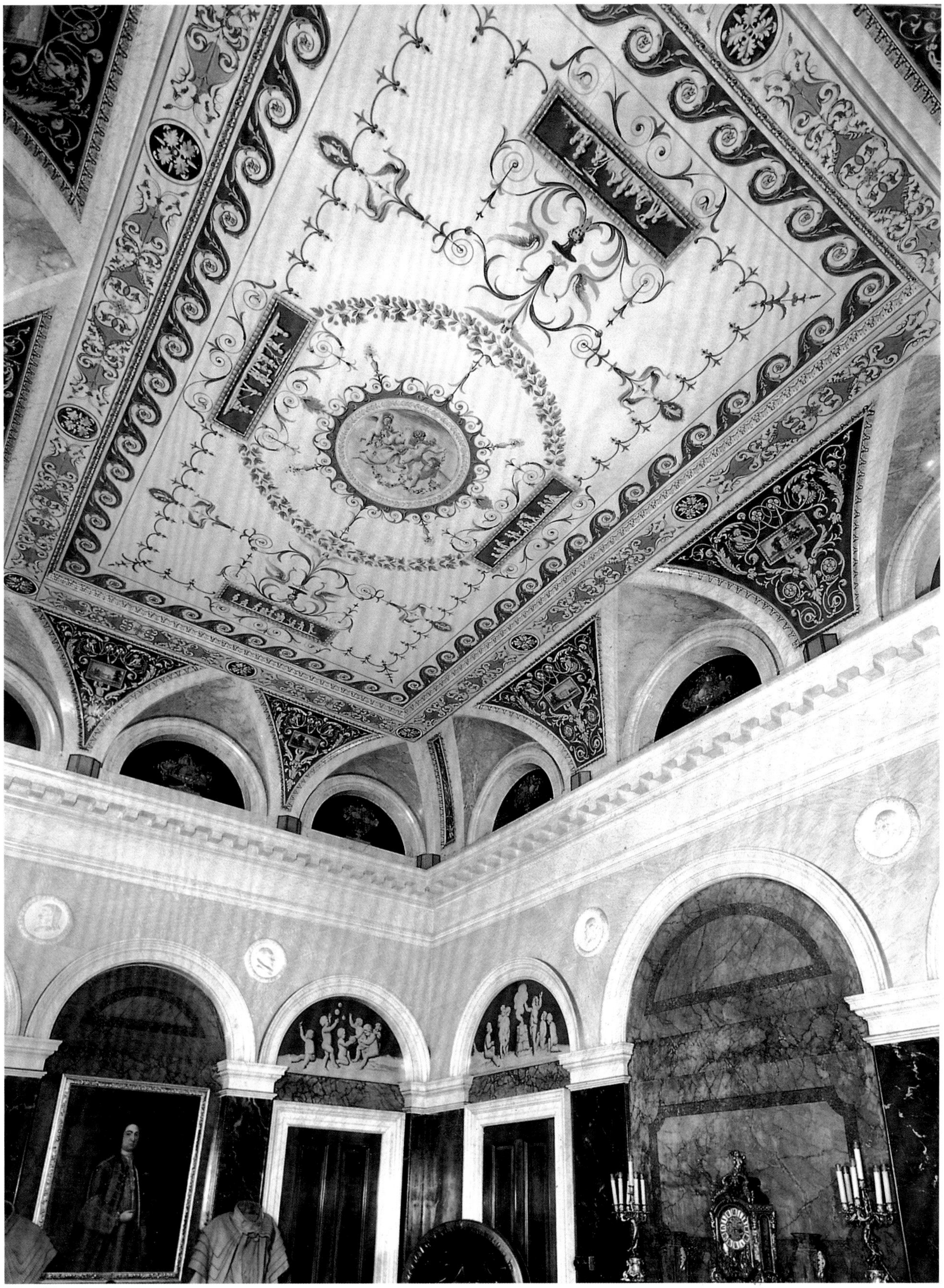

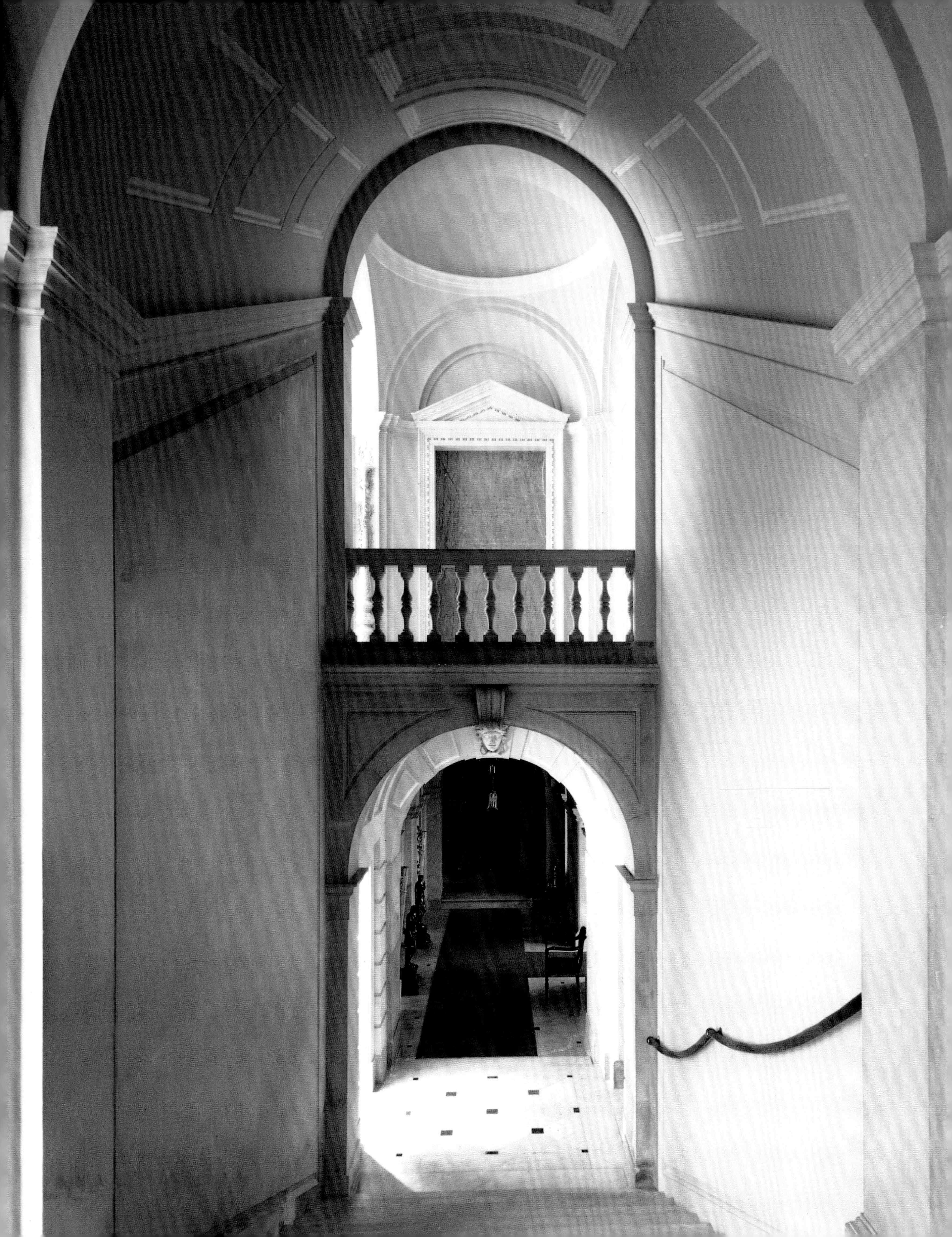

◦ KINGSTON LACY, DORSET ◦

Kingston Lacy, as remodelled and redecorated between 1835 and 1855, is an extreme example, though a rich and beautiful one, of a constant theme of this book: the ambition of one man to create a Classical setting for himself on British soil, inspired by the monuments of ancient and modern Italy. This vision was widened from the eighteenth century onwards by archaeological exploration, notably of Greek temples. Around 1800, new horizons were opened up as a result of travels to Egypt to study the civilization that lay behind that of Greece and Rome. This led to the surprising arrival in the park at Kingston Lacy in 1821 of a pink granite obelisk from the Temple of Isis on the now inundated island of Philae. The patron responsible for this was William Bankes (1786–1855), who inherited Kingston Lacy in 1834, a house built from designs by Sir Roger Pratt in 1663–65 and known as Kingston Hall until *c*.1830.

Above: *South and east fronts of Roger Pratt's house of 1663–65, as remodelled for William Bankes in 1835–41 by Barry, whose additions included the rich loggia on the east front.*

Left: *The Marble Staircase, a dramatic masterpiece in Carrara marble by Charles Barry of which Bankes justly observed, 'there is no staircase in England equal to it in effect'.*

Pratt's patron was Sir Ralph Bankes whose father, Sir Charles Bankes, Charles I's Chief Justice, bought the property in 1632–36. The house Pratt built had much in common with Coleshill, seen earlier in this book. Of red brick with stone quoins and dressings, it had mullioned casement windows, a pediment and a hipped roof with dormer windows surmounted by a balustrade and central cupola. The classic gentleman's house as invented in the seventeenth century, it was virtually the first example of this metropolitan type in Dorset. Sir Ralph's collection of pictures is also the earliest surviving one formed by the gentry rather than by noblemen or the royal family.

Sir Ralph's grandson, Henry Bankes, junior, (1757–1834), made the Grand Tour in Italy in 1778–80 and met Robert Furze Brettingham and John Soane, who were there as Royal Academy students. Soane made drawings for remodelling Kingston Lacy in Rome in 1779, but Bankes gave the commission to Brettingham whose mother was the daughter of Matthew Brettingham, executant architect of Holkham Hall. The principal survivals of Brettingham's alterations at Kingston Lacy of 1784–91 are the library and the ballroom, now the saloon, which has a shallow, barrel-vaulted ceiling painted with Wyattesque

BACK TO GREECE AND FORWARD TO ROME · 101

arabesques. This elegant Neo-Classical decoration was almost certainly carried out by the ornamental painter Cornelius Dixon in 1790–91 on the basis of drawings that Bankes brought back from Rome. It was probably done in rivalry with the similar, high coved ceilings of 1772–80 by James Wyatt at nearby Crichel. The Savonnerie carpet in the saloon at Kingston Lacy, originally ordered by Napoleon for Saint-Cloud, was bought by Henry Bankes at the sale in 1823 at Fonthill Abbey, where William Beckford had placed it in the Grand Drawing Room. A scholar as well as a collector and a man of taste, Bankes was a Trustee of the British Museum from 1816 and the author of *A Civil and Constitutional History of Rome, from the Foundation to the Age of Augustus* (2 vols, 1818).

His second son and heir, William Bankes, the principal figure in our story, inherited his artistic tastes and became an archaeologist, artist, designer and collector. He was educated at Westminster School and from 1803–38 at Trinity College, Cambridge, where he embellished his rooms over Queen's Gate, Great Court, with stucco Gothick decoration incorporating his family heraldry, which still survives. His uncle, Sir Watkin Williams-Wynn, 5th Baronet, who had made him his heir, encouraged him in this process by sending him engravings of Gothic cathedrals. Attracting gossip by burning incense in his rooms while choirboys sang for him, he became a lifelong friend of Byron, who was also at Trinity from 1805–57. He later described Bankes to John Murray as 'My collegiate pastor, master and patron' who 'rules the Roast – or rather the Roasting – and was father of all mischiefs.'

He followed William Beckford and Byron by travelling to Portugal and Spain in 1812–14, but extended his Grand Tour dramatically in 1815 by visiting Cairo and travelling down the Nile; while in 1816 in Bedouin dress he was one of the first Europeans to visit Petra. He was in Egypt again in 1818–19, spending a month at Abu Simbel copying the wall paintings inside the great temple of Rameses II. His collection of Egyptian antiquities survives at Kingston Lacy as the sole British, post-Napoleonic collection of its kind still in the house to which it was brought. He made important records and measurements of the monuments of Egypt, which survive at the British Museum and Dorset

Above: *The entrance hall, with a strongly emphasized Doric Order, was formed at basement level by Barry. It leads through the arches to the inner hall and the approach to the fabulous Marble Staircase.*

Right: *At the half landing of the Marble Staircase, a glazed loggia opens into the garden and a domed lobby houses bronzes by Baron Marochetti, including Lady Bankes (left), and King Charles I (right).*

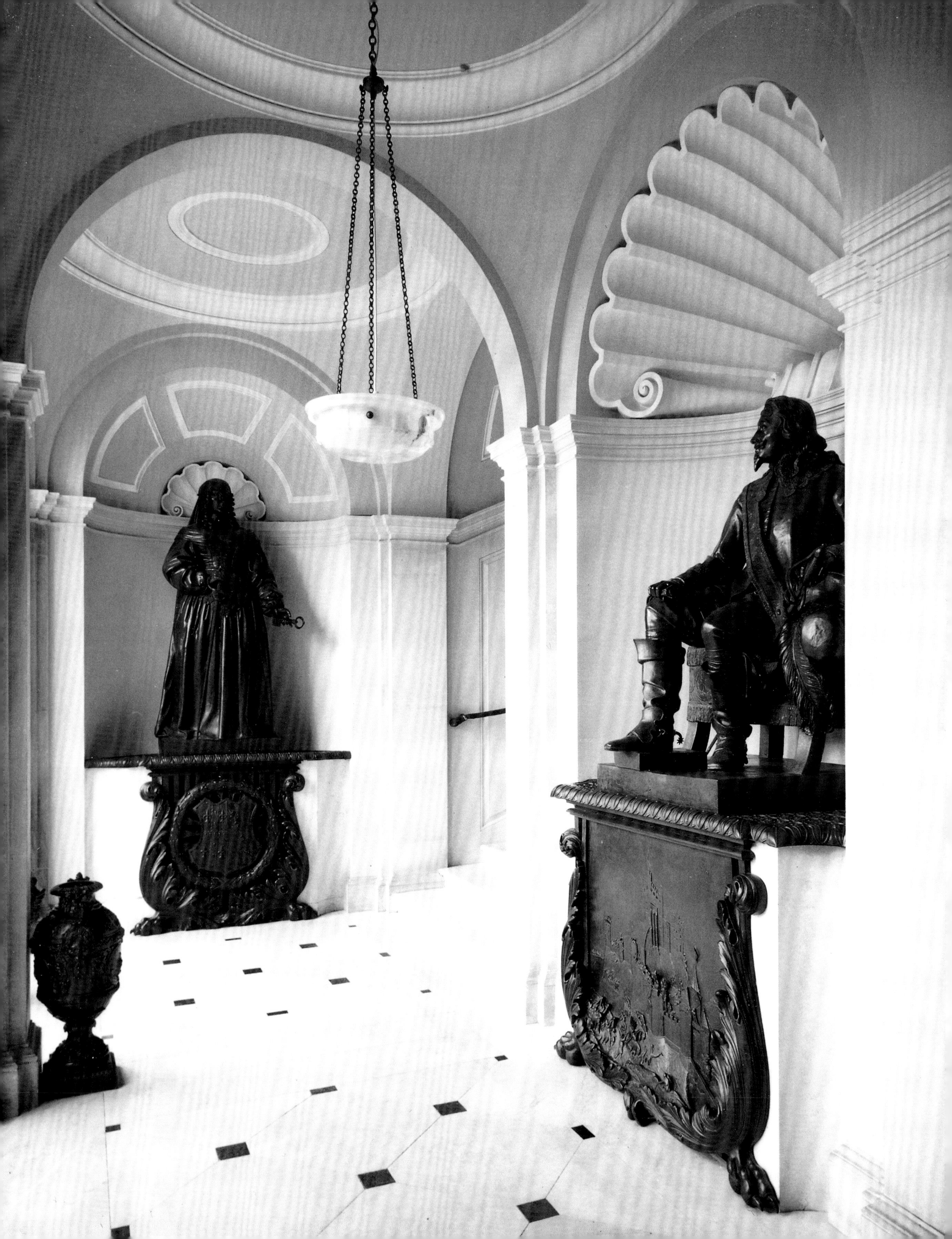

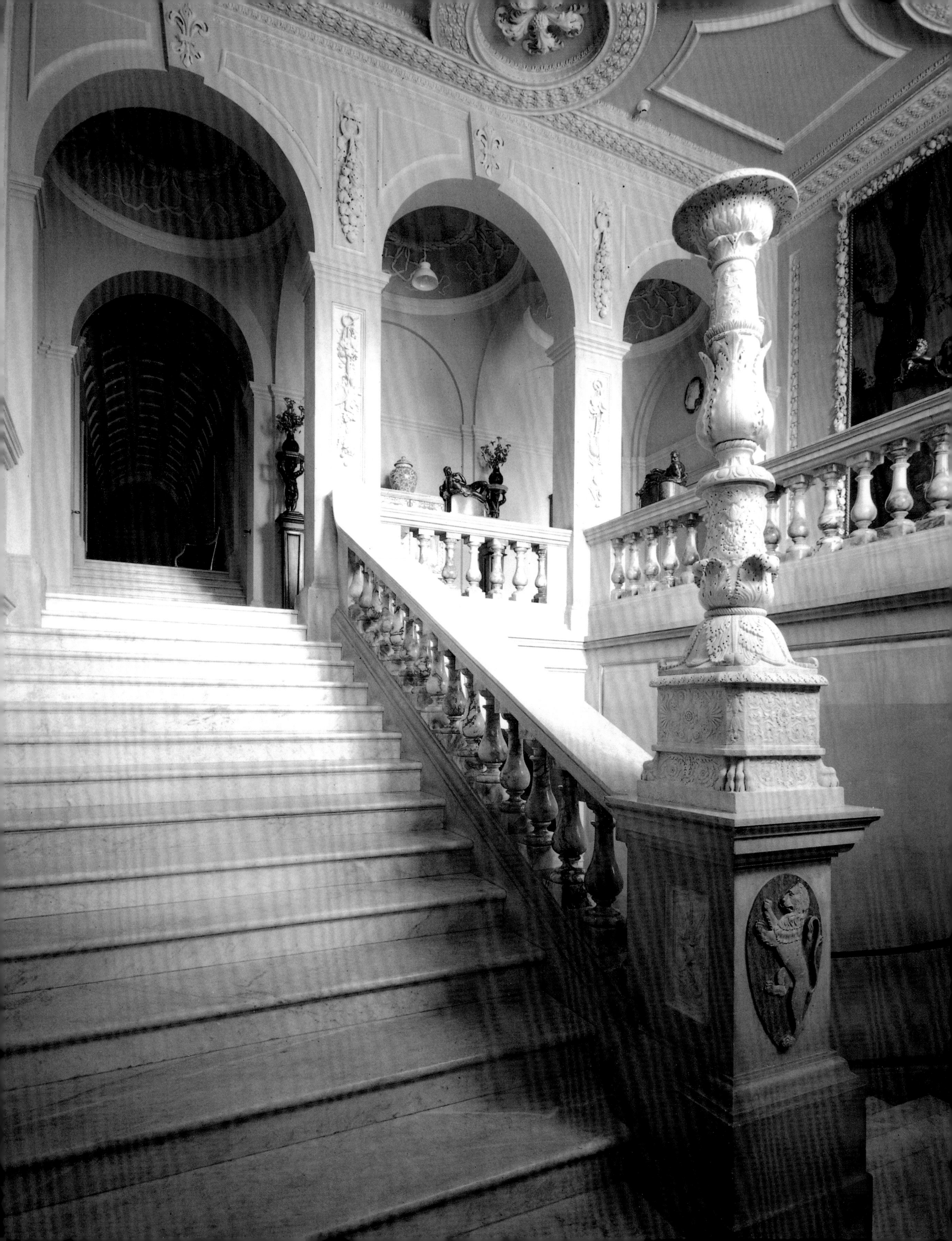

County Record Office, while his transcriptions of the Greek texts on the base of the obelisk he brought from Philae played a small but not insignificant part in the deciphering of hieroglyphs in 1822.

In Egypt in January 1819, he met the young architect, Charles Barry, who, like him, had been studying architecture there as well as in Syria and Italy. In the winter of 1819, Bankes stayed with Byron in the Palazzo Mocenigo in Venice, and in 1821 Barry sent him a drawing, which he had made of the temple at Karnak. Bankes will doubtless have admired the Travellers' Club in Pall Mall, built from Barry's designs in 1830–32 with a façade inspired by Raphael's Palazzo Pandolfini in Florence. It was to Barry that in 1835 he entrusted the task of encasing Kingston Lacy in Chilmark stone in a more elaborate version of the original. This involved raising the attic storey and adding a new balustrade, cupola, and tall corner chimneys, while the interiors were completely remodelled in a richly Italianate fashion.

Above: The third flight of the upper Marble Staircase rises in the centre of the well, where it turns by the sumptuous marble copy of an antique Roman candelabrum. The alabaster balustrade supports bronze sculptures.

Left: The three-arched screen leads to the top landing with its three domes. The ceiling is appropriately based on that of a bedroom at Coleshill by Roger Pratt, the architect of Kingston Lacy.

In June 1833, Bankes was charged with committing 'an unnatural offence' in a public convenience near St Margaret's Church, Westminster, where the churchyard was a noted meeting place for homosexuals. He was acquitted but in August 1841 he was arrested for buggery with a soldier of the Footguards in Green Park. He jumped bail and escaped before he could be tried, but since sodomy carried the death penalty until 1861, according to the barbaric laws of the day, he was forced to live abroad for the rest of his life. Barry's work for him at Kingston Lacy was completed in 1841 but, remarkably, Bankes continued to conduct extensive work on the interiors and furnishings until his death in Venice, unmarried and childless, in 1855.

Believing the house to be by Inigo Jones, though it is now known to be by Roger Pratt, he had already visited with his father Grange Park and Amesbury Abbey, both then attributed to Jones. He now went to Wilton, Lees Court and the Queen's House at Greenwich, to gain further ideas for giving an authentic flavour to the sumptuous remodelling of his house. However, his most striking contribution, Barry's Roman staircase of Carrara marble leading up to the state rooms, was more Italianate than purely Jonesian. Barry lowered the ground by 8 feet on the north side of Pratt's house to create a sub-basement with an entrance hall, an arrangement he had seen at Amesbury Abbey.

106 · THE NINETEENTH CENTURY

From the relative darkness of this new stone hall with its sombre Doric Order, a few steps take one to the left through an arcade into the gleaming marble staircase which, following Italian Renaissance custom, consists of short flights with tunnel vaults ascending round a solid square core. John Cornforth described in *Country Life* in 1986 how the relation between the arcaded entrance hall and the staircase is handled with 'a nice sense of flow through the use of the arcade and the combination of materials, stone giving way to marble just as Caroline England fuses with Baroque Rome.'

In a letter to his brother in 1837, written before Barry's staircase was completed, Bankes wrote, 'there is no staircase in England equal to it in effect, not even Wardour, and not any that surpass it in Italy. I delight in the rich Eastern external Loggia which is finished, but I do nothing but walk up and down the inclined planes of the Staircase.' The domed circular staircase to which he refers at Wardour Castle, Wiltshire, (1770–76), is by James Paine and is by far his finest work but it is nothing like that at Kingston Lacy, which owes something to that at Grange Park and more to that of 1640 by Martino Longhi the younger at the Palazzo Ruspoli in Rome. Bankes sent to Rome for 'a measured plan and location' of this staircase, with its two very sparsely decorated tunnel-vaulted flights with steps of Parian marble leading to a more decorative loggia on the first floor. It is hard to see why the Ruspoli staircase should have appealed so greatly to him, though it had unaccountably acquired the reputation in the seventeenth century as 'one of the four marvels of Rome.'

The rich Italianate loggia with plate-glass windows to which he refers at Kingston Lacy was an idea by Barry. It is on the half landing of the first flight, where at mezzanine level it forms the garden entrance on the east front. From here there is a dramatic view back, up to the arch opening on to the first-floor landing and down to the lower entrance hall. On the first-floor landing is a sequence of three domed spaces with five marble door-cases carved in 1846 by Michelangelo Montrésor, a marble mason from Verona; while the candelabra flanking the central door into the saloon were carved from Bankes's own designs by Salesio Pegrassi, whom he regarded as the heir to Grinling Gibbons. From this landing is another spatial surprise, for the third flight rises centrally within the well of a much larger, open, rectangular upper hall with an alabaster balustrade and bronze statues and busts. Barry took the design of the ceiling from one by Pratt at Coleshill, which Bankes sent Barry to visit since he only knew the house from engravings. In the circular compartment in the centre is a *trompe l'œil* painting of *putti* playing beneath a cupola of vine trellis, which Bankes bought in Venice in 1849, believing it to be by Giorgione. The top landing here, with its three domes, is approached dramatically through an open screen of three arches.

Of the interiors on the *piano nobile*, the new dining room was formed by Barry in the 1830s, with a ceiling inspired by that of the great chamber at Coleshill, and four pairs of double doors carved for Bankes in boxwood in Venice by Vincenzo Favenza in 1849–53 and inspired by

The spectacular Spanish Room, or 'Golden Room', is a symphony of harmonious gilding, including that of the coffered ceiling from a Venetian palazzo, the leather wall hangings and the new frames for the Spanish pictures.

BACK TO GREECE AND FORWARD TO ROME · 107

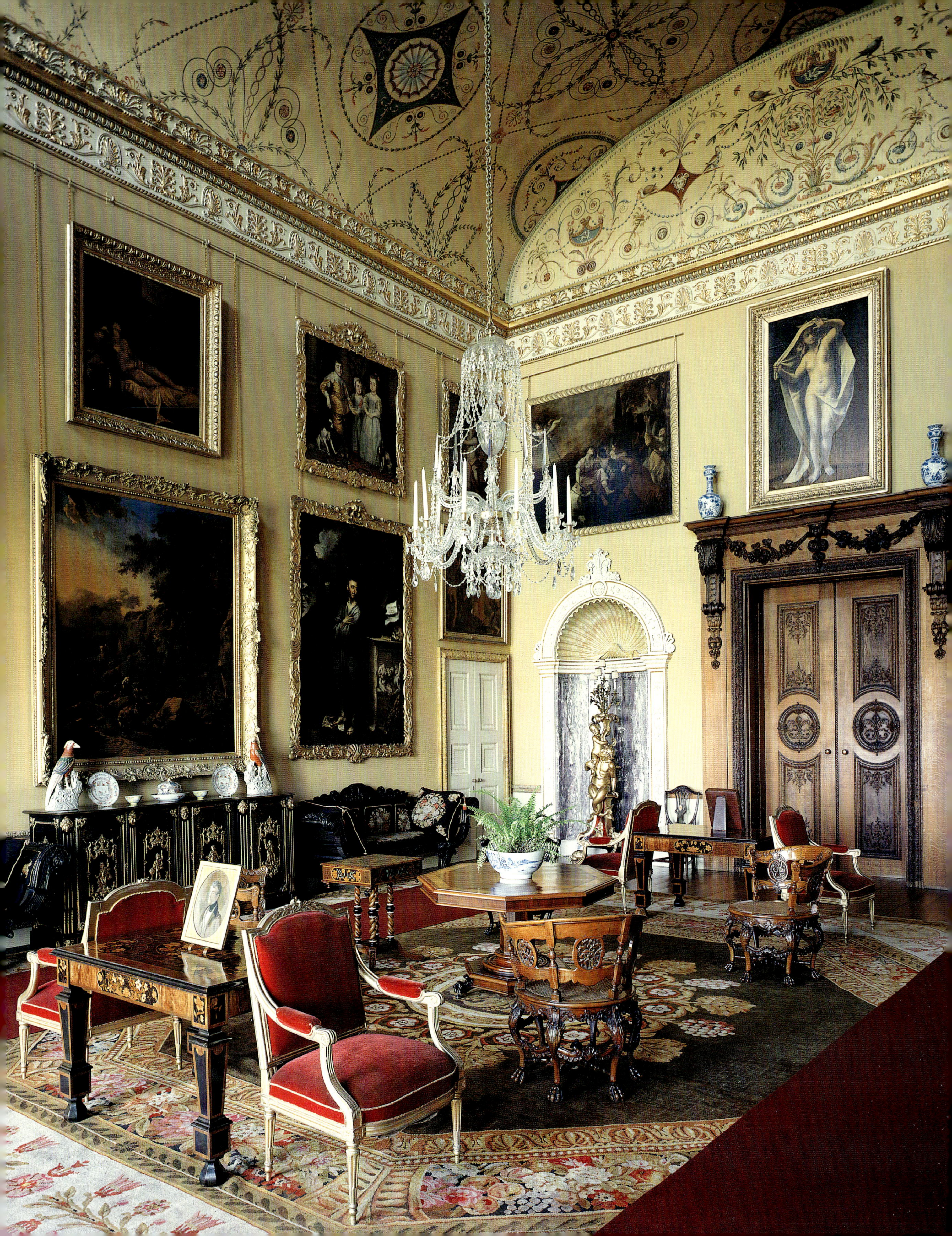

Renaissance reliefs of *putti* and angels singing and playing instruments. The room also contains a painting of *The Judgement of Solomon*, which Bankes bought in Venice in 1820, urged on by Byron. Then thought to be by Giorgione but now attributed to Sebastiano del Piombo, it is set in a palatial interior with a coffered ceiling and marble columns, which fitted well with Bankes' own tastes.

Barry raised the ceiling of the drawing room, designing the new one on the basis of a drawing made for Bankes of one he had seen at Lees Court, Kent, then attributed to Inigo Jones. The architraves of the four doors and the tablets for the north wall, all of yellow marble of Torre, were executed in Verona in 1846 by Montrésor. The room contains family portraits by Van Dyck, Lawrence and Romney, while in the saloon hang paintings by Titian, Rubens, Giulio Romano, Salvator Rosa and Berchem. The pair of oak doors between the drawing room and the saloon, with the arms of the Farnese Pope Paul III, is supposed to have come from the Vatican. Typical of Bankes's attention to detail is a letter to his brother George sent from Lucca in 1844, complaining of the restoration of these doors with the addition of 'oak knobs in a room where there is gilding!!'

The genesis of the Spanish Room, the most elaborate in the house, was probably Bankes's purchase in 1838 from a London dealer of a coffered and painted ceiling said to have come from an interior by Scamozzi of 1609 in the Palazzo Contarini degli Scrigni, Venice. The central section of the ceiling as installed at Kingston Lacy, though, is a version or later copy of a ceiling by Veronese from the Palazzo Pisani in the Campo San Stefano, Venice. Bankes had the walls of the Spanish Room hung with one hundred and twenty pieces of gilt embossed and gilded leather from the Palazzo Contarini, which he had restored in Venice in 1851. The rich effect of the room is heightened by the presence of paintings by Murillo and from the studio of Zurburan, as well as by the three pairs of doors with twelve panels painted on pear wood, six on a gold base representing the summer months, and six on bronze for the winter. These he described in a letter to his sister in 1851 as 'a work which has been in hand upwards of three years, done entirely from my own designs.' They were a personal contribution to a place which, uniting themes from houses such as Wilton, Coleshill and Grange Park, is the perfect statement of the Classical ideal on English soil.

Left: *The elegant saloon survives from Brettingham's alterations of 1784–91. Its Wyattesque painted ceiling represents an earlier and lighter Italianate taste than that of William Bankes from 1835.*

Below: *Pratt's south front, originally of red brick, was encased in stone by Barry, who added the cupola and balustrade to replace those removed in the eighteenth century, but made them richer.*

BACK TO GREECE AND FORWARD TO ROME · 109

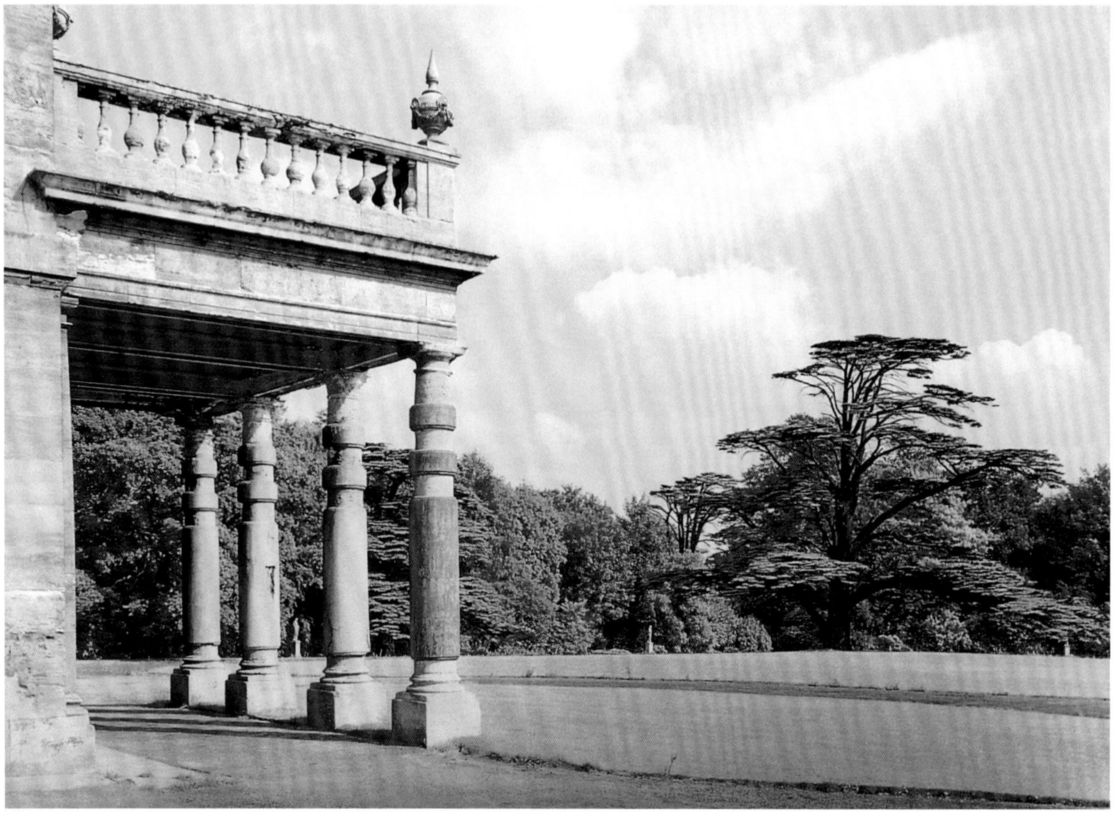

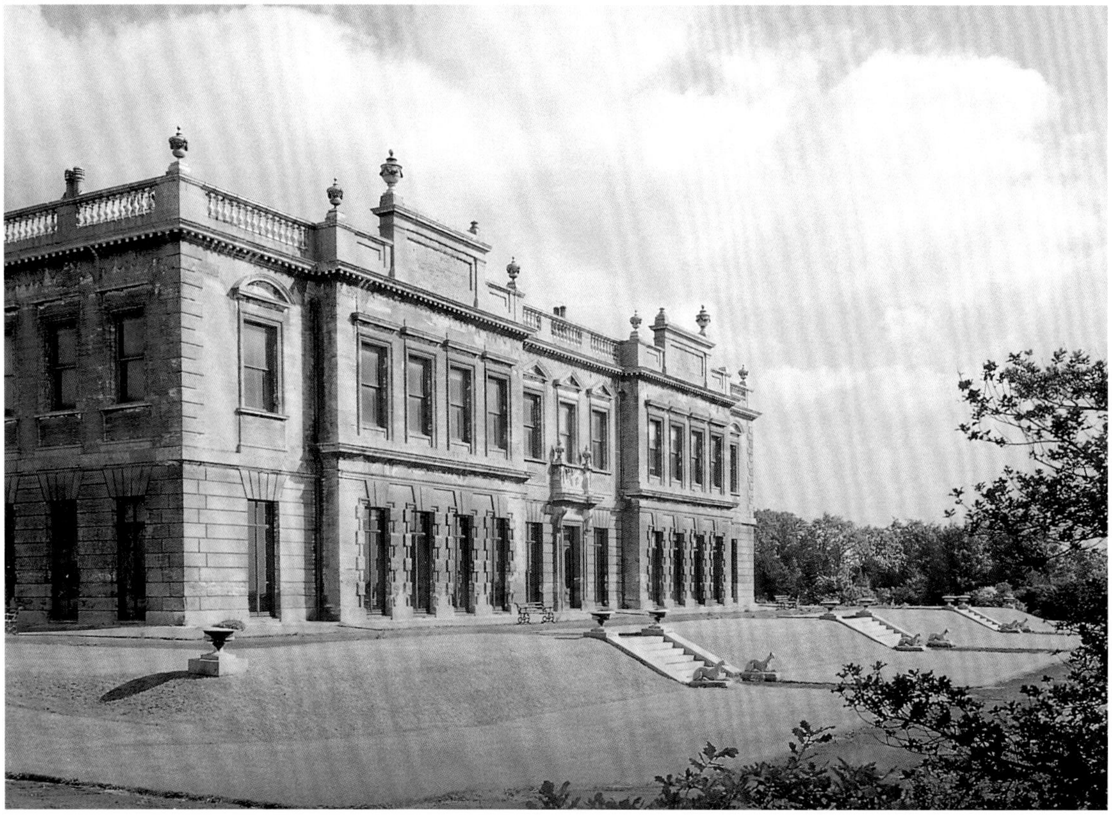

⸱ BRODSWORTH HALL, YORKSHIRE ⸱

In the story of the long love affair with Italy and Classical culture traced in this book, Brodsworth takes us beyond Kingston Lacy into the High Victorian Age. Its creator, Charles Sabine Thellusson (1822–85), who had the same single-minded aesthetic passion as William Bankes, inherited Brodsworth Hall, a huge Georgian house with a coal-mine on its estate, in 1859 when the House of Lords finally settled the long disputed will of his great-grandfather, a city banker of Swiss origin, Peter Thellusson, who had died in 1797. His estate now went to his great-grandsons, Lord Rendlesham and Charles Sabine Thellusson, whose share included Brodsworth, where he decided to demolish the old house and replace it with a grand Classical palazzo. Born in Florence and spending part of his youth in Paris and Belgium, he employed as his architect Giovanni Casentini, an Italian architect and sculptor from Lucca, whom he had presumably met in Italy. His designs were executed in 1861–63 by a minor English architect from London, Philip Wilkinson.

The façades of Brodsworth Hall have a touch of Classical austerity, rare for the 1860s, while the composition lacks the asymmetry which would be more typical of the period – even the low service wing at the rear which makes the house T-shaped is hidden by a shrubbery. The south garden front is thirteen bays long but only two storeys high, with a crowning balustrade punctuated with urns. The façades are provided with false windows so as to preserve Classical symmetry where they were not required by the plans of the rooms within. The whole place was conceived and largely completed within a short period, including the formal garden and its fountain. The house is set on a raised terrace of grass banks where successive long flights of steps are decorated with shallow urns and greyhounds of grey marble.

Above: View from the west hall towards the south hall at the centre of the house, both arranged as a museum to display Charles Thellusson's collection of Italian marble sculpture, much of it chosen by Giovanni Casentini.

Left (above): Porte-cochère on the east entrance front of the house built from designs sent from Italy by Casentini, heir to Italian architects like Leoni, who had designed English country houses in the eighteenth century; (below): The south garden front, thirteen bays long, has a symmetry untypical of country houses of the 1860s, but reflecting the urban palazzi of Italy rather than the country villas.

112 · THE NINETEENTH CENTURY

The opulent interiors form a museum for Charles Thellusson's collection of mainly Italian nineteenth-century sculpture, recalling the role of the Villa Borghese as a sculpture museum. What helps makes Brodsworth all but unique is the unity between the house and its contents, for its architect, Casentini, was largely responsible for the choice of the sculpture displayed in it. This is a little reminiscent of the process by which, as we saw earlier in this book, the sculpture gallery at Holkham Hall was rising while the sculptures to fit its niches were being acquired in Rome. The collection at Brodsworth comprises fifteen large figures and eight smaller ones, the former bought by Thellusson at the Dublin International Exhibition of 1865, where all but two of them were exhibited through Casentini, acting as an agent for other sculptors. Notable for the high quality of their craftsmanship and materials, they have a strong narrative element and range from the coy through the sentimental to the mildly erotic, being mostly partially draped female figures with exposed breasts.

The halls and circulation spaces were finished in imitation painted marbles of different colours, notably green and red porphyry and golden yellow Siena marble, arranged in panels. The effect of the marble figures partly depends on the skill with which Thellusson placed them through the house, where their gleaming whiteness is set off by the darker colours of the painted marbleised walls and the textures of the rich silks and velvets. Several of the figures are also reflected in mirrors, some framed between the columns.

In the large entrance hall, containing minor pieces of sculpture, a double screen of columns of terracotta pink *scagliola* opens into the even larger inner hall, within which the main staircase rises. This key space houses two of the principal sculptures: *Girl on a Swing*, a complex piece full of vertical movement by Pietro Magni (1817–77), a promoter of the new realism from Milan, and *Education*, a group of a woman and a boy being taught to pray by Giuseppe Lazzerini (1831–95), from a family of sculptors practising in Carrara from the late eighteenth century to the Second World War.

From the inner hall one passes through a small lobby into the south hall, a remarkable space that is approached through another double screen of eight columns, this time of yellow, Siena marble *scagliola*. There are as many as sixteen columns in this room, contrasting in colour and texture with the crimson silk which originally hung on the walls and which still survives in the adjacent drawing room. Nestling in this columnar forest are two large female sculptures by Lazzerini, *Nymph going to Bathe* and *Vanity*.

The two drawing rooms opening into each other at the south-west corner of the house glow with rich red curtains in silk and velvet, while the chairs are also of crimson and gold, and there are two pairs of Corinthian columns of white *scagliola* with gold and grey capitals. All this and the crystal chandeliers are reflected in tall gilt mirrors, but the decorative plasterwork in an eighteenth-century French taste has the growing coarseness of the time. It is interesting to note that the curtains, carpets and furniture throughout the house were all provided

The two drawing rooms, hung with red damask, are separated by white scagliola *Corinthian columns. The house was both built and furnished in 1861–63, so these opulent Victorian interiors form part of a planned unity.*

BACK TO GREECE AND FORWARD TO ROME

by a single fashionable Mayfair firm, Lapworth Brothers of Old Bond Street.

The west hall, which is a generous corridor outside the drawing rooms, is the climax of the sequence of painted halls. Arcaded with white painted pilasters and marbled and stencilled Classical patterns, it serves as a background for sculptures backed by gilt-framed mirrors. At the end of this long space is the dramatically placed *Sleeping Girl* by Giosuè Argenti, unusually lit from behind by a large internal window with a painted glass border. Here, too, is *Eve with Cain and Abel* after an original by Auguste-Hyacinthe Debay, and two smaller pieces by Pietro Franchi. Round the corner in the north hall is a copy of the *Venus Italica* by Canova and a small version of Bartolini's *Fiducia in Dio* of 1834, products of the tradition from the Ancient Romans onwards of replicating famous sculptures.

The sculptural theme in the house was carried with striking consistency of aim into the garden, for which Casentini supplied much sculpture from the Carrara area of Italy in 1866: fifteen marble statues placed in niches in the yew hedges, as well as the fountain, urns and eight greyhounds for the terraces. The garden, which has recently been restored as far as possible to its condition in the 1860s, could not be better summarized than in the guidebook to the house published by English Heritage in whose care it has been since 1988: 'The new garden was very much a product of the third quarter of the nineteenth century. It contrasted areas of high formality, of seasonal bedding, a fountain, statuary and dense shrubberies, with areas of studied, rustic prettiness, of climbing roses, arbours, little vistas, a cascade and quaint garden buildings.'

Above: *Detail of the west front with the fountain chosen by Casentini, who filled the gardens with 'Marble Works Statues etc' sent from Italy, including the urns, greyhounds, and even the terrace steps.*

Right: *One of the white marble statues brought to the formal gardens from Italy in 1867. In the standard handbook on Classical pictorial imagery, Cesare Ripa's* Iconologia *(1593), a woman lifting from her face a mask of a younger one represents Deceit.*

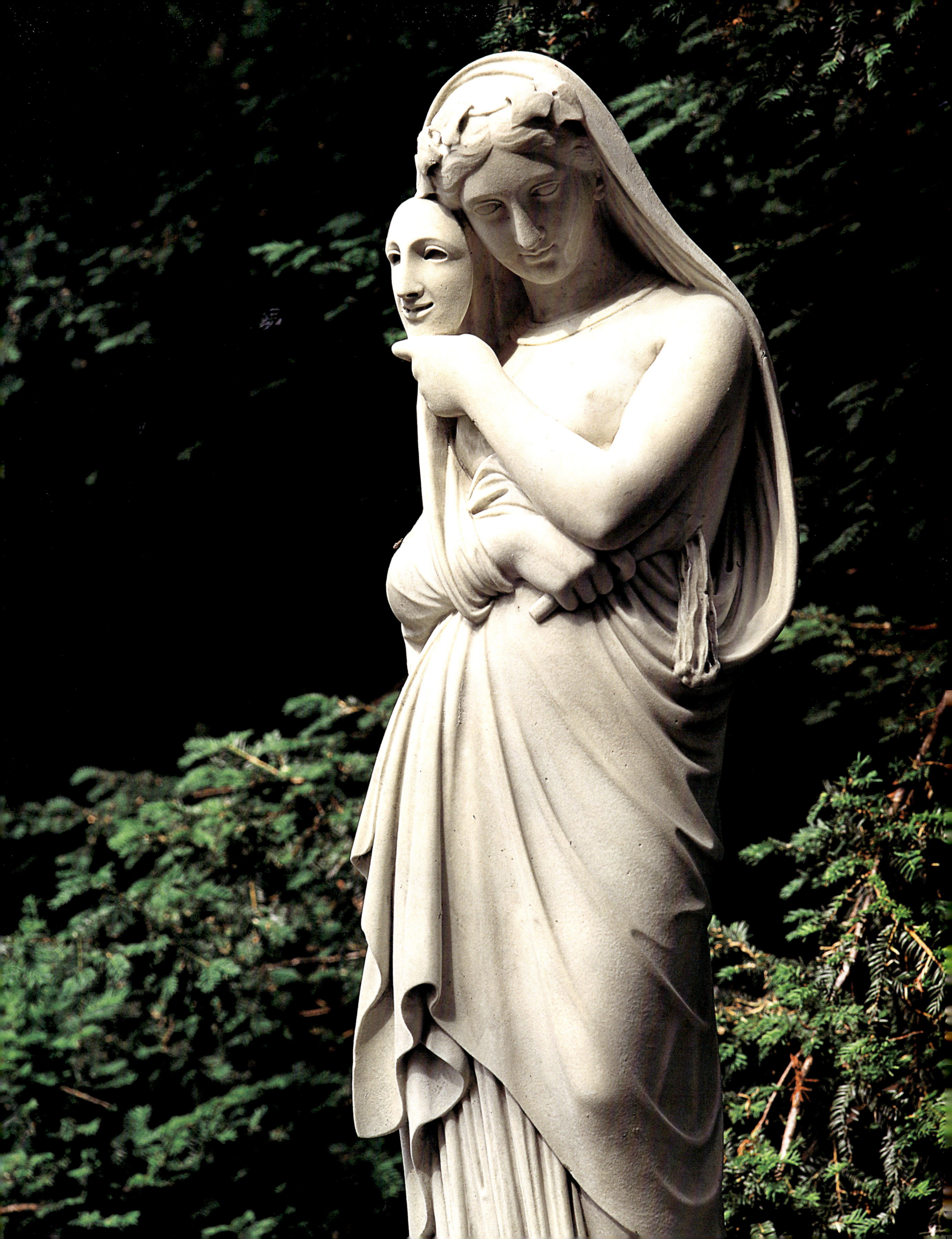

116 · THE NINETEENTH CENTURY

GOSFORD HOUSE, EAST LOTHIAN

Gosford House, one of the most palatial houses in Britain, was built about fifteen miles east of Edinburgh in 1790–1800, from designs by Robert Adam. One of its main purposes was to house the picture collection assembled by the 7th Earl of Wemyss (1723–1808), which included Italianate country-house paintings, works by Vouet and Chardin, as well as Dutch paintings by Hobbema, Jordaens and Jacob, and Salomon van Ruisdael. The main block of Adam's house, comprising drawing room, circular saloon and dining room, provided a space 136-foot long and two storeys in height, the central saloon being 46-foot high, including the dome. After Adam's death in 1792, Lord Wemyss altered the design to create more light for showing his pictures by widening the windows of these galleries along the west, garden or sea front, with its views towards the Firth of Forth. Writing in *Country Life* in 1971, John Hunt complained that this change 'had the regrettable effect of reducing the grace and fluency of Adam's proposed elevation.' However, the alteration can be seen as an improvement, for its gargantuan scale was better suited to the vast size of the whole house than the detailing of Adam's architecturally timid façades which were a tired echo of Kent's Holkham, with a series of Palladian windows set in reveals with semi-circular heads.

The house was not completed in Lord Wemyss's lifetime and he never lived in it, finding it damp. He was succeeded in 1808 by his grandson, the 8th Earl, who also chose not to live in it but hung the paintings in the central block, and commissioned several designs for the completion of the house, including one from Smirke in a Greek Revival manner and one in the Gothic style, probably by James Wyatt.

Above: *The west garden front of this colossal house built by Adam in 1790–1800 is less well known than it should be because his wings, demolished c.1810, were replaced in 1883–91 to a more ambitious design.*

Left: *The new south entrance front of the 1880s by William Young is an undeniably magnificent composition, even if it seems almost impossibly grand for a private house.*

BACK TO GREECE AND FORWARD TO ROME · 117

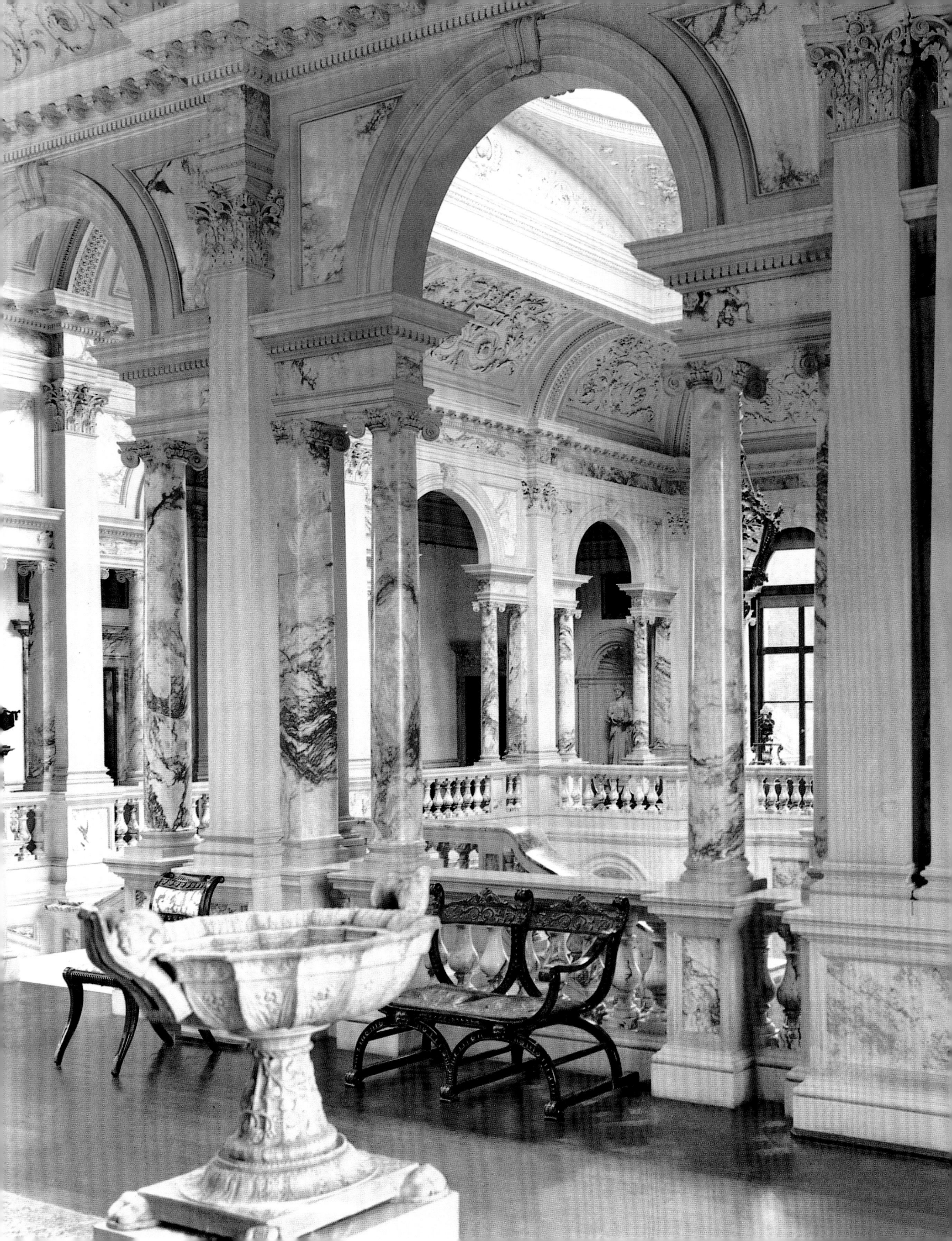

Instead of executing these, he demolished Adam's two side wings, which left the central block unsupported and isolated for over half a century. It was not until 1883–91 that the wings were replaced for the 10th Earl of Wemyss (1818–1914) who succeeded in 1883. He began collecting while he was at Christ Church, Oxford, as a contemporary of Ruskin, and on his first visit to Italy in 1842 he bought a Correggio and a Romanino. He became a Trustee of the National Portrait Gallery for ten years from its foundation in 1856, and his own collection included work by Masolino, Dolci, Maratti, Murillo and Zurburan, as well as Mannerist works by Sodoma and Pontormo. With enthusiasms including the Venetian School of the Italian High Renaissance, his acquisition of a Tintoretto was an appropriate accompaniment to the Palladian Marble Hall he later created at Gosford.

To complete Gosford, the 10th Earl chose in 1883 the prolific Scottish architect, William Young (1843–1900), who began work in the same year on the Glasgow Municipal Chambers, an opulent and eclectic pile, which earned him the commission in 1899 for the Old War Office in Whitehall. The monumental scale of these public buildings was echoed at Gosford, where he improved the west front by creating a rusticated terrace and twin staircases, a composition in scale with the huge windows of the galleries. His two, new large wings to north and south were in a richly Italianate manner, with plenty of Palladian windows to harmonize with Adam's work. The north wing contained guest bedrooms and domestic offices round a central kitchen, while the south wing was a self-contained family house to which he transferred the main entrance, which had originally been in the east front.

This ambitious new south wing, approached through its own curtain-walled entrance court, contains the Marble Hall or staircase hall, which flanked by two blocks of reception rooms and bedrooms, is one of the most exciting interiors in any nineteenth-century British country house. A balustraded Imperial staircase, with steps of Italian marble, rises to the balustraded gallery with open screens of Palladian arches on all four sides. Again, these recall those proposed by

Above: In an unusual configuration, the two arms of the theatrical double staircase in the Marble Hall shelter an Italian Renaissance marble chimneypiece.

Left: Young's Marble Hall has Palladian arched openings matching the windows of the entrance front outside. The walls are lined with polished Caen stone and the columns and balustrade are of pink and white Derbyshire alabaster.

BACK TO GREECE AND FORWARD TO ROME · 119

120 · THE NINETEENTH CENTURY

Adam for the west front, though Young's are closer to those on Palladio's Basilica in Vicenza. The opulent effect is heightened by the colour contrast between the Caen stone used for the main structure, including the Corinthian pilasters rising to the coved ceiling, and the richer Staffordshire alabaster chosen for the balustrades, Ionic columns and wall panels. All three Orders are deployed with Doric on the ground floor supporting the staircase arch, which shelters a somewhat incongruous inglenook chimneypiece with a relief copied from Donatello's bas-relief plaque of St Cecilia.

Lord Wemyss recorded his relationship with William Young in his memoirs, 'He has designed, I have planned.' Indeed, Young provided three designs for the Marble Hall before Lord Wemyss was satisfied. Young's central dome is suspended from cast-iron girders concealed behind coffered plaster panels by Jackson's, with carving in appropriately deep relief yet delicate in detail. The ironwork is a product of the engineering skills of Sir William Arrol (1839–1913), the self-made, Scottish-born civil engineer and Liberal MP, whose work included the Tay and Forth Bridges.

The house was ready for occupation by Lord Wemyss and his large family in 1891 but little use was made of it between 1914 and 1940, and it was briefly run as an hotel by the 11th Earl in the 1930s. During its occupation by the army in the Second World War, part of the central block was gutted by fire, and a few years later the north wing was unroofed following the discovery of dry rot. It was thus heroic of the 12th Earl to return to live in the house in 1951 at a time when many other owners abandoned houses that were much less damaged. The family occupied the south wing which had escaped the fire and where the furniture and pictures had been stored. The central block was re-roofed in 1987 and further restoration work has been carried out since, so that the 7th and 10th Earls of Wemyss's vision of creating a new synthesis of Italian Classical architecture and painting for modern living survives into the twenty-first century.

The coved, compartmented ceiling in the Marble Hall is surmounted by a dome, incorporating steel-work beams. In an operatic coup, the columnar screen leads into the gallery, a long transverse space, lit from the ends.

BACK TO GREECE AND FORWARD TO ROME · 121

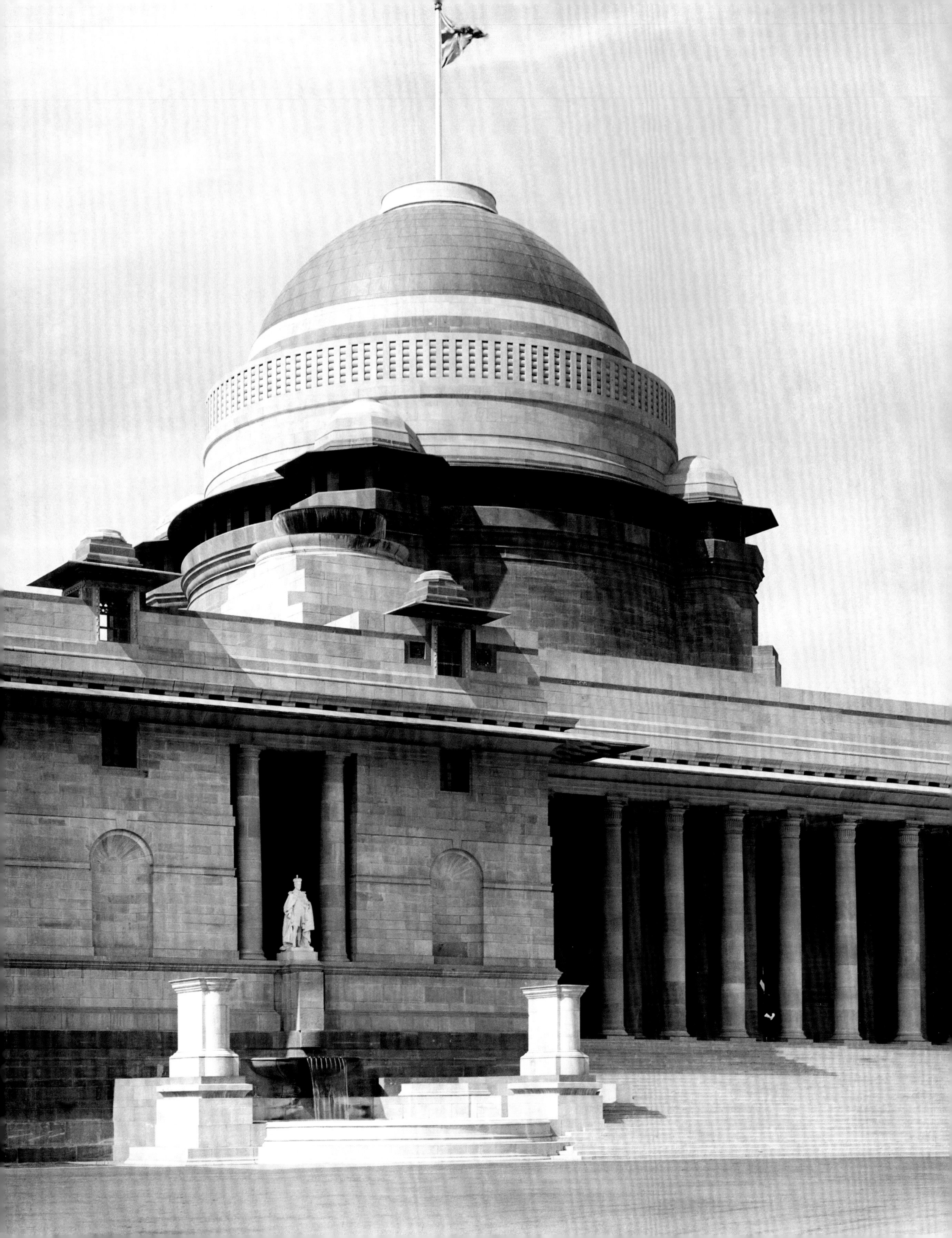

IV

THE TWENTIETH CENTURY: PRE-WAR VARIETIES OF CLASSICISM

The houses we have seen so far were almost exclusively the product of a system in which members of the nobility and gentry, holding public office at parliamentary and county level, saw themselves as largely responsible for the social, economic, cultural and political welfare of the nation. Their country seats were powerhouses from which they carried out the public duties which justified their élite status, dispensed hospitality, commissioned architects and artists, and oversaw the farming on their estates, thus contributing to their own prosperity as well as to that of the country. This system lasted from the Middle Ages until the opening years of the twentieth century when it was brought to an end by the great agricultural depression of the 1870s and by the growing power of the state, leading to vastly increased taxation, including death duties, which had an immeasurably damaging impact on country houses and their estates.

Though the houses we shall see in the remainder of this book are no longer centres of power, the desire to create a fine house in the country is so deeply engrained that it has fully survived the collapse of a social order that had lasted for centuries. The Classical language of architecture has been no less adaptable, having appealed to patrons in every possible political system, including Ancient Greek democracy, the Republic as well as the Empire of the Romans, Renaissance popes, English Whig landowners, and the régimes of the Soviets and Nazis.

At the start of the twentieth century, just when it might have seemed that all possible changes had been rung on the theme of houses inspired by the ancient and modern architecture of Italy, a home-produced genius sprang up from a different tradition. This was Sir Edwin Lutyens, rivalling Wren in genius and a prolific country-house builder, whose work features prominently in this chapter. He wrote of the Classical Orders: 'They have to be so well digested that there is nothing but essence left ... the perfection of the Order is far nearer nature than anything produced on impulse and accident wide. Every line and curve the result of force against impulse through the centuries.'

His Viceroy's House, New Delhi (1912–31), in some ways the greatest English country house ever built, was a personal, abstract synthesis of the Classical language that represents the essence not the accidents of Classicism. It thus features few Classical mouldings or features out of pattern books, while his version of Ancient Greek entasis means also that there is hardly a single vertical or horizontal line in this great masterpiece.

Lutyens' Viceroy's House, New Delhi, a serene yet inventive Classical masterpiece, is one of the great buildings of the world. In the portico is a marble statue of the King-Emperor, George V, by Bertram Mackennal of 1913.

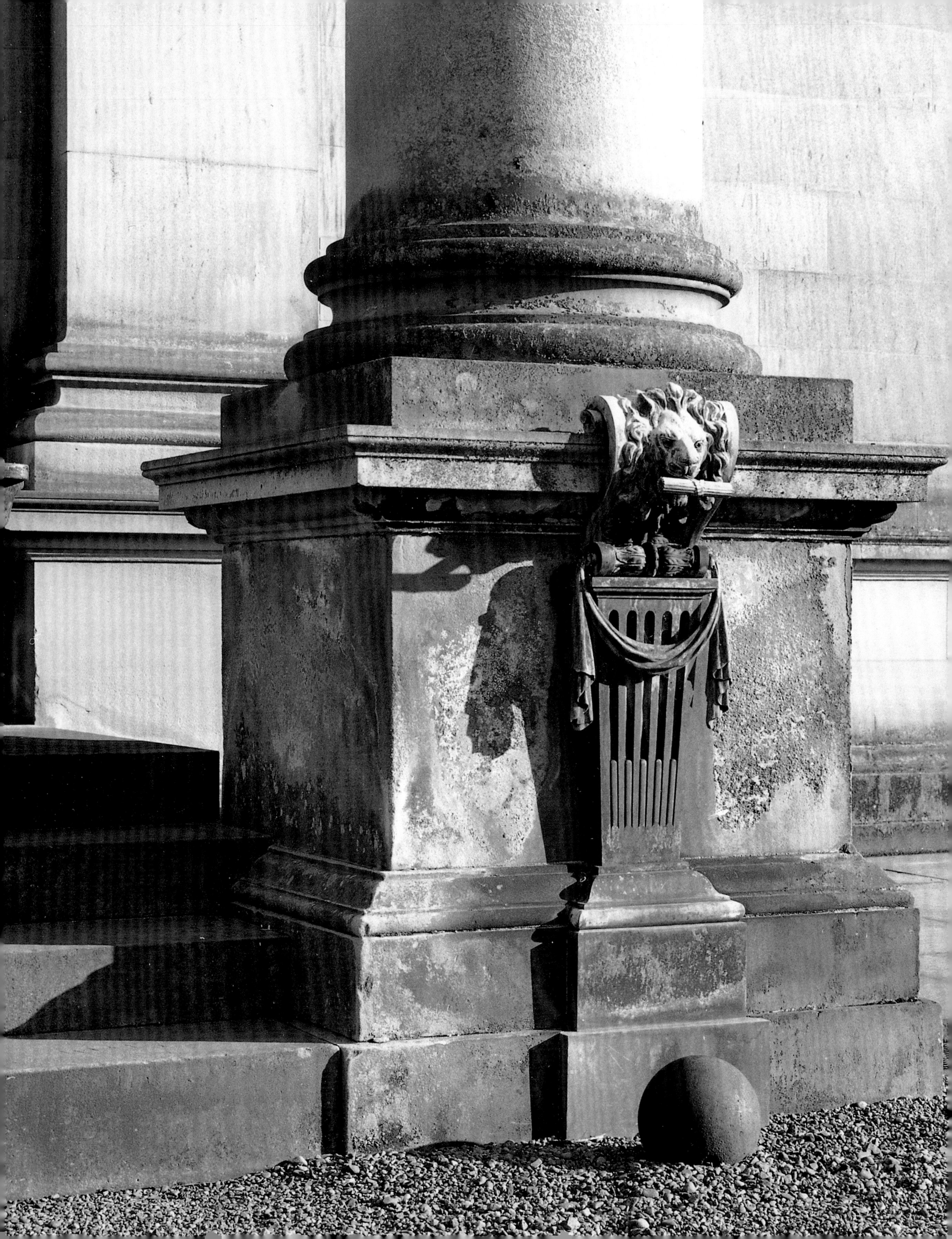

MANDERSTON, BERWICKSHIRE

Our search for the perfectly consistent Classical house has been dominated by patrons who looked directly to Italian precedent, but in the twentieth century we find a patron who felt it entirely appropriate to look to Robert Adam in the eighteenth century for inspiration, on the grounds that while in Rome Adam had more than adequately studied Classical sources.

The aggrandisement of the eighteenth-century house at Manderston from 1901 was in striking contrast to the complete rebuilding of Gosford House, which, as we have just seen, had begun exactly ten years before. There, with Victorian confidence the new wings of the 1890s were in a heavier and more exuberant style than that of the original Adam mansion. By contrast, a new sensibility at Manderston kept the flavour of the exterior of the old house when it was greatly enlarged in 1901–05 for Sir James Miller, 2nd Baronet (1864–1906).

The eleven-bay, long country house built by an unknown architect in the early 1790s had been bought in 1864 by Sir James's father, Sir Richard Miller, who had amassed a fortune of several million pounds from Baltic and Russian trade, and later from industrial interests in Manchester. He was a Liberal MP, as a result of which Gladstone ensured a baronetcy for him in 1874. He remodelled Manderston in the 1870s, adding a *porte cochère* and an incongruous high, French mansard roof. On his death in 1887, his son inherited his title, house and fortune, enabling him to move in a smarter social set than his father. He married in 1893 the Hon. Eveline Curzon, daughter of the 4th Baron Scarsdale and sister of the future Viceroy of India and 1st Marquess of Curzon. She was brought up in the Adam splendour of Kedleston where Sir James proposed to her, a circumstance not without influence on the work he was to carry out at Manderston.

A well-known race-horse owner, Miller began at Manderston by building extensive stables in 1895 of which Giles Worsley, sometime Architectural Editor of *Country Life*, wrote in 2004: 'Built round a quadrangle in an elegant Adamesque manner, these were a conscious

Above: The new entrance front 1901–05 of a late Georgian house completely remodelled and enlarged regardless of expense for Sir James Miller, 2nd Baronet, by John Kinross, who echoed externally the style of the original house.

Left: Bell-pulls on the column pedestals take the elegant form of bars held in the mouths of lion masks resting on tapered, fluted pilasters with swags in the style of A.-J. Gabriel.

PRE-WAR VARIETIES OF CLASSICISM · 125

homage to the great age of the Georgian stable, but with all the luxury associated with the Edwardians.' Below sophisticated segmentally vaulted ceilings, the stalls are of teak with solid brass posts while the names of the horses are picked out in gold on long marble panels. The architectural refinement of the stables was characteristic of their architect, John Kinross (1855–1931). After travelling and sketching in Italy in 1880–81, he published *Details from Italian Buildings, Chiefly Renaissance* (Edinburgh, 1882), a book which attracted the favourable attention of the millionaire architectural patron, the Marquess of Bute, for whom he carried out extremely sensitive restorations of Pluscarden Priory, Morayshire, and Falkland Palace, Fife.

In 1901, Miller invited Kinross to enlarge the main body of Manderston, involving demolition of the entrance front with its projecting side wings, adding a new wing, a service court and a basement, as well as rebuilding the roof to remove the French mansards. When Kinross asked Miller what the remodelling of Manderston should cost, his boastful reply was, 'it really doesn't matter.' It was thus fortunate that Kinross exercised restraint by retaining the late Georgian flavour of the best parts of the existing house, for though his new entrance front was larger than the original one, he kept the garden front with its elegant, three-bay curved bow in the centre, adding to it a wing with a similar bow. His windows are set cleanly into the ashlar with no fussy architrave mouldings, and there are exquisite Classical details in a French Louis XVI manner on the entrance front, including the swagged portrait medallion of the huntress Diana and the lion-mask bell pulls below the column bases, two working by hand and two by foot, which also feature in the stable yard.

The attenuated Ionic columns of the entrance portico have unusual capitals with fluted necking bands, which appear on an eighteenth-century design for the house by John Webster and may have been derived from Eydon Lodge, Northamptonshire (1788–89). This was by James Lewis (c.1750–1820), who published it in his *Original Designs in Architecture* (vol. II, 1797). Kinross tautened the design by making the portico unpedimented and reducing the entablature to just the frieze,

---

Above: The marble floor and chimneypiece in the hall echo details at Adam's Kedleston, as requested by James Miller, Baronet, whose wife's family home it was. The huge dome was entirely the contribution of Kinross.

Right: The corridor opening out of the hall, with its rich Doric Order, leads to the staircase with a wrought-iron balustrade inspired by that at the Petit Trianon, Versailles, by Gabriel.

126 · THE TWENTIETH CENTURY

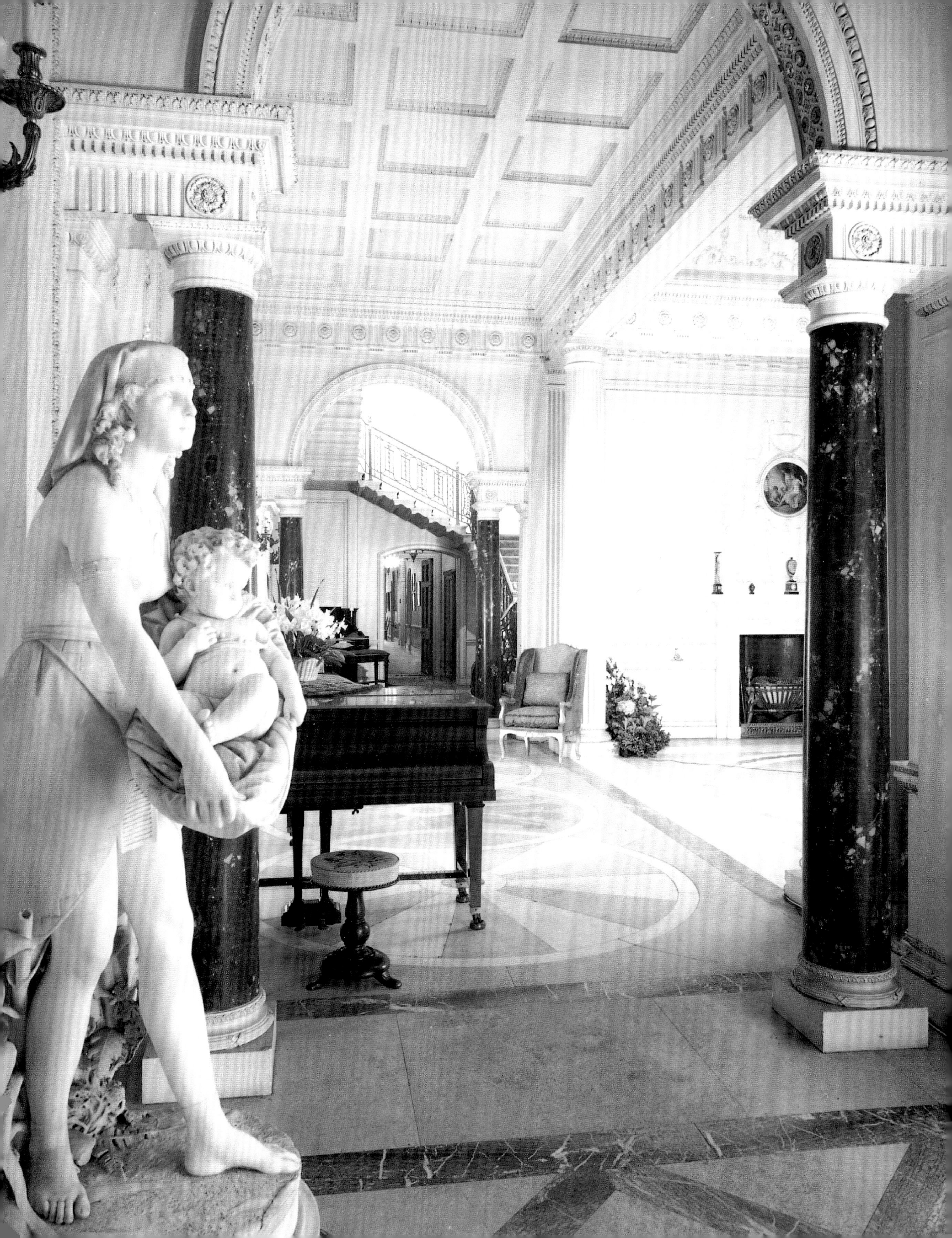

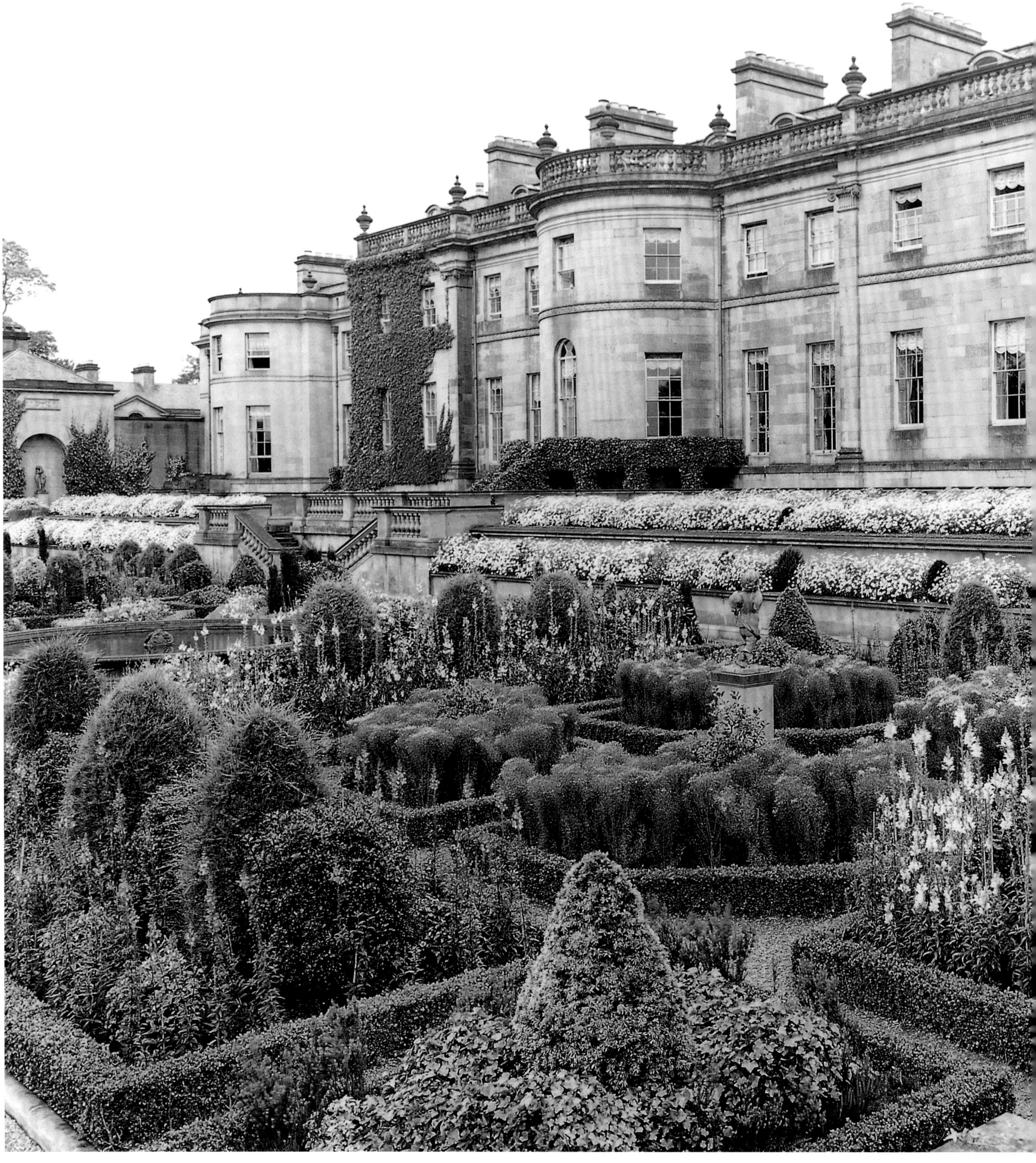

richly ornamented with *paterae* and swags. The crowning balustrade is broken in the centre by a large tablet based on an Ancient Roman sarcophagus decorated with a Vitruvian wave scroll. Adam used this on the one-storeyed portico at Newby Hall, Yorkshire, and in triumphal gateways at Croome Court and at Syon, where he illustrated it in his *Works in Architecture* (vol. 1, 1773).

The exquisite interiors of Manderston reflect the wish to overthrow what was felt (at the start of the reign of Edward VII) to be the rich heaviness of the Victorian Age, in favour of a return to the lightness and sophistication of eighteenth-century French and English design. The task of creating this effect at Manderston was entrusted to the Anglo-French firm of Charles Mellier and Co., of Albemarle Street, Mayfair, fashionable cabinet-makers and interior decorators, who employed French craftsmen here and at other commissions. Their proposals for furnishing and decorating Manderston include plans of 1805 showing the exact position of the furniture provided by them, sometimes exact copies of earlier pieces.

Kinross had also been required by Miller to create interiors that echoed features of Adam's work at Kedleston, his wife's family home. For example, both the chimneypiece and the floor in the hall derive from the Marble Hall at Kedleston, the former with an overmantel in which tall female figures in stuccowork support a circular painting, the latter with a circular motif of inlaid marble. The ballroom ceiling is similarly inspired by that in the dining room at Kedleston, and niches in the circular morning room are variants of those in the saloon at Kedleston, where the wall sconces with Wedgwood plaques are echoed in the portico bedroom at Manderston.

Kinross looked for inspiration in work by Adam other than at Kedleston: for example, in the hall at Manderston the Doric Order echoes that in the entrance hall at Syon and the stuccowork below the dome in the Second Drawing Room at Derby House, Grosvenor Square; the organ by the door to the drawing room is inspired by that in Sir Watkin Williams-Wynn's house in St James's Square. These sources were all illustrated in the Adam brothers' *Works in Architecture*, which were republished in 1900 in both Paris and London as part of the revival of interest in Adam's work by architects and decorators. Architecturally, Kinross's work at Manderston is in no way a copy of anything by Adam: the breathtaking hall with four corner columns below a high dome is his own invention, as is the spatial flow in which rooms are approached not from the hall but from passages and ante-rooms forming picturesque vistas. In a rare departure from Adamesque precedent, the wrought-iron balustrade of the grand staircase was inspired by that at the Petit Trianon, Versailles, by Ange-Jacques Gabriel of 1761–68. Kinross also created extensive formal gardens on a sloping site south of the house, where below a terrace adorned with stone vases is a series of broad and elaborate parterres with clipped hedges centred on a fountain.

Kinross retained the central curved bow on the garden front of the Georgian house, adding a wing with a similar bow on the left. Below, terraces with steps lead down to an elaborate formal garden.

PRE-WAR VARIETIES OF CLASSICISM · 129

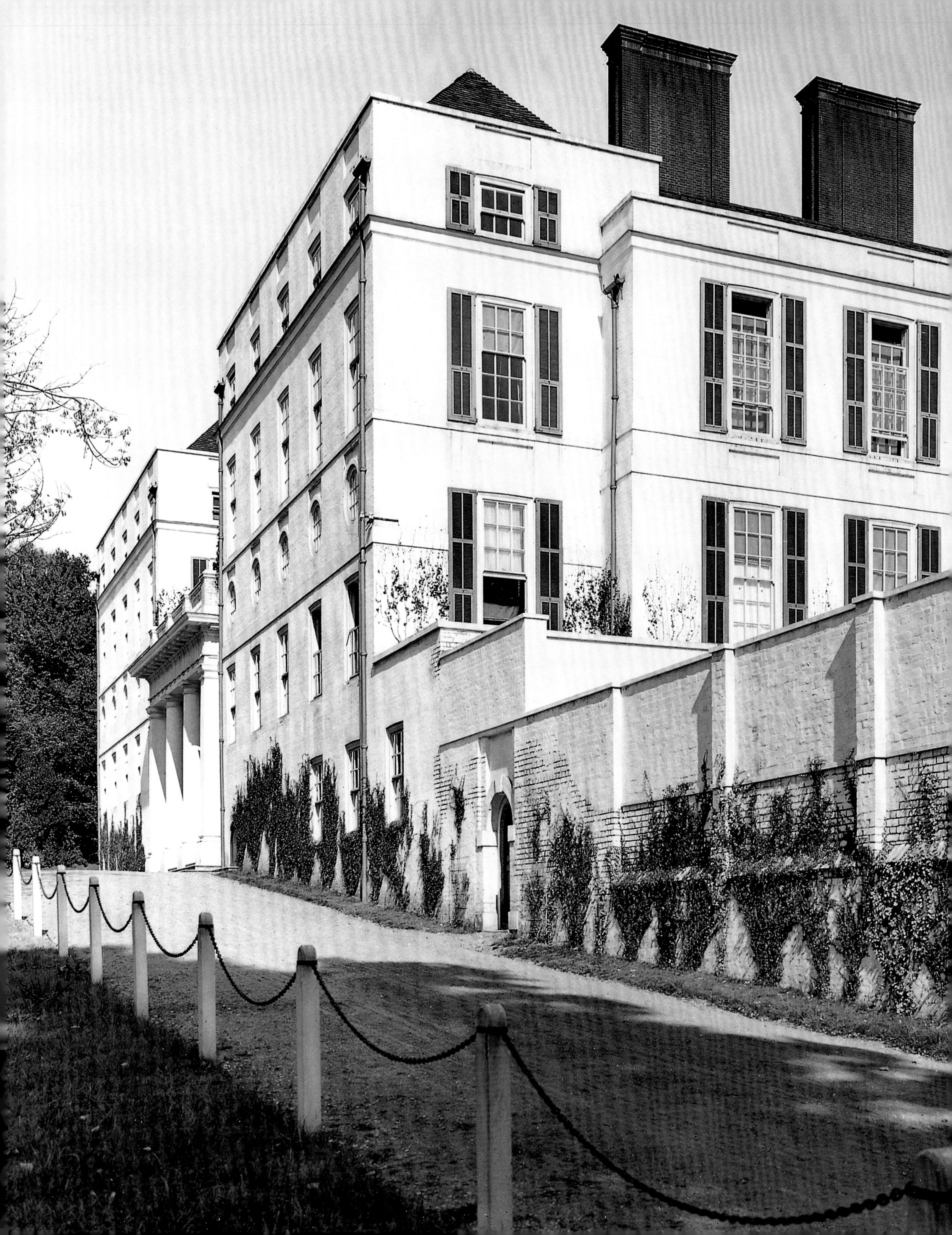

NASHDOM, BUCKINGHAMSHIRE

The majority of houses in this book have been driven by a patron with a passion for the Classical language of art and architecture, but through the forceful powers of his invention and personality, Edwin Lutyens provided a Classical house at Nashdom for a patron who seems to have had few ideas of her own, other than wanting a plushy setting for parties.

Nashdom was designed in 1905–08 at a turning point in the career of one of England's greatest architects. After a series of subtle Arts and Crafts masterpieces from 1897–1902, notably Orchards, Munstead Wood, Tigbourne Court, Deanery Garden and Little Thakeham, Lutyens' discovery of an architecture based on the timeless vocabulary of the Classical Orders came as a revelation. He explained this in 1903:

Left: *Commissioned from Lutyens in 1905 by the wealthy, Scottish-born Princess Alexis Dolgorouki, married to a Russian émigré, the towering house of white washed brick is approached dramatically up a steep slope.*

Below: *Looking along the dining room from its screened Ionic end towards the glass-domed, double-height, Winter Garden. The enfilade of interlocking reception rooms, including the circular drawing room at the far end, is 106-foot long.*

'The way Wren handled it was marvellous. Shaw had the gift. To the average man it is dry bones but under the mind of a Wren it glows and the stiff material becomes as plastic as clay.' He believed that 'You cannot copy,' for 'It means hard labour and hard thinking … [so that] If you tackle it in this way the Order belongs to you, and any stone being mentally handled must become endowed with such poetry and artistry as God has given you.'

One of his first Classical houses, Heathcote, Yorkshire (1906), was a masterly exercise in the powerful Doric of Michele Sanmichele, as in his Porta Palio, Verona (1548–59), with its recessed rusticated wall layers. But what Lutyens brilliantly showed at Nashdom was how the Classical Orders could govern the character and proportions of a design without being sprayed all over it. Though Nashdom is a largely unadorned pile of whitewashed brick, the key is set by its Doric entrance loggia, which determines the height of the first two floors of the entrance front. It has been compared to the loggia at Peruzzi's neo-antique Palazzo Massimo, Rome (*c.*1532), though that lacks the full triglyph frieze that Lutyens provided at Nashdom.

PRE-WAR VARIETIES OF CLASSICISM · 131

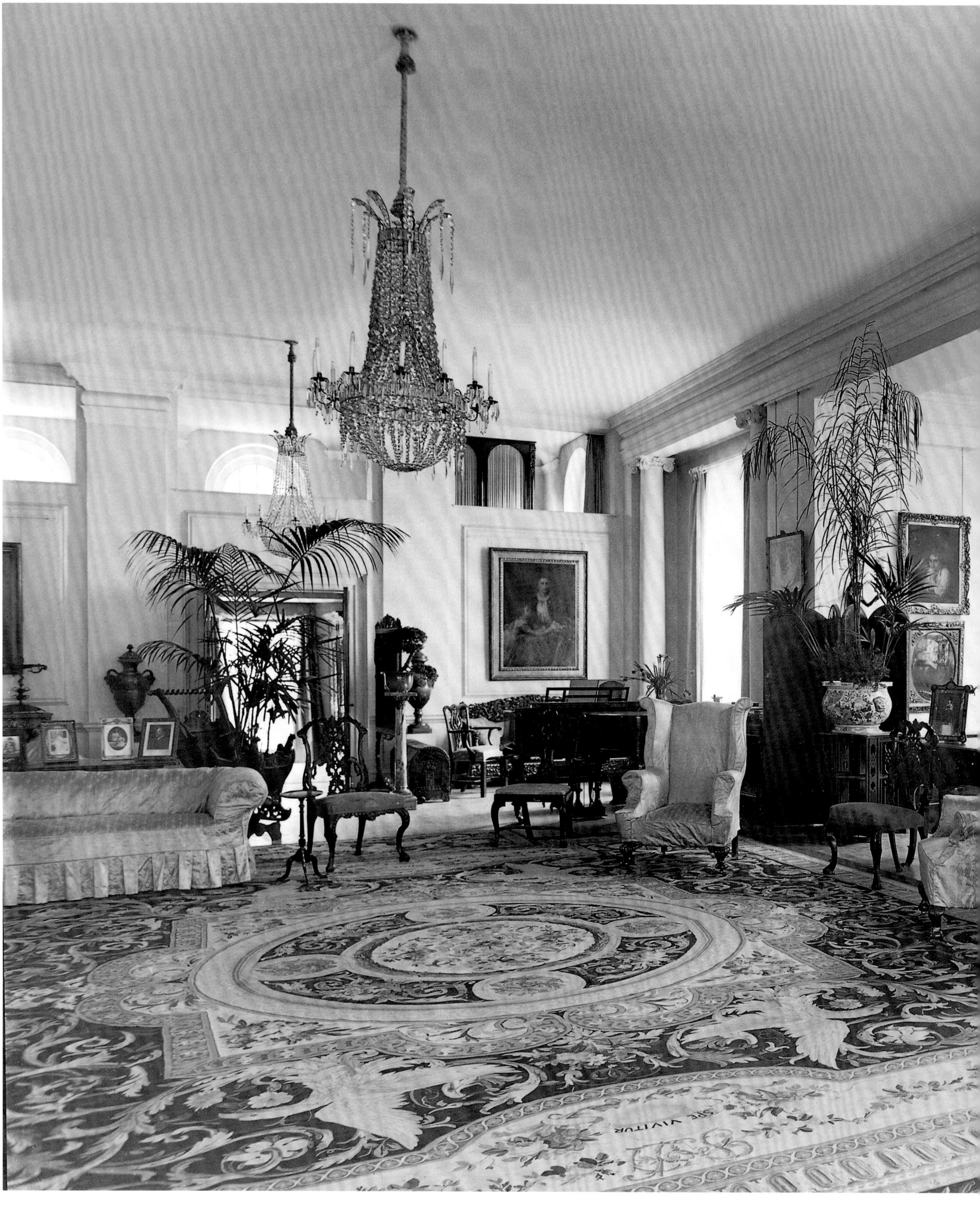

two columns. It is the centre of an axis 106-foot long consisting of reception rooms, all of different shapes but opening into each other in the way in which the Princess wanted for her big parties. Though this was at variance with Lutyens' customary preference for surprise and ingenuity in planning, he was able to create an unusual circular drawing room which, like the circular bedroom over it, has exceptionally thick walls to allow for deep window embrasures and to create diffused light. As Jane Ridley suggested in *The Architect and his Wife: The Life of Edwin Lutyens* (2002), 'Lutyens mocked the Princess's "pretentious French furniture" with the "austere detailing" of these rooms.' However, against his better judgement, she did manage to get into the Ionic dining room her circular dining table with a goldfish pool and small bubbling fountain in the centre, surrounded by 'delicate flowers in their seasons' and lit by concealed electric lights.

Partly to thwart the desire of the Princess for a staircase with a red plush handrail, Lutyens chose to place it rising between solid walls in half flights, following Italian Renaissance fashion, rather than in the open well, which he normally preferred in large houses. But he could not resist allowing the half landing to expand into an astonishingly large space, 18-foot by 10-foot, which, typical of his wit, served ambiguously as half writing room and half landing. Other unusual and generous features on the first floor include a corridor, 8-foot wide, and a 25-foot long studio, with three north-facing windows.

The spectacular gardens contain two monumental staircases with a flavour of Persepolis or Versailles at the end of a 20-foot high retaining wall, between the upper lawn and the lower garden. The vista of the upper lawn is terminated by a small Classical temple, which ingeniously screens the electricity-generating house behind an arch breaking into a pediment. The entrance lodge, a small masterpiece, is a complex composition with canted wings and a central archway, flanked by Doric columns supporting an entablature that breaks into the eaves of the roof.

Prince and Princess Alexis Dolgorouki both died within ten years of the completion of the house in 1909, and in 1926 it became, improbably, an Anglican Benedictine monastery for which an unattractive wing was added in 1967–69. The monks have now left and the house has been adapted as apartments.

Above: Though Georgian in detail, the garden front is a novel composition, its balancing halves expressing the separate suites of the Prince and Princess, and the dip in the centre accommodating the Winter Garden dome.

Left: Lutyens' imagination and feeling for mass are well shown in this giant staircase linking the upper lawn and lower garden at the end of a 20-foot high retaining wall.

136 · THE TWENTIETH CENTURY

VILLA VIZCAYA, FLORIDA

This stunningly beautiful house and garden, created in 1913–15 for James Deering (1859–1925), reflects one of the main themes of this book, the love affair of a demanding patron with the Classical forms of Italy, especially as expressed in the great period from the Renaissance to the Baroque. William Bankes of Kingston Lacy would be a close parallel to Deering, who was similarly a bachelor with taste as well as wealth. A contemporary who claimed he had 'a mind as exquisitely cultured as one could imagine', added, 'I do not believe it is possible to find in all the aristocracies of Europe a nature really more distinguished than that of Mr James Deering.' His fortune came from the family manufactory of agricultural machinery, which had pioneered the combine harvester. He suffered in later life from pernicious anaemia, hence the choice of Florida for a villa for winter residence.

The architect was nominally Francis Burrall Hoffman, Jnr, but the whole project, down to the last detail in both the house and gardens, was the vision of Paul Chalfin (1873–1959), who had been associated with Elsie de Wolfe at her celebrated New York Studio of Interior Decoration. She had introduced Chalfin to Deering when he went to her for advice in 1910. After Harvard, he had been trained as a painter at the Ecole des Beaux-Arts in Paris in the atelier of Jean-Léon Gérôme, winning a scholarship to the American Academy in Rome in 1905. Conscious of the need of the services of a trained architect, Chalfin recommended Deering to employ the young Hoffman, also a Harvard graduate, who had been a pupil at the Ecole des Beaux-Arts in Paris of Henri-Adolphe-Auguste Deglane. He began his career in the New York office of Carrère and Hastings before starting his own practice in 1910.

Chalfin and Deering travelled in Europe before 1913 to find models for villas, selecting the Villa Rezzonico, near Bassano del Grappa, in the Veneto, built in 1678–82 from designs by Baldassare Longhena. Its two-storeyed main front of seven bays, flanked by taller towers, was followed for the design of the east front at Villa Vizcaya, overlooking Biscayne Bay. The whole place was intended to provide a narrative as though it were on an Italian estate occupied and renovated by several generations of a family. The element of narrative fantasy, which had featured in the English Picturesque, had similarly played a part in Soane's creation of instant Roman ruins in the grounds of his own villa, Pitzhanger Manor. In the quest for over-night mellowness, 100,000 pantiles, many of them already nearly a century old, were brought for the roofs of the Villa Vizcaya from buildings in Cuba, while great effort was expended on toning down the external stuccowork to give the impression of having been mellowed by years of sun and rain. Much of the limestone was also imported from Cuba, the local stone being considered too coral-like to be used, except decoratively.

Hoffman planned the villa round a central open cortile with three, large open loggias in the centre of the east, south and west sides, the

The Italian Gardens were designed by Diego Suarez as a vast outdoor room and included the water staircase, recalling that at Palazzo Corsini, Rome, and shell grottoes with decorative ceilings and volcanic stone carved to imitate water.

PRE-WAR VARIETIES OF CLASSICISM · 137

first two providing superb views towards Biscayne Bay and the gardens respectively. Having visited the Veneto in 1913 to study at first hand the villas by Palladio and other architects, Hoffman had observed in many of them an intimacy and a domestic character, which he was able to reflect at the Villa Vizcaya where, despite the overall splendour, the rooms were not unduly high. Though it was in some ways the southern counterpart to the palatial houses of millionaires at Newport, Rhode Island, it yet had the atmosphere of a villa rather than a palace. Much of this atmosphere was due to Paul Chalfin who was seen by Marcus Binney, writing in *Country Life* in 1980, as playing a 'role akin to that of the *décorateur* in certain 18th-century Baroque palaces, a kind of artistic director or coordinator who was responsible for the over-all effect as well as for designing interiors and supervising furnishings.'

Chalfin and Deering had acquired historic chimneypieces, doorcases, *boiseries*, ceilings and wrought-iron grilles, which were temporarily stored and arranged in tentative room settings on several floors of a Manhattan warehouse before being brought to Villa Vizcaya. Here, Chalfin incorporated them with skilful additions and alterations of his own in a series of rooms in a range of styles from Renaissance through Baroque and Rococo to Neo-Classical and Empire. The aim was to create something beautiful rather than narrowly accurate from an historical point of view. The three loggias with their patterned marble floors are effectively semi-outdoor drawing rooms on a scale without Italian precedent. Nonetheless, the east loggia has late-eighteenth-century pine doors and marble architraves brought from the Palazzo Torlonia in Rome, a touch that would have pleased William Bankes at Kingston Lacy. The loggia on the south garden front was given a late-eighteenth-century Neapolitan character, a more southern touch as befits the climate of Florida.

The gardens, which it overlooks, were laid out from designs by Diego Suarez (1888–1974) who was born in Bogota, Colombia, but, thanks to his Italian mother, was trained in architecture at the Accademia delle Belle Arti in Florence. Becoming interested in garden design, he worked at Villa La Pietra, near Florence, for Arthur Acton

Right: *The Rococo music room, a North Italian assembly, showing the fruits of Deering's vast collection of historic furniture, fabrics, boiseries, ceilings and chimneypieces, arranged with taste and authenticity in interiors in different styles.*

Below: *James Deering's sitting room in the Italian Directoire style, the masterpiece of Paul Chalfin, who had travelled in Europe with Deering to seek inspiration and was the artistic coordinator of the house, as built from Hoffman's designs in 1913–15.*

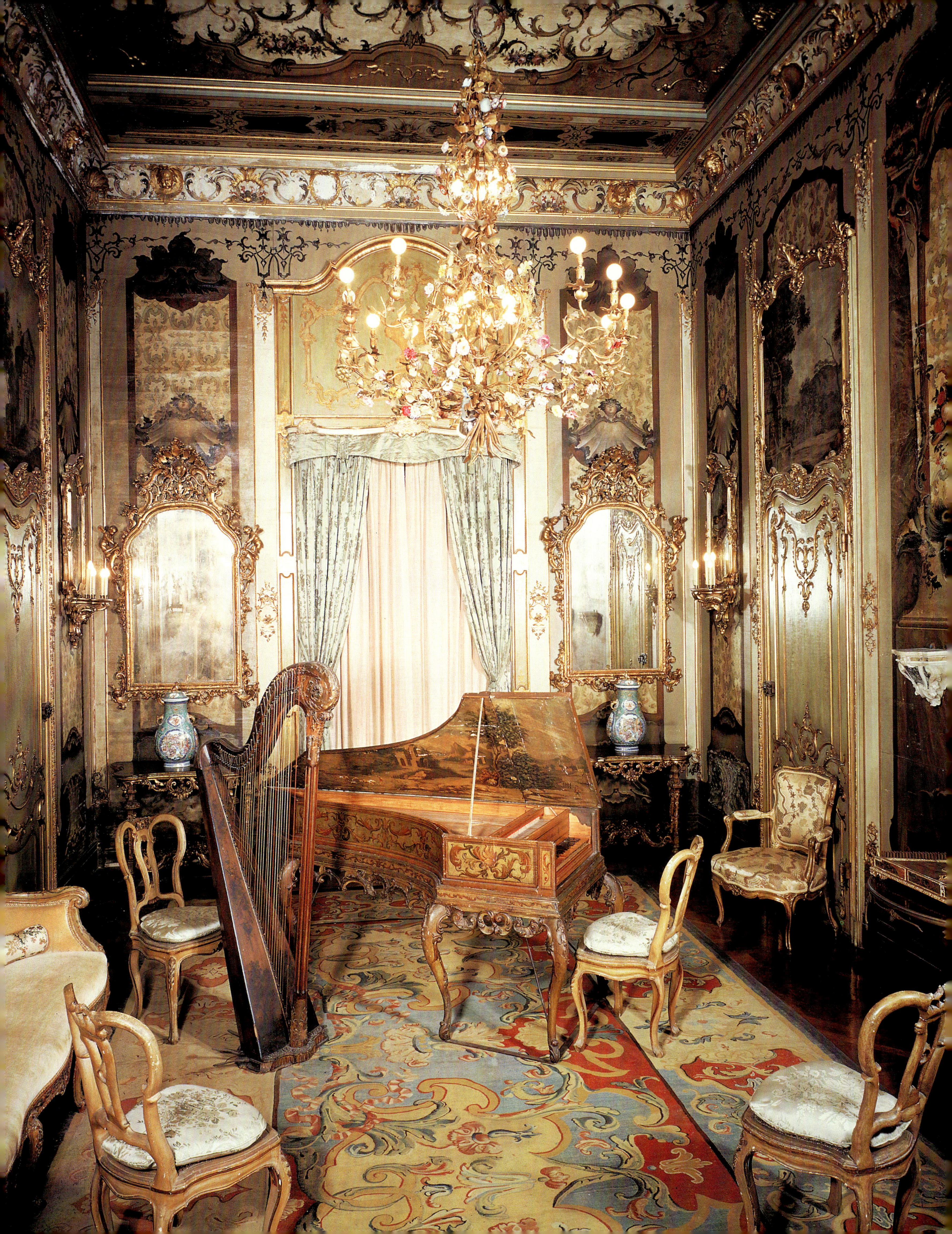

who, with his American heiress wife, was creating a formal Italianate garden at the villa from 1904. This was subsequently maintained by their son, the aesthete and author, Harold Acton. Deering and Chalfin met Arthur Acton who arranged for Suarez to show them a range of nearby villas and gardens, and introduced them to Anglo-American society in Florence of which Geoffrey Scott's book, *The Architecture of Humanism* (1914), was a product.

The spectacular garden, which Suarez created at Villa Vizcaya from 1914, radiates out in a fan pattern from the loggia on the south front, branching off to a subsidiary circular area, a complex pattern not unlike those envisaged by Robert Castell in his fanciful plans of Pliny's gardens in his *The Villas of the Ancients Illustrated* (1728). The walled secret garden, with rusticated pilasters and a shell-headed grotto, was inspired by that at the Villa Gamberaia near Florence. The great water staircase recalls the water theatre by Carlo Maderno of 1702–25 at the Villa Torlonia, Frascati, itself in the tradition of the Islamic water stair, as at the Generalife, Granada. A large rubbish mound, accumulated during dredging in the bay near the house, gave Suarez the astonishing idea of using it as the basis of a vast stone barge, with a surrounding balustrade capped with obelisks and statues by the leading American sculptor, A. Stirling Calder (1870–1945). This glamorous creation was inspired by Isola Bella on Lake Maggiore, where the gardens covering the whole island were in the form of a barque or barge. Visitors to Villa Vizcaya could be ferried in gondolas from the stone barge along a canal cut through the mango swamp to the two-storeyed *casino* on the mount at the far end of the whole garden.

The farm section of the estate lay west of the main residence, on the other side of the road that was to become South Miami Avenue. Here, Hoffman created a series of buildings resembling a small North Italian village, a subtle essay in instant Picturesque history to which there is a close parallel at Hever Castle, Kent, created for another wealthy American, William Waldorf Astor. In 1903–07, Astor provided a series of interiors in an early Renaissance style inside the moated, fourteenth-century castle and built a cluster of guest cottages and offices in stone and half-timber round a series of courtyards on the other side of the moat, creating the impression of a small Tudor village.

The nieces of the childless James Deering inherited Villa Vizcaya on his death in 1925 and within ten years were opening it to the public in the winter as an experiment. It was bought in 1952 by the local authority, now Miami-Dade County, and survives today as a museum of the decorative arts, though to maintain the external stonework and the gardens has proved a major challenge in the humid and hurricane-prone climate with its salt air.

Looking from the glazed doors of the loggia on the south front towards the mount and the two-storied casino. *Work continued until 1921 on the gardens where the hedges were of pine to suit the climate.*

PRE-WAR VARIETIES OF CLASSICISM · 141

⊙ GLEDSTONE HALL, YORKSHIRE ⊙

Nashdom was perhaps the most capricious house Lutyens designed, a contradictory and paradoxical place where nothing is what it seems. By contrast, Gledstone Hall, Yorkshire (1925–27), has a perfect balance with few fireworks but just the repose which the Classical language can bring. Every detail inside and outside, however large or small, bears the stamp of Lutyens' creative mind so that, with the total unity between it and its architectural gardens, it could claim to be the most masterly and refined house in this book. Indeed, it is impossible not to agree with A. S. G. Butler, who summed it up in the *Lutyens Memorial* volumes in 1950 as 'a design of matchless distinction. There is an almost royal quality in it too; and a faint resemblance to Compiègne comes especially from the low wing walls suggesting guard-rooms to a small palace.'

Gledstone was built for Sir Amos Nelson (1860–1947), a wealthy cotton-mill owner at Nelson in Lancashire, who bought the old Gledstone Hall with a 5,000 acre estate near the Yorkshire border in 1919. Almost certainly by Carr of York of *c.*1770, this was a fine house with a seven-bay front, the three central bays canted, and with two, smaller two-bay pavilions. Immediately adjacent to it was an enormous quadrangular stable block with a cupola and a circular arcaded courtyard. Nelson's original intention was to reconstruct this house, a commission he gave in November 1919 to a local architect, Richard Jacques. When the large scale of the task became clear, Nelson suggested that he might like to work with an architect of wider reputation. Jacques, like Nelson, knew Lutyens' Heathcote, under twenty miles away, so the choice fell on him.

The plans for reconstruction were soon abandoned on grounds of cost and it was decided to build a new, slightly smaller house for not more than £40,000, half a mile away on a higher site. In fact, it was to cost £120,000! Surely only Lutyens could persuade an owner that it would be cheaper to build an entirely new house than restore an existing one, but one of the aims was to find a site on which a garden

---

Above: *On the entrance front, a monument of faultless Classic calm, Lutyens inclined the walls slightly inwards like the columns of the Parthenon, concealed downpipes, and formed the immense roof of stone slates diminishing in height.*

Right: *In a domed oval lobby opening off the vaulted ground-floor corridor, the dynamic bronze group,* Au Loup!, *by Louis Hiolin, matches the lively patterns of the floor in black, white and dove grey marble.*

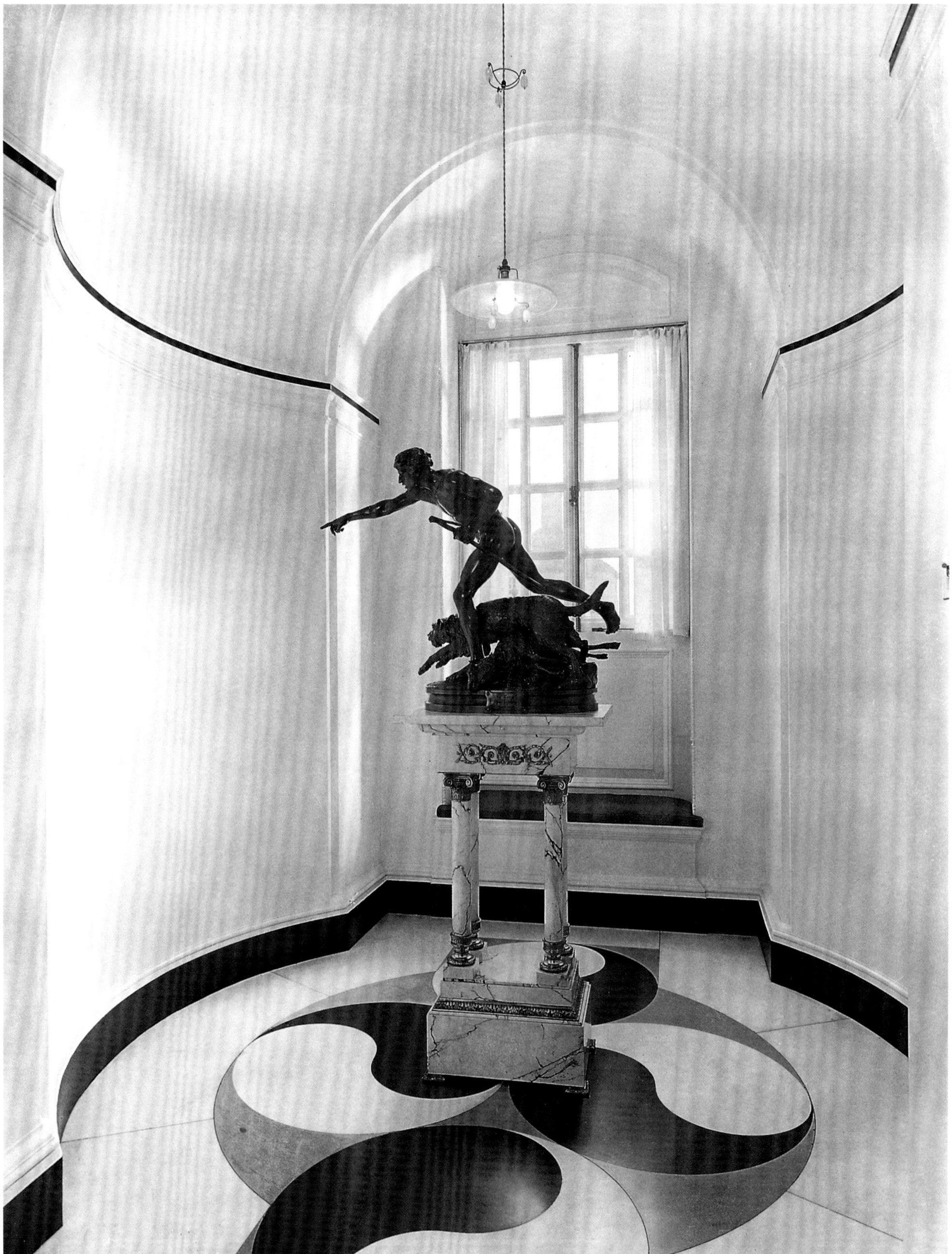

worthy of the noble moorland setting could be made. When Nelson demolished the old house in 1925–27, bringing doors and fine chimneypieces to its replacement designed by Lutyens, he fortunately spared the stables, a fine piece of architectural geometry, which Lutyens must have appreciated.

In 1920, Nelson and his wife were on the same ship to Bombay as Lutyens, who was on his way to Delhi to work on designs for the Viceroy's House. He was also persuaded to make designs for Gledstone while on board, and it is no coincidence that an early sketch shows it with the sense of mass and the canted walls of Viceroy's House. Described by Lutyens as 'a pleasant cotton spinner', Nelson was thought to resemble him in appearance as well as in manner. The cotton industry fell into temporary depression while Gledstone was rising, but Nelson concealed his financial strain from Lutyens so that the place was fortunately completed in every particular, apart from the two apple houses and cottage at the southern end of the gardens.

The house is set in the rolling Pennine landscape on the brow of a shallow rift in the hillside at West Marton, about eight miles west of Skipton. As A. S. G. Butler observed, 'One gets the impression on the spot that the buildings and the landscape are modelled into each other and that no other position or shape of a house is possible.' It has a broad axial approach, orchestrated spatially into two parts, the first defined by a balancing pair of entrance lodges, each a cube with a pyramidal roof culminating in a central chimney stack, a scheme he later echoed at Middleton Park, Oxfordshire, and at the British Embassy, Washington. Beyond these is a long *clair-voie*, or grille, with central entrance gates, all of wrought iron and creating the palatial French air noted by Butler. This forms one side of a forecourt with buildings on three sides, that facing us being the entrance front of the house with its Palladian Ionic portico of free-standing columns, the only one of its kind on a Lutyens house in England. The large arched opening in its side walls, derived from the Portico of Octavia in Rome, may be based on those at St Paul's, Covent Garden, though Lutyens was probably unaware that here they were not by Inigo Jones but were introduced in a rebuilding of 1878–82.

One of the most memorable features of Gledstone is its immense stone roof of Cotswold stone slates from Gloucestershire, diminishing in size as they rise. Lutyens insisted that its mass should not be interrupted by any dormer windows, nor is the purity of the walls compromised by plumbing and waste pipes, for they are concealed within. The walls are inclined inwards as they rise and the depth of each course of the creamy stone is diminished, as at Viceroy's House, Delhi, and his Midland Bank. The tall first-floor windows giving the air of a French château do not light the large rooms of a *piano nobile* as they suggest, but simply the staircase, linen room, a bathroom and a bedroom, a typical Lutyens game. The windows are also prolonged downwards by wooden aprons to stress the verticality of the entrance front, which is in contrast with the more domestic and horizontal note struck by the garden front with its two, one-storeyed loggias with Doric columns.

With its inventive balustrade and black coved ceiling, the staircase has steps alternately in black and white marble, with one of the risers extended to form the dado in a celebrated example of Lutyens' wit.

PRE-WAR VARIETIES OF CLASSICISM · 145

146 · THE TWENTIETH CENTURY

Another game is played indoors on the staircase where the steps are alternately in black and white marble and one of the risers is extended to form the dado, while another marks the level of the first floor and is continued round the stair hall to form the widow sills. The cove of the ceiling is black while there is much black, white and dove grey marble in exhilarating patterns in the entrance hall, corridors and lobby to the dining room. It is somewhat chilly for a house on high ground in Yorkshire, but doubtless Sir Amos Nelson, like the patron in Alexander Pope's *Epistle* to Lord Burlington, 'Of the Use of Riches', was 'Proud to catch cold at a Venetian door.'

'*Metiendo Vivendum*', ('by measure we live'), was Lutyens' motto and it is nowhere better expressed than at Gledstone where, as at Viceroy's House, the axial planning of the house is continued into the architectural garden. Skilfully handling the gentle slope of the land southwards, he was able with striking originality to create a long canal, dramatically sunk to look like a dock or harbour and flanked by two bastions over 200-foot long. These provide welcome shelter from the Yorkshire winds and terminate in flights of steps leading up to pergolas like pavilions. At the foot of these, the canal finishes in a magical touch with a circular basin in which the rim is almost flush with the water.

Gertrude Jekyll, now aged eighty-three, provided the planting in 1926 as her last commission for Lutyens, but she never came to the house and her impressionist work, involving seven hundred and twenty-nine different plants, was not entirely appropriate to the architecture or the climate. Nonetheless, she made an heroic attempt, writing justly: 'The formally designed garden that is an architectural adjunct to an imposing building demands a dignified unity of colouring rather than the petty and frivolous effects so commonly obtained by the misuse of many colours.'

Above: *With its generous Doric loggias, the south garden front has an appropriately more domestic flavour than the imposing entrance front yet commands a breathtaking view from the terrace along the formal canal.*

Left: *The astonishing canal or sunken rectangular pool is flanked by bastions over 200-foot long with double bordered walks on their top, which were planted, with some difficulty in this northern climate, by Gertrude Jekyll.*

PRE-WAR VARIETIES OF CLASSICISM · 147

THE BRITISH EMBASSY, WASHINGTON

This famous Embassy by Sir Edwin Lutyens, on one of the tree-lined avenues of greater-Washington, was planned from the outset to resemble a country house. While it was being built in 1928–30, New Delhi, which Lutyens designed as a garden city of low-rise buildings, was nearing completion. As the most prolific architect of country houses as well as of Viceroy's House, Delhi, and as the only British architect to be awarded the Gold Medal by the American Institute of Architecture, Lutyens was the natural choice for the new Embassy.

Nevertheless, these were difficult years in which to undertake so ambitious an enterprise, one problem being the enormous British debt to the United States, which had accumulated during the First World War; another was the Crash of 1929. The parsimony of the Treasury forced Lutyens to scale down the whole design by ten per cent, a process which led him to produce four successive schemes. This resulted in some awkwardness in planning, including several rooms being too small in size, insufficient bedrooms, and the eventual omission of even a laundry and a lift.

The architect Charles Moore, Chairman of the Commission for Fine Arts in Washington, observed of Lutyens' drawings for the Embassy that they 'seem to be a happy expression of a style of architecture which the Fathers of the Republic brought with them.' This reflected Lutyens' awareness that East Coast settlers in the seventeenth century had adopted the style and the red brick of buildings by contemporaries of Wren, his favourite architect, as seen in the College of William and Mary at Colonial Williamsburg. He hoped that the great brick chimney stacks rising out of the immensely high-pitched roofs of his Ambassador's Residence at Washington 'will be as impressive as those which stand as sentinels on the roofs of Chelsea Hospital – one of Wren's most dignified buildings.' The traditional plantation houses of Virginia seem also to be echoed in the Ionic portico on the south front, which Lutyens made double depth to provide a welcome shady loggia for retreat from the summer heat.

He responded with characteristic brilliance to the difficult site, which is irregularly shaped and steeply sloping. His solution was a totally novel plan comprising of three building blocks, the first of which is the Chancery, a three-sided quadrangle of offices open on the east to Massachusetts Avenue. In an element of the surprise, which always appealed to Lutyens, the Chancery largely conceals the much bigger Ambassador's Residence, from which it is linked by a smaller wing containing the Ambassador's study. Facing south, this wing has an axis at right angles to the Chancery, but the fact that the ground rises to the west enabled Lutyens to make the principal ground floor of the Ambassador's Residence on the same level as the first floor of the Chancery. In the monumental, three-volumed *Lutyens Memorial* (1950), his pupil A. S. G. Butler explained in detail the complex disposition of volumes

The monumental Ionic portico at Lutyens' Embassy is unusually not on the entrance front but the garden front, where the shady depth provided by its double columns brings welcome relief from the summer sun.

PRE-WAR VARIETIES OF CLASSICISM · 149

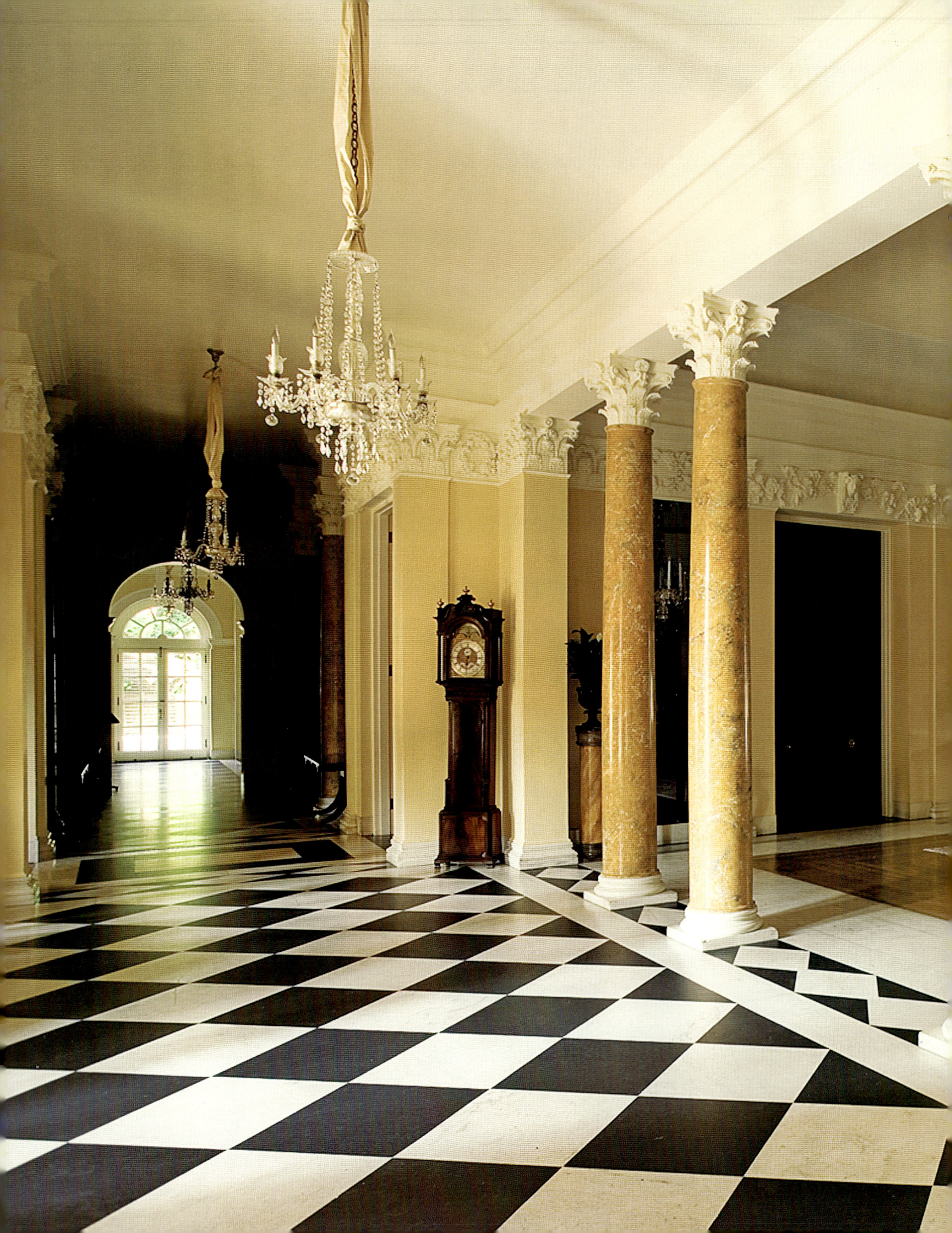

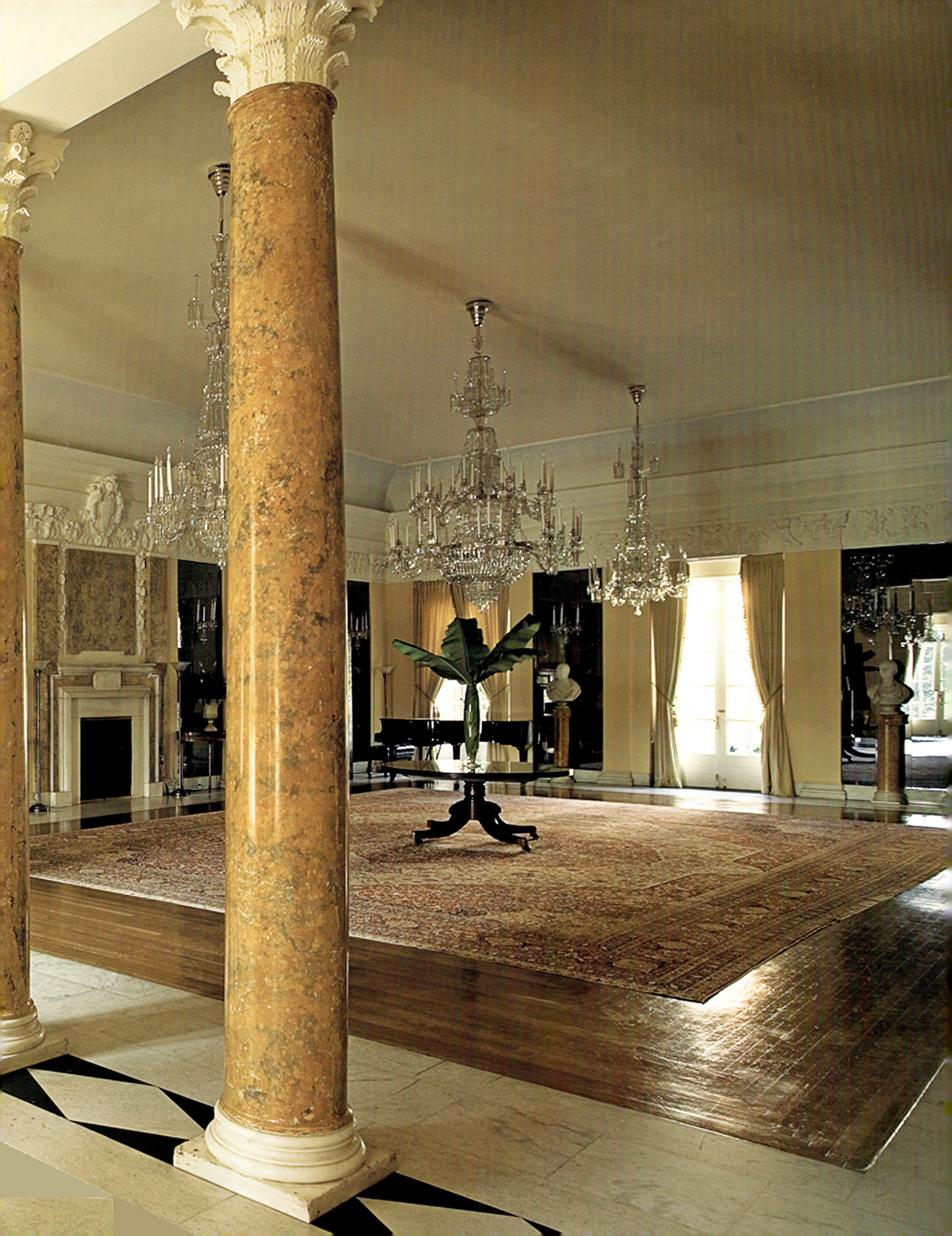

152 · THE TWENTIETH CENTURY

and the internal planning, observing, 'A prevailing symmetry is very apparent. It is felt through the knitting together of axial lines at right angles to each other.'

The Chancery and Embassy have their own entrance approaches, in which motor cars taking large numbers of guests to receptions in the Ambassador's Residence proceed along the main entrance drive which passes in a tunnel below the Ambassador's study, where they are set down at the entrance to the main staircase. A similar arrangement on a vaster scale had been one of Lutyens' innovations in planning the circulation at Viceroy's House, New Delhi.

The Ambassador's study, the most important of all the interiors and placed at the heart of the whole complex, is richly panelled with fluted Corinthian pilasters. A perfect cube, it is a noble tribute to Inigo Jones with generous Palladian windows commanding views of the entrance drive passing beneath it, as well as of the gardens, the Potomac valley and the dome of the Capitol.

The great entrance hall is one of Lutyens's most thrilling spaces, for the staircase on a T-plan rises up to meet an internal flying bridge of stone and marble, which connects the Ambassador's study with a huge corridor, 130-foot long, running along the whole Residence from east to west. To provide variety despite its great length, Lutyens designed this corridor as a series of connecting spaces separated by arches and piers, and opening in the centre through two screens of Corinthian, Siena marble columns into the great hall or ballroom on the north side and the portico on the south.

Lutyens rarely provided his country houses with full-scale porticoes but the one at the Ambassador's Residence, generously detailed with pulvinated frieze and modillion cornice, recalls that at Gledstone Hall. He chose to relax the mood at Washington by omitting the modillion cornice of the entablature on the wings flanking the portico, a trick he borrowed from Palladio at the Villa Capra. He plays a characteristic Lutyens joke with these wings by incorporating two, floating Ionic capitals which crown neither columns nor pilasters. Further games indoors include huge doors opening on to shallow cupboards and, by contrast, small hidden doors giving on to the grand circular staircase leading up to the bedroom floor. This enchanting cantilevered stair has an iron balustrade of a uniquely whirling form.

Every feature of Lutyens' masterpiece in Washington bears his own personal stamp: its rhythms, proportion, masterly control of the Doric, Ionic and Corinthian Orders, and its geometrical massing, including concealed guttering so that the roof is flush with the cornice below rather than projecting. It would have been impossible but for his adoption of the symmetry and discipline of the Classical language of architecture, which acts not as a straitjacket but as a stimulus to the creation of the beauty and harmony celebrated in this book.

Previous pages: *The view west towards the garden along the cross corridor, which opens dramatically into the great ballroom through a screen of Corinthian columns.*

Left: *The imposing T-plan main staircase, with its inventive ironwork balustrade, rises to meet the flying bridge, which enables the Ambassador to pass directly from his study to the cross corridor.*

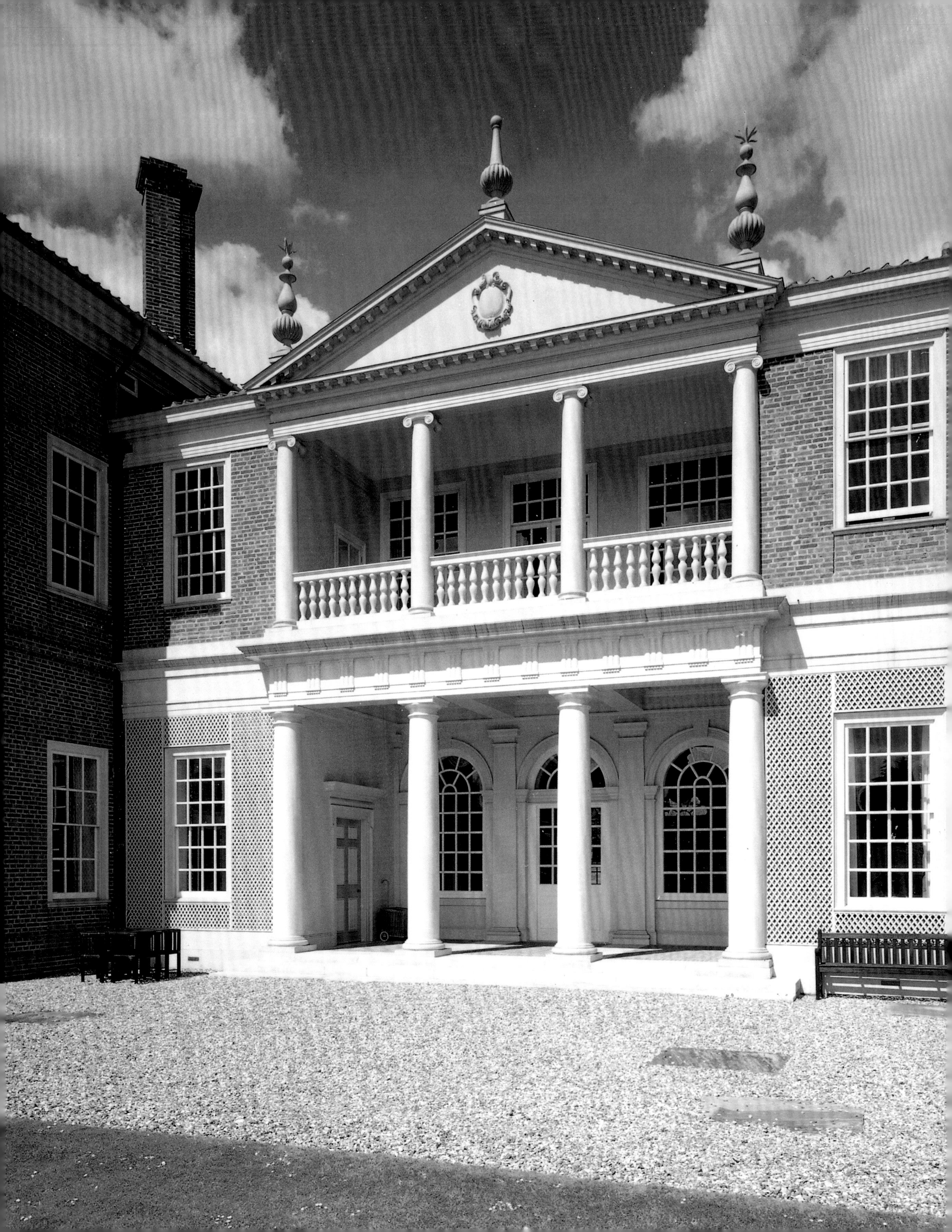

V

INTO THE TWENTY-FIRST CENTURY: CLASSICISM REBORN 1960 TO THE PRESENT DAY

The difficulties that the country house faced, notably from taxation and social change, led to the demolition of between three and four hundred major houses between 1919 and 1939. The destruction after the Second World War was even more extensive, John Harris calculated that in 1955 one house was demolished every two and a half days. Scarcely less damaging was the rise of the architectural ideology of the Modern Movement, which, reaching its apogee after 1945, believed that it was essential to abolish all references to the Classical language to create an architecture fit for 'modern man'. Few in 1955 would have predicted the renaissance in Classical country-house building that took place from the late 1970s. This was made possible not only by a return to prosperity but by a fact, forgotten by the Modernists, that Classicism is hydra-headed and will thus always renew itself.

Two distinguished architects who refused to adopt the language of Modernism after the Second World War were Francis Johnson

The garden front of Raymond Erith's King's Walden Bury, Hertfordshire, with a hint of the American Colonial style, was an early sign of the imminent revival of Classicism when it was begun in 1969.

(1911–95) and Raymond Erith (1904–73). Before the War, Johnson saw himself as part of the mainstream of architecture then prevailing in most countries, a plain, simple, but often quite monumental Classicism, which was more a reaction against Victorian and Arts and Crafts architecture than against Modernism. For him, contemporary work in Copenhagen, 'sound, clear brick architecture', as he called it, represented Classicism as 'the natural and graceful way in which to build.' Examples in Yorkshire include his remodelling of Settrington House (1963–68), with a portico of baseless, Roman Doric columns, and Whitwell-on-the-Hill (1970–72), featuring elegant curved bows in the early manner of Soane.

King's Walden Bury, Hertfordshire (1969–71), by Raymond Erith and Quinlan Terry, was widely believed at the time to be the last major Classical country house that would be built, yet it was followed by Terry's Waverton House, Gloucestershire (1978–80), Newfield House, Yorkshire (1979), and Merks Hall, Essex (1984–86), and many more since. Work by leading architects, John Simpson, Robert Adam and William Whitfield are illustrated here, but there are many others who uphold the eternal torch of Classicism.

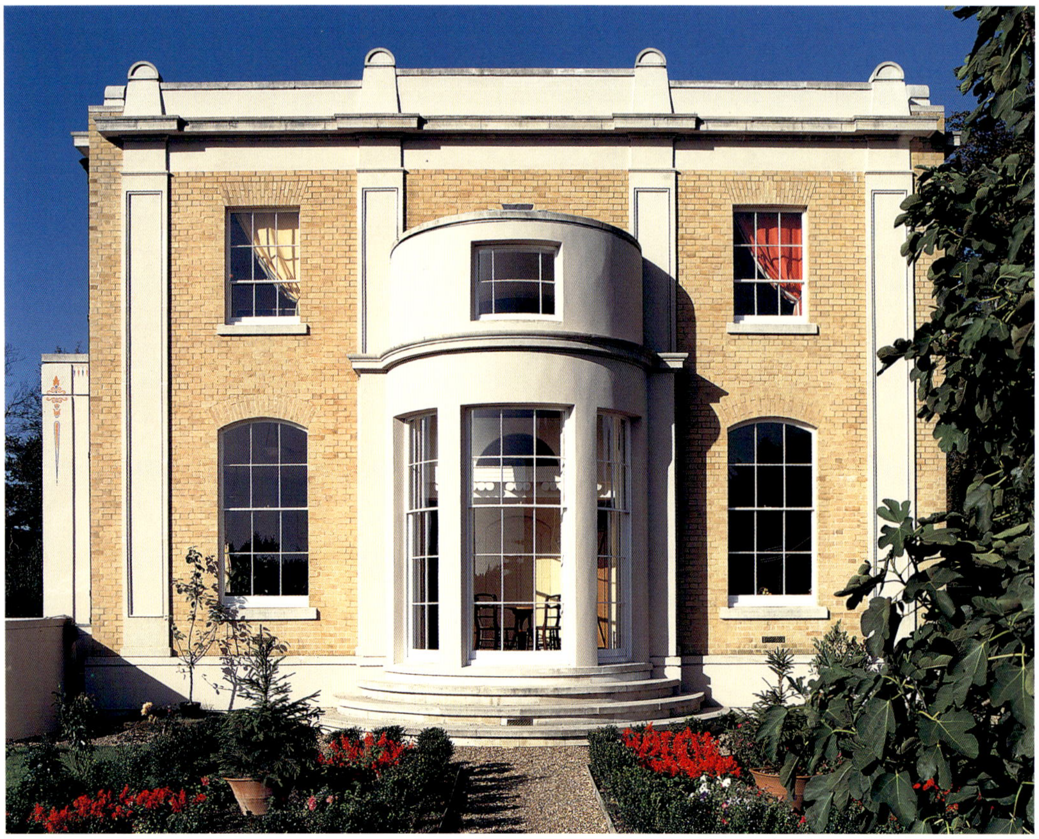

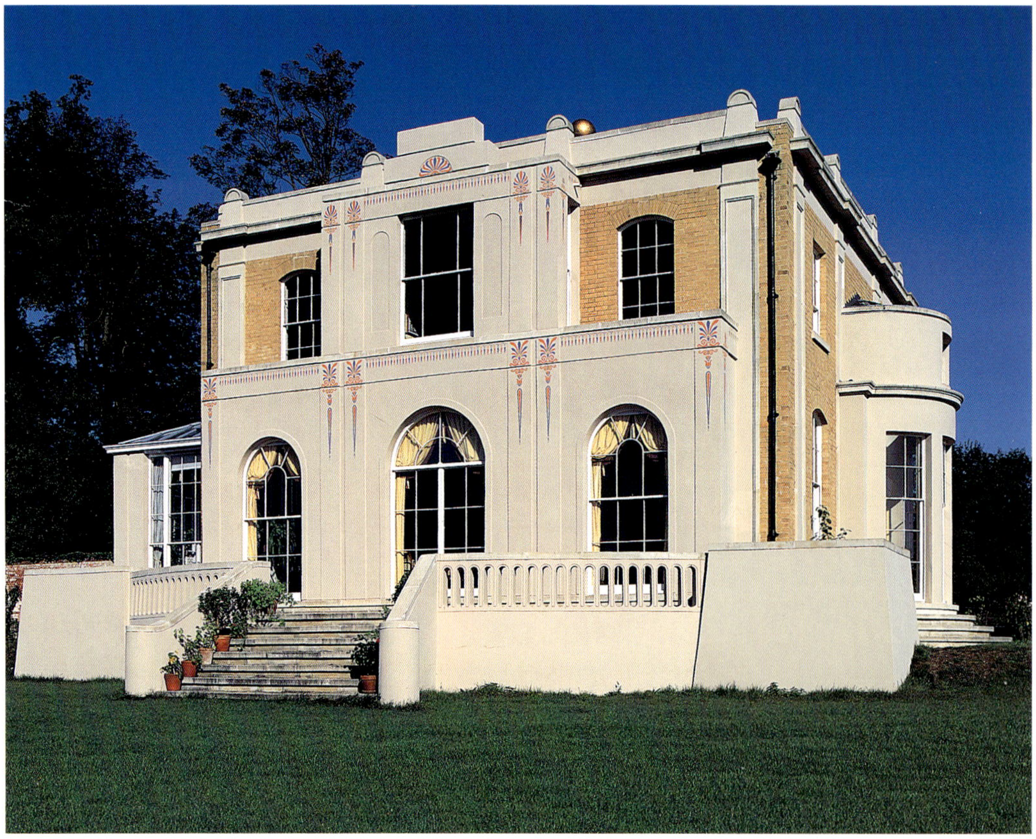

ASHFOLD HOUSE, SUSSEX

Ashfold House of 1988–90, though the work of a young architect, has a remarkable consistency of aim, displaying all the hallmarks of John Simpson's mature work: the combination of spatial poetry with minute attention to detail in which not even the design of a light-switch is overlooked. It demonstrates his recognition that modern technology can be integrated seamlessly into the house, for architecture is not truth: it involves the creation of beauty in which concealment and surprise can be as valuable as 'honesty'.

Ashfold was designed by John Simpson with his brother and partner, Michael, for their parents, John and Lydia. John Simpson senior was himself an architect. 'My parents wanted a house that would be easy to maintain', John explained, adding, 'Not so daunting a commission. Nobly, they left the great intangibles of space and proportion to me. My main objective was to give an impression that it is larger than the basic two-and-a-half-thousand square feet. Space is the most elusive of all architectural illusions.'

The springs of inspiration for this house will be recognized as lying in the work of John Soane. For example, Simpson has taken the theme of Soane's typical pilaster strip and cleverly played four variations on it, one on each face of the house. The north entrance front of Ashfold distantly echoes the entrance front of Soane's country house, Pitzhanger Manor, Ealing, of 1800–03, while the south front recalls the entrance front of Soane's house and museum of 1815 at No. 13, Lincoln's Inn Fields. Soane, who stood at the cusp of Classicism and the modern world, despised modern architecture for what he condemned as its visual poverty, its crude, commercially driven materialism. Simpson shares this outlook so that his constant ambition, like Soane's, is to create 'the poetry of architecture.' For both, this is inseparable from the knowledge and practice of Classical architecture.

Above: The sitting room where Simpson designed the chimneypiece and all the furniture, including the monumental cupboards housing electronic equipment.

Left (above): On the east front the giant semi-circular window lights the breakfast room. All four elevations of this subtle house on a square plan are different, the north entrance front having echoes of Soane's Pitzhanger Manor; (below): The south front, with the three round-headed windows of the drawing room, reflects the façade of Soane's house in Lincoln's Inn Fields.

CLASSICISM REBORN · 157

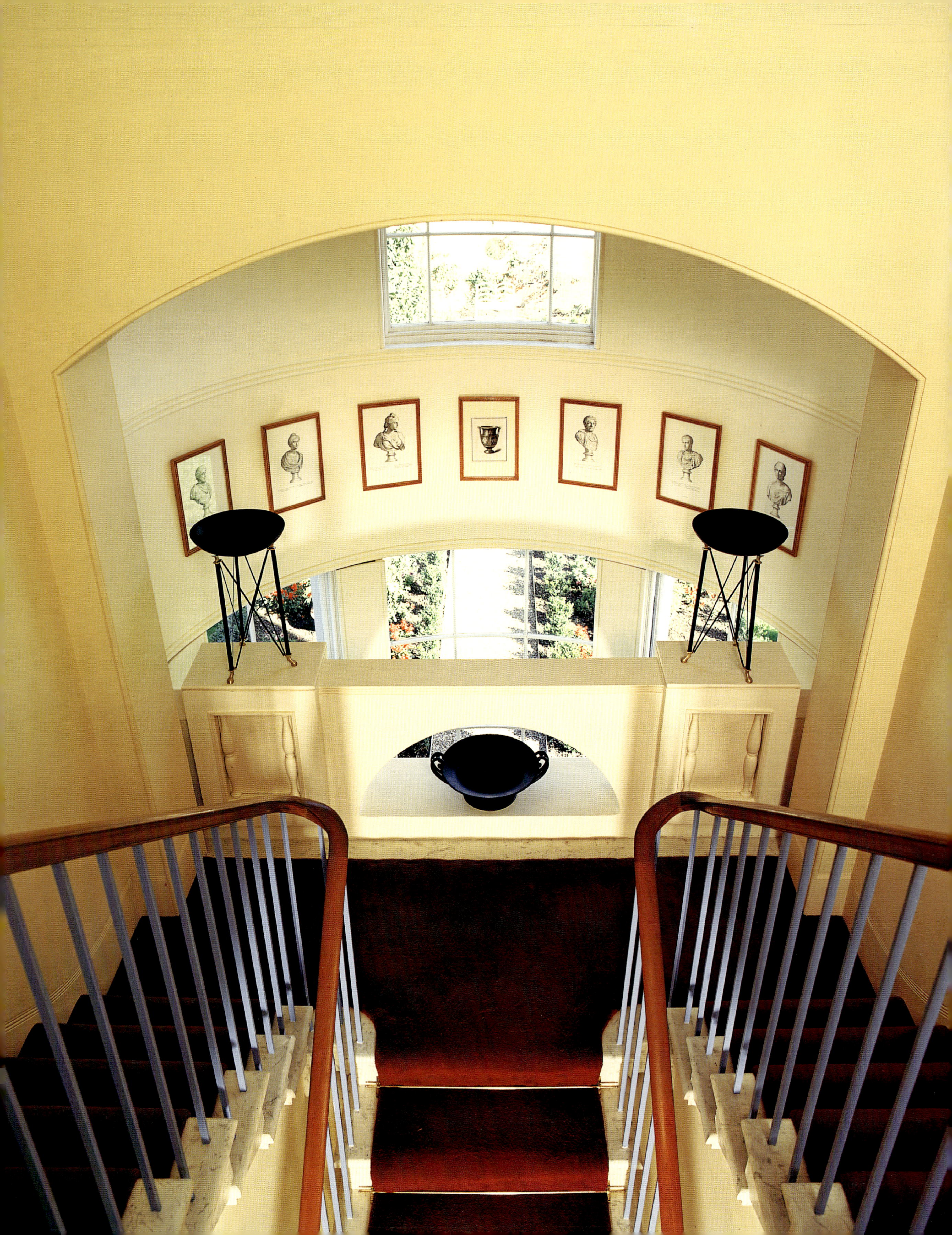

Soane saw architecture as a hierarchy that ran from the primitive hut and the simple vernacular architecture in which he excelled, to the most sumptuous public buildings in the Classical style. 'Art', Soane memorably declared in his Royal Academy lectures, 'cannot go beyond the Corinthian order.' But in the hierarchy from hut to temple, neither could be appreciated without awareness of the existence of the other; in other words, the simple stripped Classicism of Soane's most modest works only have meaning when set against the richness of the full deployment of the Classical Orders in his more ambitious ones.

Soane was equally a child of his time in that he exploited new developments in technology as much as possible. In parts of his own house in Lincoln's Inn Fields, he used the most up-to-date forms of central heating then available so as to abolish solid walls and chimney-pieces, allowing space to flow freely. Simpson exploits the surer heating methods of the modern world at Ashfold so as to place an open hall, rising the full height of the house, at the heart of the building. This is not sealed off by solid walls from the rest of the house; nor is there any need to provide buffer zones against draughts in the form of subsidiary lobbies. A German system of underfloor heating, with a heat recovery boiler, makes unsightly radiators unnecessary.

Above (left): View along the main axis to the drawing room beyond the central hall with a glazed circular dome, recalling Soane's top-lit tribunes; (right): From the upper level of the hall, where a balcony sports inverted Michelangelesque balusters, we look across the library to the Sussex landscape.

Left: A tantalising glimpse of the breakfast room from the half landing on the staircase.

The hall at the centre of Ashfold, lit by a glazed circular dome, recalls the top-lit tribunes which Soane placed in similar positions, such as his now destroyed one at Tyringham Hall, Buckinghamshire, of 1793–1800. The hall or tribune at Ashfold has a generous arch on each side, of wood painted and detailed to resemble horizontally channelled stone rustication, a device Simpson borrowed from Sir Robert Taylor, whose work Soane remodelled at the Bank of England. One of these arches provides a dramatic frame for the staircase, the approach to which contains slim jib doors on either side to conceal the entrances to a bathroom and the kitchen.

As we mount the stairs we can look down from the half landing into the breakfast room, ingeniously contrived out of little more than the space provided by a massive semi-circular bay window on the east front. This kind of spatial complexity is unusual in modern Classical houses, yet it is here that we should recall the comparatively modest dimensions of Ashfold. Simpson explains that 'Smallness of size tends to concentrate the mind to some extent.' He believes that 'On a big building, there would have been less justification for playing the kind of tricks we did at Ashfold.' One of the most thrilling of the 'tricks' at Ashfold is the way in which space flows in all directions from galleries round the upper storey of the hall. Here, each side of the gallery features in its lower part a bookcase disguised on its outer front as a sarcophagus with inverted Michelangelesque balusters, flanked by Soanean piers with acroterion heads. Above these, we can look out to the pastoral Sussex landscape in which the house is set. Simpson explains, 'I wanted to build up a series of views within the house to add to the illusion of space.' In fact, he developed the techniques of Regency Picturesque architects, who landscaped the interiors of a house in the same way as the designers of parkland. That this was Soane's practice is confirmed by his friend, John Britton, perceptively prefacing his book on Soane's house and museum in Lincoln's Inn Fields (1827) with the advice on garden design that Alexander Pope gave to Lord Burlington: 'Let not each beauty ev'rywhere be spied when half the skill is decently to hide. He gains all points who pleasingly confounds, surprises, varies and conceals the bounds.'

The views throughout this house do, indeed, provide endless unexpected surprises and contrasts. From the front door, an arch frames the hall up a short flight of steps, while a further arch leads axially to the drawing room, its own arched windows leading to the garden: all this can be comprehended from the moment we enter the house. The axis at right angles contains the staircase, which leads to the gallery from which the bedrooms in each corner of the house can be approached. At every level the various parts of the house fit satisfyingly together like the most skilful piece of clockwork.

The drawing room, occupying the whole of the south front on the ground floor, is flooded with light from windows on three sides, those on the garden front featuring the arched forms that recur throughout the house. Ceilings, so often forgotten by modern architects, are everywhere worthy of attention at Ashfold. Here, the drawing-room cornice, made up *in situ* like those throughout the house, consists of the running small balls seemingly invented by Soane in the drawing room of his house in No. 13, Lincoln's Fields, in 1792.

Simpson explains that modern heating arrangements make more practical the Regency love of full-length windows. The shutters in the drawing room, unconventionaly, fold back not into the window embrasure, but into the wall on either side. The side curtains are attached to the shutters and move with them. Further ingenuity appears in the sitting room, where the chimneypiece is flanked by sarcophagus-like cupboards which contain video and television equipment. Even in the kitchen, all the labour-saving, high-tech devices are concealed within massive cupboards, articulated with Doric columns.

The house is built throughout from soft ochre, handmade bricks from Lincolnshire, with each of the four façades treated differently. This is a Picturesque practice as exploited, for example, by James Wyatt at Dodington Park, near Bath, in 1798–1813. The north front has the triumphal arch theme of Pitzhanger; the east front is dominated by a commanding, centrally-placed glazed bow; the south front breaks forward in a slight projection, faced in stucco stencilled with polychromatic Classical decorations; while from the west front projects a large conservatory containing handsome furniture designed by Simpson along lines inspired by Thomas Hope. Since Simpson gave the detailing of the interiors a pared-down character similar to much of the work of Soane, he felt that Classical furniture of a fairly emphatic quality would be required. Finding nothing quite appropriate in shops, he became a furniture designer.

Filling the south front with windows on all three sides, the drawing room serves three functions: there is a dining table at one end, a grand piano at the other, and seating in the middle.

CLASSICISM REBORN · 161

LVCEAT

SOLAR HOUSE, WAKEHAM, SUSSEX

Solar House, built from designs by Robert Adam in 1999, stands out as superficially less Classical than any of the other houses in this book. It certainly lacks conventional Classical ornament, but it is nonetheless the product of an architect and a patron committed to demonstrate that there is nothing un-modern about Classicism. Moreover, since building Solar House, Robert Adam has been responsible for some large and purely Classical mansions with fully detailed traditional porticoes, such as Witley Park, Surrey, and Ashley Park, Hampshire.

The energy-efficient house at Wakeham is an experimental house built by Harold Carter on behalf of his late mother, the Hon. Mrs Hugh Carter, who initiated the project. A daughter of the 2nd Viscount Cowdray, she trained as a radiologist and became a pioneer in the study and use of solar energy on which she published numerous articles. In association with her son, the architect and solar heating expert, Ray Maw, and Robert Adam, she had substantially agreed the design of Solar House before her death in 1993. Carter describes himself, half-ironically, as a 'modernist' but argues that the simplicity and purity at the heart of Classicism makes it the ideal framework within which to create clearly modern buildings. He believed that other modern attempts at energy-efficient buildings were needlessly hideous. He was thus delighted to find in Robert Adam an architect who could combine the simple language of Classicism with the engineering requirements for the substantial south-facing windows, a portico for shade, and the circulation of solar-heated air. Designed to balance the technical requirements of the use of solar energy with Classical design for the first time, the house combines new technology with

Above: With its massive horizontal rustication, the entrance front recalls the abstract geometry of Neo-Classical architects like Ledoux and Gilly. The wind towers rising like alert ears on the skyline provide a lively note of contrast.

Left: The simplified almost primitivist entrance has something of the severity of the Greek Doric portal at Millichope Park. 'Luceat' ('let there be light'), refers to the energy-efficient technology of the house.

CLASSICISM REBORN · 163

traditional building forms and materials 'to enable technology to be humanised and to allow the classical tradition to develop', as Robert Adam puts it.

One of the many surprises of this house is that, though seemingly built of masonry, it is in fact of timber-frame construction coated with a natural-coloured render, which uncannily resembles stone. Only the door and window surrounds are of stone. Largely constructed with building materials from the adjacent landscape, its timber frame was originally to have been clad in brick. Planning consent was granted in 1993 for a brick house, but energy efficiency made a highly insulated timber and render construction more appropriate. Many old local buildings including those nearest to the new house are stucco-faced.

To prevent heat loss, fenestration is kept to a minimum on the north-facing entrance front. This character is further stressed by the massive doorway with the canted sides prescribed by Vitruvius. Above it is the Latin word, 'LUCEAT' ('let there be light'), carved by Rory Young, an inscription referring to the dependence of the house on the sun and also intended as 'a punning reference to the Requiem mass.' The extremely deep bands of rustication add a lightness to the entrance front by diminishing in height as they rise.

The principle of solar heating at Solar House is that sixty per cent of the south-facing garden front is glazed so that it can allow the sun to heat the massive slate floor of the large double-storey hall. This hall distributes solar-heated air to the main living rooms on the ground floor and the bedrooms on the first floor before emerging naturally at roof level. Cool air is also drawn in through hidden ducts at ground level so that the whole house acts as a kind of giant chimney, the air being discharged above the roof by means of two shafts each with louvred sides. These wind-assisted ventilation outlets are combined with chimney stacks and, besides being functional, serve as picturesque tower-like features in the landscape, marking out the presence of a house of consequence. The system adopted here is not that of central heating, which keeps all areas to a uniform heat. Solar House, by contrast, is more 'organic', as it is essentially flexible. Thus, on warm or on cold but sunny days, the sun is sufficient to heat the central hall which is therefore used on those days or when it is warm enough to open the doors. If it is necessary to heat or to cool the side rooms, an internal door is opened to let the heated air or, fresh air, if cooling is required, to circulate by way of high-level vents which connect to the roof vents. On dull, cold, or wet days, the central hall is only used if a fire is lit in it. On those days, the side rooms are used, for these are efficiently heated due to both their design and insulation.

Since the solar heating is passive, there is a minimum of mechanical equipment. External walls and the roof are heavily insulated, while the warm-air circulation is silent and simple, unlike most high-tech heating solutions with their electronically-operated window blinds, which are noisy and liable to break down. The windows are fitted with simple, manually-operated shutters or blinds for use at night.

The small entrance lobby seems larger because it is screened from the central hall by a wall of glass separated into three divisions by simple mouldings, as in the Red Hall of Schinkel's Schloss Glienicke, Berlin, of the 1820s. This gives one a dramatic view of the main double-height hall, its walls painted white to reflect the heat. The black slate floor on an insulated bed also retains heat, which it releases at night. The hall is surrounded by a gallery, supported on large brackets that double as light-fittings. The room creates something of the feel of a courtyard, for its slate floor is continued into the deep portico outside so that when the glass doors are open the two spaces become one. The south-facing windows of the dining room and study do not have glazing bars because they feature triple glazing of Swedish manufacture, which is an integral part of the energy-efficient design.

The house contains just the principal hall, study and combined kitchen and dining room on the ground floor, with four small bedrooms and three bathrooms on the first floor, which are grouped in a U-shape round the gallery in the central hall. This becomes a continuous circuit since it is carried across the portico on a balcony with a steel mesh floor.

The portico is at the back or garden front of the house, unlike those of Palladio who clapped the temple porticoes of the ancient world on to the fronts of his villas. It is at the back because its considerable depth and deep roof serve the necessary practical function of keeping too much sunlight from falling on the largely glass front, whose size comes into its own in the winter. The portico thus protects the hall from too much sunlight in the summer, but in winter when the sun is low, its very thin metal columns obstruct the sun as little as possible so that the room can be bathed with light. Robert Adam has made a special study of 'slender order columns', often neglected by historians but in a tradition going back to the buildings depicted in Pompeiian frescoes and taken up in the 1850s by Alexander 'Greek' Thomson in interiors admired by Robert Adam, such as St Vincent Street Church, Glasgow.

As an experiment in low-energy living, Solar House both is and looks experimental and unconventional, yet the adoption of the Classical language provides a welcomingly familiar note. Thus, the portico has something of the depth and power of that of Hawksmoor's at Christ Church, Spitalfields, of 1714. The striking lotus-leaf capitals of the columns at Solar House distantly recall those on the porch of the Tower of the Winds, the famous monument in Athens of the mid-1st century BC. Those at Solar House are of stainless steel, but if this might initially seem an inappropriate material, it should be recalled that the Corinthian capital, according to Vitruvius, was invented by the famous Athenian sculptor, Callimachus, who was known for his bronze work. The city of Corinth was a major centre of bronze making in the ancient world so that bronzes could be referred to as 'Corinthian work'. In his book, *Classical Architecture: A Complete Handbook* (1990), Robert Adam has himself suggested of the Corinthian capital that 'a bronze original could provide an explanation for both the name and the way the leaf decoration seems to be applied like repeated castings to a central core.'

Such details demonstrate that the Classical language is not a constraint but a stimulus to power and novelty. Every age has to rediscover the language of Classicism for itself and often to adapt it to new functions. In that sense, the Classical language is always new yet enables us to enjoy the privilege of being heirs to a great civilization, in contrast to the Modernists, who attempted to obliterate memories of the past.

Above: *Commanding views towards the South Downs, this memorable building, which once seen is not forgotten, is a striking tribute to its architect and patron. Once again, it echoes Ledoux whose cubic villas or* maisons de campagne, *often with belvedere towers, surrounded his Ideal Town of Chaux (1804).*

Below: *View into the sun-filled south-facing portico from the main two-storeyed hall with its floor of heat-retaining black slate.*

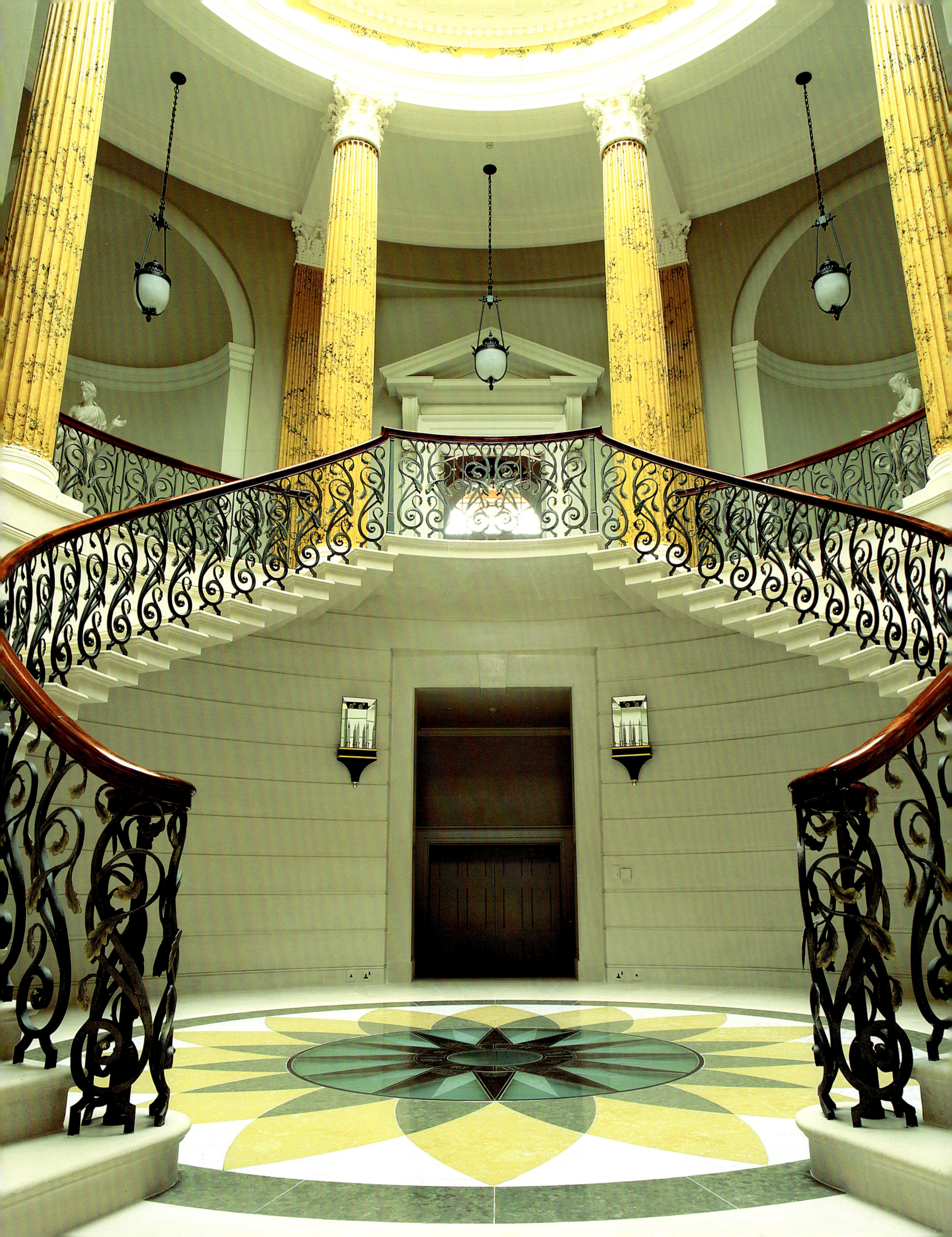

◦ TUSMORE PARK, OXFORDSHIRE ◦

This Classical palace built in 2003–05 is an unusual concession to fine design by its architect, Sir William Whitfield, a Modernist of the old school, who was responsible for Brutalist concrete additions in 1964–70 to the Institute of Chartered Accountants, an Arts and Crafts masterpiece of 1890–93 by John Belcher and Beresford Pite, with a Genoese Baroque flavour, enriched with much figure sculpture. Tusmore was rightly hailed by John Martin Robinson in *Country Life* in 2005 as a Classical house which is 'perhaps the grandest since Manderston.'

Tusmore Park was built by Wafic Saïd on the site of an imposing Palladian mansion of 1766 by Robert Mylne, with a pedimented portico of engaged Ionic columns on the east entrance front and another on the west front of free-standing Ionic columns. It is worth recounting briefly the subsequent history of Tusmore, as it is all too typical of the vicissitudes of country houses in the nineteenth and twentieth centuries. Remodelled by William Burn for the Earl of Effingham in 1858, it was bought in 1929 by Vivian Hugh Smith, later 1st Lord Bicester, for whom Imrie and Angell returned it to its eighteenth-century appearance in the 1930s, adding a terraced sunken garden. In 1961, it was demolished by the 2nd Lord Bicester, who replaced it in 1962–64 with a new and smaller house by Claude Phillimore. His Arundel Park House, built in 1958–62 in the park at Arundel Castle for the Duke of Norfolk, had been an important early revival of Palladian planning in post-war British architecture. Phillimore's new Tusmore Park incorporated chimneypieces by Mylne from the old house, while the Georgian stables as well as the Edwardian outbuildings, including lodges and formal terraces by Imrie and Angell, were also retained.

In 1987, the estate of 3,000 acres was acquired by Mr Saïd for its location and mature parkland, not for its architecture, since Phillimore's house, only one third of the size of Mylne's, failed to match its imposing setting. Mr Saïd therefore approached Philip Jebb to design a new house for the site. However, Jebb, who had built North

Above: The magnificent symmetry of the entrance front centres on its monumental, hexastyle Corinthian portico, paralleled by James Wyatt's portico at Dodington Park, Gloucestershire (1798–1813).

Left: The superb domed staircase draws inspiration from one of the most beautiful of the eighteenth century, that by James Paine at Wardour Castle, Wiltshire.

CLASSICISM REBORN · 167

168 · INTO THE TWENTY-FIRST CENTURY

Port, East Lothian (1978–79), in a Regency manner for the Dowager Duchess of Hamilton, died in 1995 before his scheme for Tusmore could be fully developed. While planning consent was being sought for replacing the house by Phillimore with a new one on its footprint, four major firms of architects were invited to submit designs. But their proposals were not in line with Mr Saïd's ideas. He wanted a Classical Palladian house, with two storeys on one side and three on the other, which would blend better into the landscape and be practical to live in.

Sir William Whitfield came to Tusmore when acting as Mr Saïd's architectural consultant at the Oxford University Saïd Business School (designed by Dixon Jones). Mr Saïd explained his ideas and Sir William produced a sketch of the Classical house he wanted, and so, despite being retired, was persuaded to be the architect of Tusmore House. The final design was expanded by ten per cent, which meant that parts such as windows and doors had to be expanded proportionately in correct Classical manner.

The house is built of a warm, cream Burgundian limestone while the capitals of the columns and of the two Venetian windows on the west front, with its canted bay inspired by Sir Robert Taylor, are also of stone. Otherwise there are no carving in stone and no string courses, for the mass of the wall surfaces, into which the first-floor windows are cut without architraves, is sufficiently imposing without ornament, though the generous pulvinated frieze all round the house provides a satisfying touch of curvaceous strength.

By placing the main entrance at ground level, Sir William avoided the inconvenience of the frequent Georgian disposition of an entrance at *piano nobile* level reached up an external staircase. Staff accommodation and the swimming pool are concealed below the artificially raised forecourt in front of the house. It is worth noting that in this twenty-first century house, forty per cent of the space is taken by the servicing and mechanical services.

The comparatively small and simple entrance hall leads to a contrasting interior of breathtaking spatial originality. This is the great circular saloon and stair hall, where twin cantilevered flights with wrought-iron balustrades lead down from the saloon level, with more steps leading down into the garden hall. Above the six, fluted Corinthian columns and entablature of Siena marble *scagliola*, and balustrade and *scagliola* urns, is a shallow-domed ceiling from which light floods down from the central oculus.

The stair hall is an echo of that by James Paine at Wardour Castle, Wiltshire (1770–76), which, as we have seen, William Bankes compared to the Marble Staircase he created at Kingston Lacy in the 1830s. Paine took the theme from the unexecuted design of 1759 for the staircase at York House, Pall Mall, by Sir William Chambers, which was partly inspired by a dramatic Baroque source, Bernini's church at Ariccia (1662–64). For his circular domed staircase at Home House, Portman Square (1773–76), Robert Adam was able to draw on the example of his two rivals, Paine and Chambers.

Of course, the stair hall at Tusmore goes beyond those at Wardour and Home House with the complexity of its two sets of flights, of

The splendid dining room includes the traditional pair of columns, here of the Corinthian Order, screening the service end.

which the lower leads down to the garden hall behind the canted bay in the centre of the west front. Articulated with Roman Doric pilasters and with a polished marble floor, the garden hall was described by John Martin Robinson as 'an austerely treated space comparable to an Italian *sala terrena*.' Serving as the principal access to the garden, it also leads into the large family living room. Because the entrance front of the house is raised on an artificial terrace so that it is two-storeyed, the west garden front, without this terrace, is three-storeyed, allowing direct access from the lowest storey to the garden.

On the *piano nobile* the reception rooms, all 22-foot high, form an enfilade round three sides of the central rotunda or stair hall. The South Drawing Room, its windows articulated with Corinthian pilasters, has a high coved ceiling with a central oval panel flanked by rectangles, a model inspired by Inigo Jones. The West Drawing Room serves as a link from the South Drawing Room to the dining room, which, with its table seating twenty-four, virtually fills the north side of the *piano nobile*. It includes the traditional pair of columns, here of the Corinthian Order, screening the service end, while its ceiling is inspired by those we have seen earlier in this book at Coleshill. The handsome, mid-Georgian chimneypiece, flanked by consoles, includes a frieze carved with the grapes of Bacchus, god of wine, a familiar decorative theme for a dining room. This was originally at Ashburnham Place, Sussex (demolished 1959), as remodelled in 1757–61 by Stephen Wright and the local architect, John Morris.

Attention has properly been given to the relation of this large house to its eighteenth-century landscaped park and gardens. These were developed in three principal phases, beginning with a formal, early-eighteenth-century scheme with a rectangular canal, the long water, parallel to the west front, and radiating lime avenues forming a *patte d'oie* to the east. After this came the typical landscaped park of the 1760s in the manner of 'Capability' Brown with clumps of trees and eye-catchers, such as the surviving balustraded bridge and temple. Finally, Lord Bicester added stone terraces and clipped yews in the 1930s, which have now been revivified, while the landscape has also been renewed to a plan by Colvin and Moggridge, with a new lake on the south and a formal vista centred on the entrance portico.

Our account of Tusmore as a house rich with resonances has required references to architects such as Palladio, Jones, Pratt, Paine and Adam, all of whom we have met before in this book. Tusmore won the Award for the Best New Building in the Classical Tradition from the Georgian Group in 2005, just two years after the same award had been given to another superb Palladian building, Ferne Park, Dorset, by Quinlan Terry.

The canted bay on the west front recalls designs by Robert Taylor, thus adding another name to those of Palladio, Jones, Pratt, Paine, Adam and Wyatt, of whose work this house is an inventive synthesis.

CLASSICISM REBORN · 171

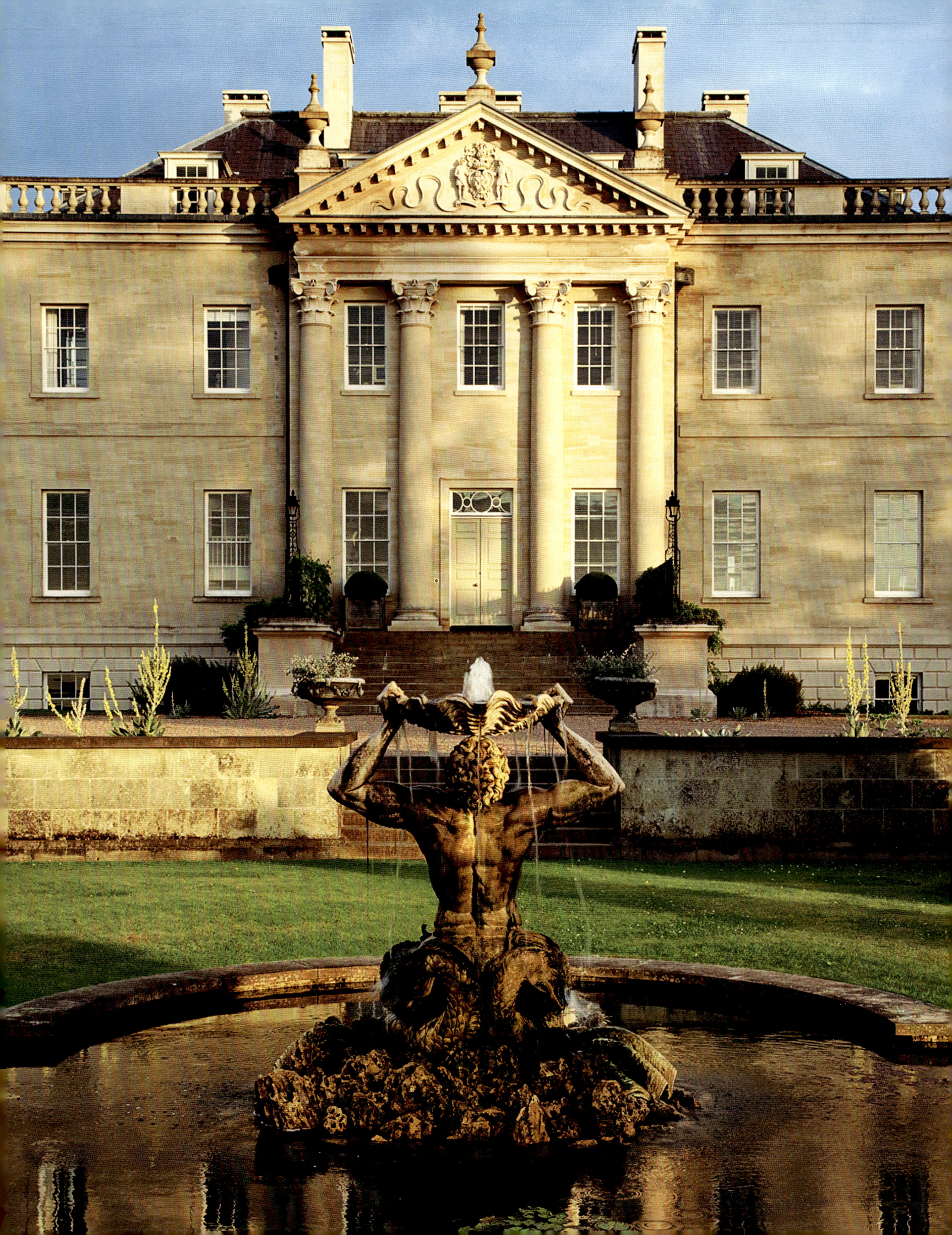

◦ FERNE PARK, DORSET ◦

The house built in 2000–2002 for Viscountess Rothermere, the third on its site, replaces a plain Georgian mansion built in 1811 by Thomas Grove, whose family had lived there from 1561. It was enlarged by the Grove family in the same style in the mid-nineteenth century, and further additions were made by a new owner in 1903. In 1914, Ferne and the nearby estate of Ashcombe, over the Wiltshire border, were bought by the 13th Duke of Hamilton, whose wife came from an old Wiltshire family. Founder of the Scottish Society for the Prevention of Vivisection in 1912, she ran Ferne in the Second World War as a sanctuary where wealthy Londoners could house dogs that might be at risk from bombing raids. It continued as an animal sanctuary after the War but fell into disrepair and was demolished in 1965.

Long before seeing the site of Ferne, Lord Rothermere was keen to build a new house, an ambition that was the catalyst for the project. His wife suggested what she thought was an impossible list of *desiderata* for such a house, including that the site should have beautiful views, and that there should be some old buildings and stables to develop. When they visited Ferne, they found that, remarkably, it fulfilled all their needs. Lady Rothermere was familiar, through a family connection, with King's Walden Bury, Hertfordshire, built for Sir Thomas and Lady Pilkington by Raymond Erith and Quinlan Terry in 1969–71. She was thus aware that a new and modern country house could be built with traditional materials in the Classical language. It turned out, by coincidence, that the local planning authority required that any new house at Ferne should be built of local stone, Classical in design, and not larger than the previous house on the site.

The intention of the Rothermeres, with their five children, was to create a permanent family home that was not enormous, but would be plain, strong, and not dominated by lavish ornament. They saw that it would be important to relate the house carefully to its incredibly beautiful site, high up in a landscape with stunning views across Wiltshire and Dorset. The view north, towards Wardour Castle, is dramatic,

Above: The south-facing garden front, lacking columns, has a deliberately more domestic flavour than the grand entrance front. The balustraded terrace before it, rich with flowers and plants, opens directly from the drawing room.

Left: Over the portico of engaged Composite columns on the entrance front, the pediment is entirely filled by the vigorously carved family coat of arms surrounded by flying ribbons, in the manner illustrated by Palladio.

CLASSICISM REBORN · 173

rising to hills of almost mountainous profile, while the prospect south into Dorset is rather softer. Thus, the house Quinlan Terry designed for them featured contrasting façades: the more ambitious north front has a pedimented portico of engaged columns in the Composite Order, richest of the Classical Orders, approached up a monumental flight of steps, while the quieter south front is almost entirely astylar and has a long, sunny terrace filled with garden furniture and plants.

Lady Rothermere first met Quinlan Terry through her friends, Lord and Lady Rayleigh, for whom he had built an elegant Palladian summer house at Terling Place, Essex, in 1998. She was also familiar with Came House, Dorset, a fine Palladian mansion of 1754–62 by the master-builder, Francis Cartwright, with a five-bay, pedimented entrance front in Portland stone, crowned with a balustrade. She suggested this to Terry as a model for Ferne, another source of inspiration being Castletown Cox, Co. Kilkenny, Ireland, of *c.*1770, by David Ducart, an engineer and architect of Italian origin of whom little is known except that he settled in Ireland, where he designed several country houses. Terry was familiar with Castletown Cox, having worked on it for its present owner.

Lady Rothermere also pays great tribute to *Country Life*, suggesting that, though starting with no particular passion for architecture, she soon acquired one through her constant perusal of its pages, which provided inspiration for the architecture and interiors of Ferne, as well as for its gardens and garden buildings and their relation to the park and landscape. This is in happy continuation of the tradition by which many of those who employed Sir Edwin Lutyens and Gertrude Jekyll to create houses and gardens for them had been stimulated by seeing their work illustrated in *Country Life*.

Deeply rooted in the soil, and fitting harmoniously into its vast landscape, Ferne is a solid and enduring construction, during the creation of which Lady Rothermere has become a convinced believer in the permanent validity of the Classical language of architecture. The house is a symphony composed of four stones, all but one of which, in accordance with the wishes of the planning authority, are local. The façades are in Chilmark stone, the Jurassic oolitic limestone used in Wiltshire for Salisbury Cathedral in the thirteenth century, Longford Castle in the sixteenth century, and Wilton House in the seventeenth. The rusticated basement and the ornamental details, including the columns, entablature and pediment with its giant Rothermere coat of arms carved by Andrew Tansey, and even the chimneys, are all in Portland stone from Dorset. The third local stone, of the post-Jurassic period, is the sandstone known as Upper Greensand from the Shaftesbury district, which has a delicate colouring of a pale, greenish-grey. This was the ashlar used in eighteenth-century Dorset for major buildings such as Blandford church and Vanbrugh's Eastbury. The only non-local stone is the durable York stone, used for the staircase on the entrance front and for the paving of the south terrace.

The entrance portico has engaged columns in the Composite Order, as in the Arch of Titus in the Forum in Rome. It is approached at Ferne up a broad flight of steps, equal in width to the portico and protected on each side by long cheek walls, which are the same height as the basement or podium of the whole house. This arrangement echoes Ancient Roman buildings, such as the Temple of Antoninus and Faustina in the Roman Forum. This was illustrated in the influential *I Quattro Libri dell'Architettura* (1570) by Palladio who was the medium between Ancient Rome and modern England, for it was he who transferred this arrangement of steps from temples to houses in all four of the porticoes of his celebrated Villa Rotonda near Vicenza.

To stress the plain geometry of his composition, Terry greatly simplified the rich Composite Order, for example by leaving plain and uncut the two tiers of acanthus leaves on its giant capitals, which are over 6-foot high. Again, there is a precedent in Palladio, who also left them uncarved in his largest church, San Giorgio Maggiore, Venice. A feature of Came House and of many similar Palladian houses is that the three windows on the top floor between the capitals of the columns are notably smaller than those in the flanking bays. The Rothermeres were anxious to avoid this crowding and imbalance, so that Terry made all the upper windows of the same generous size. Further simplicity is achieved by confining modillions, the scrolled brackets below the cornices of the Corinthian and Composite Orders, to the pediments on the north and south fronts, rather than running them emphatically round the entablature of the entire building, as at Came House.

The south front, though much plainer than the north, is enlivened by the balustrade on the terrace, where the alternate flat and pointed placing of the balusters echoes the Baroque rhythm of those at the Ca'Pesaro, Venice, by Baldassare Longhena, of 1649 onwards. There is a practical reason for this, because current nannying regulations in Europe forbid the placing of balusters, or banisters, with spaces between them sufficiently large for a child's head to enter.

The plan of the main floor, or *piano nobile*, at Ferne Park has a grand Georgian simplicity with no corridors or awkward passages. The great, rectangular entrance hall has a stone-flagged floor and a bold screen of two, unfluted Doric columns carrying a triglyph frieze of imposing depth, which runs all round the room. The entrance hall at Castletown Cox is similarly divided by a columnar screen, though there of Corinthian columns. Opening off the hall to the right is a sitting room for Lady Rothermere, well lit with windows facing west and north. Though modest in size, this has a spaciousness due to its generous height which, in common with all the main rooms on this floor, is 15-foot.

When the house is full, the entrance hall serves as a sitting room and general meeting place, bringing people together and opening conveniently at its south-west angle to the main staircase. This has cantilevered stone steps and an ambitious wrought-iron balustrade, which echoes that at Came House. Further interest is provided to those ascending the staircase by confronting at close quarters the handsome architectural details of the large Venetian window in the middle of the west front. Castletown Cox also features a Venetian window on its west front. The entrance hall and the dining room boast new carved chimneypieces of exceptional quality, designed by Francis Terry. On the upper floors the arrangement of bedrooms around a central landing has proved very convenient.

The cantilevered main staircase, with its elegant wrought-iron balustrade, invites ascent with its shallow steps, while its west-facing Venetian window floods it with light.

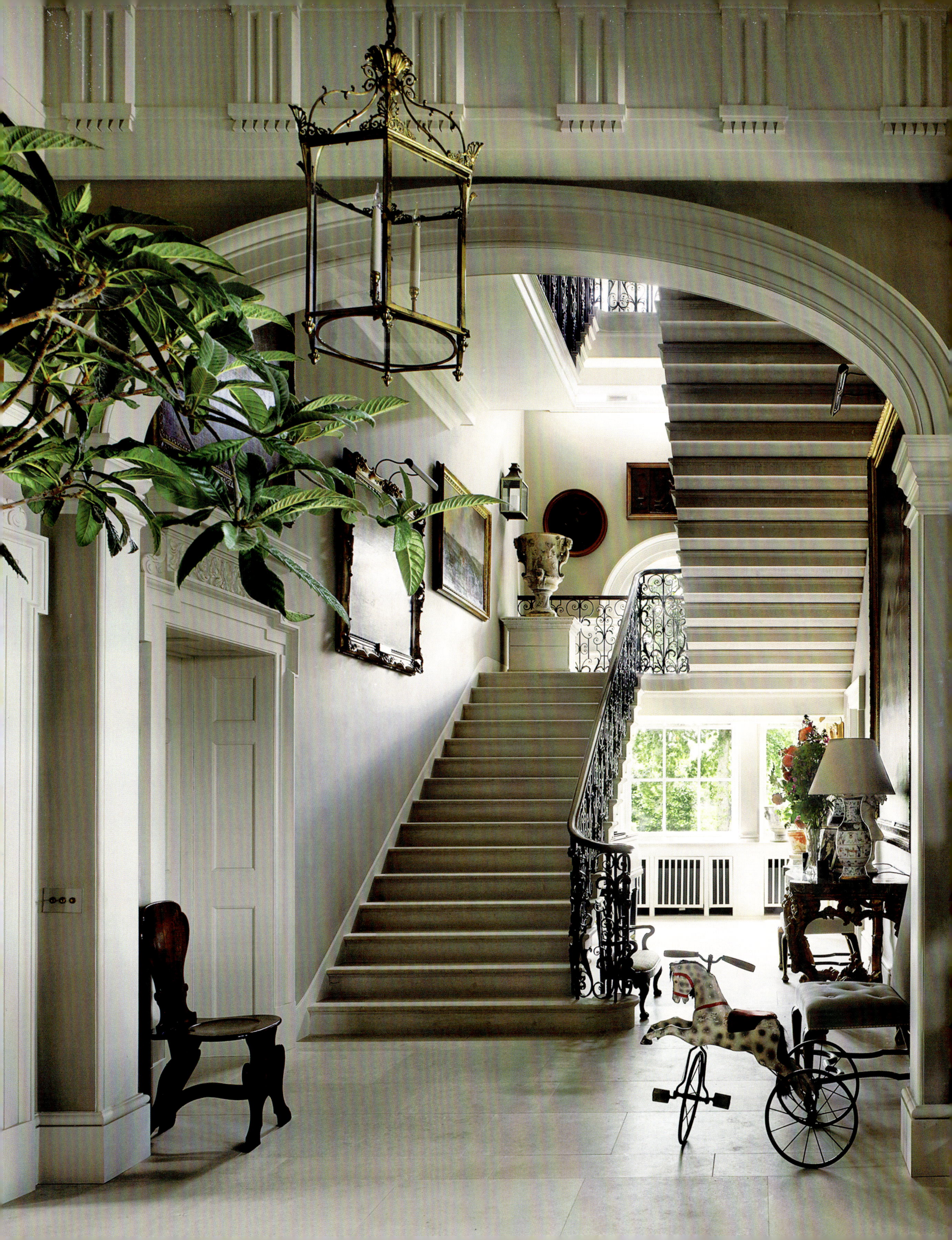

Veere Grenney Associates, interior designers, advised in the early stages, but the interiors now owe their main character to the extensive but discriminating purchases by the Rothermeres of furniture and paintings specifically for the house. Oil paintings, watercolours, drawings and engravings of an exceptionally wide range of dates and styles create the impression of a collection that has grown over many years. All the baths are old ones refurbished, but there are no coloured marbles or gold taps in the bathrooms, which are plain and discreet.

In the early stages of the vast project of creating a house, which took a year to design and nearly two to build, there was little time to consider what kind of garden it required. Extensive gardens have long been a feature of this beautiful site, as confirmed by John Britton in *The Beauties of England and Wales*, vol. xv, *Wiltshire* (1814), where he wrote of Ferne: 'A large garden is attached to this mansion; and the pleasure-grounds are laid out in a pleasant and beautiful style.' The Rothermeres gradually realized the importance of gardens on a large scale as a means of linking the house to its extended setting. They cover 20 acres but are still enclosed to the south by the surviving ha-ha of the previous house on the site. The well-known gardener, Rupert Golby, has been employed here from the start, though Lady Rothermere has now become equally passionate about garden design and planting.

Before the north entrance front, flower gardens would be inappropriate, so here a formal area with a large fountain separates the gravelled entrance approach from the park of 260 acres. For the first time since the 1920s, the park has now been extensively replanted with lime, beech, oak and chestnut trees appropriate to the eighteenth century, for Lady Rothermere does not believe in exotic species for such a setting. To extend the architecture of the house into the landscape she has planted an avenue of limes to the south and one of oaks to the

---

Above: The drawing room, incorporating an eighteenth-century chimney-piece, has elaborate plasterwork in the deep cove of Quinlan Terry's generously high ceiling.

Right: The hall combines domestic comfort with a touch of the grandeur appropriate to a large house, which is provided by its handsome screen of Doric columns with triglyph frieze marching boldly all round the room.

176 · INTO THE TWENTY-FIRST CENTURY

CLASSICISM REBORN · 177

west, content that her children and future grandchildren will see the latter in its maturity.

Another notable feature of her contribution is the many wrought-iron gateways, often on a large scale, which play an architectural role in leading from one part of the gardens to another, as from room to room. Their importance in planning the relation of buildings to their setting was understood in the seventeenth and eighteenth centuries, as at Hampton Court, Belton, Burghley, Chatsworth, Drayton, Okeover, Buckingham House and Trinity College, Oxford, but the practice has rarely been adopted in recent times. Originating in France under Louis XIV, and published in engravings by Jean Berain and Daniel Marot, the tradition was brought to England by Jean Tijou whose *A New Booke of Drawings* (1693) was the earliest publication of ironwork in English. The gateways at Ferne have been designed by Lady Rothermere and Rupert Golby on the basis of historic patterns, and made by Hughie Powell of Cotswold Decorative Ironwork, Gloucestershire.

Lady Rothermere has also given her attention to the design of modest wooden gates for the kitchen garden, which she has created to be smaller and more manageable than the original one to its east, 2 acres in size, as was customary in the eighteenth and nineteenth centuries. She has found old garden tools, notably forks and spades, of sufficiently small size to be incorporated into the gates where they form pleasing patterns, a happy joke worthy of Lutyens. The kitchen garden is overlooked on the south by a large stone building, (originally a granary, but later a dairy), which has been beautifully restored together with its cupola, which is partially a dovecote. There was no access from the west side of this building to the main garden, so the tractor house

Above: A panoramic view showing the shift in character from the gravelled forecourt to the formal garden below it, centering on the triton fountain, then the newly replanted park, and finally the distant hills above Wardour Castle, Wiltshire.

Right: Though architecturally formal, the house is not approached axially, but is discovered gradually through the natural setting of trees and parkland.

which formerly stood here has been replaced by Lady Rothermere with a handsome stone loggia with a great semi-circular arch inspired by those of the Market Hall at Chipping Camden of 1627. The opportunity has also been taken to restore the nearby stable yard where Quinlan Terry has replaced the cupola.

In 2007, Quinlan and Francis Terry built an ambitious pool house in a secluded valley to the east of the house. At the suggestion of Lady Rothermere, the north entrance front of this took inspiration from a building of $c.1738$ by William Kent of whom she is a great admirer. This is the arcaded garden building at Rousham, Oxfordshire, which early acquired the name Praeneste through its association with the Ancient Roman Republican Sanctuary of Fortuna Primigenia at Praeneste, formerly Palestrina, near Rome. This had been studied by numerous architects, notably Palladio, as a remarkable example of a terraced, landscape architecture, hugging its hilltop site.

With the exception of the broad string course and the cornice, the stone on the north front of Terry's building has been hand-tooled to give it a rough surface texture to emphasize that it is a garden building. This powerful and rather grave front overlooks a Kentian irregular lake, originally a stew pond with a cascade, which have both been recently restored. The planting of flowers round the lake has been inspired by those at the celebrated garden at Ninfa, near Rome, where Rupert Golby has worked.

Kent's Praeneste at Rousham is simply an open, arcaded passageway, but Terry's building at Ferne is far more ambitious architecturally, containing rooms and having a U-shaped garden front with a projecting pavilion, or open gazebo, at each end. The large reception room in the centre boasts a Palladian chimneypiece, designed by Francis Terry and made of stone given a distressed treatment to make it look convincingly old. This room is flanked on one side by a kitchen and on the other by changing and shower rooms. With its relation to the planting and to the long formal pool which it overlooks, the south front has something of the character of the garden front of Gledstone Hall, Lancashire, by Lutyens with its planting by Gertrude Jekyll.

In the centre of the rectangular pool, most unusually, is a life-size, seated, statue of the Enlightenment philosopher, Immanuel Kant (1754–1804), of whom Lady Rothermere has been an admirer since reading Philosophy, Politics and Economics at Oxford. She commissioned it in 2001 from Alexander Stoddart, appointed Her Majesty's Sculptor in Ordinary in Scotland in 2008. His statue of Kant creates a serious and thoughtful atmosphere in this beautiful area of retreat at Ferne, where the pool occupies part of the vast, walled kitchen garden that survived from the previous house.

A pool garden might be thought a wholly light-hearted place but the statue harmonizes with the monumental quality of the building by Quinlan and Francis Terry, where the massive stones speak of a permanence and durability uncompromised by ornamental detail. This architectonic masterpiece, one of the finest works in the careers of its architects, won the Georgian Group Award for a New Building in the Classical Tradition in 2008, just as the house itself had won the same award five years before.

Above: Beyond Alexander Stoddart's statue of the philosopher, Immanuel Kant, in the centre of the pool, we see the pool house, inspired by William Kent's Praeneste, a garden arcade of c.1738 at Rousham, Oxfordshire.

Right: Quinlan Terry's pool house departs from William Kent's model by providing a sunny, U-shaped garden front, facing south with an open, vaulted pavilion at each end.

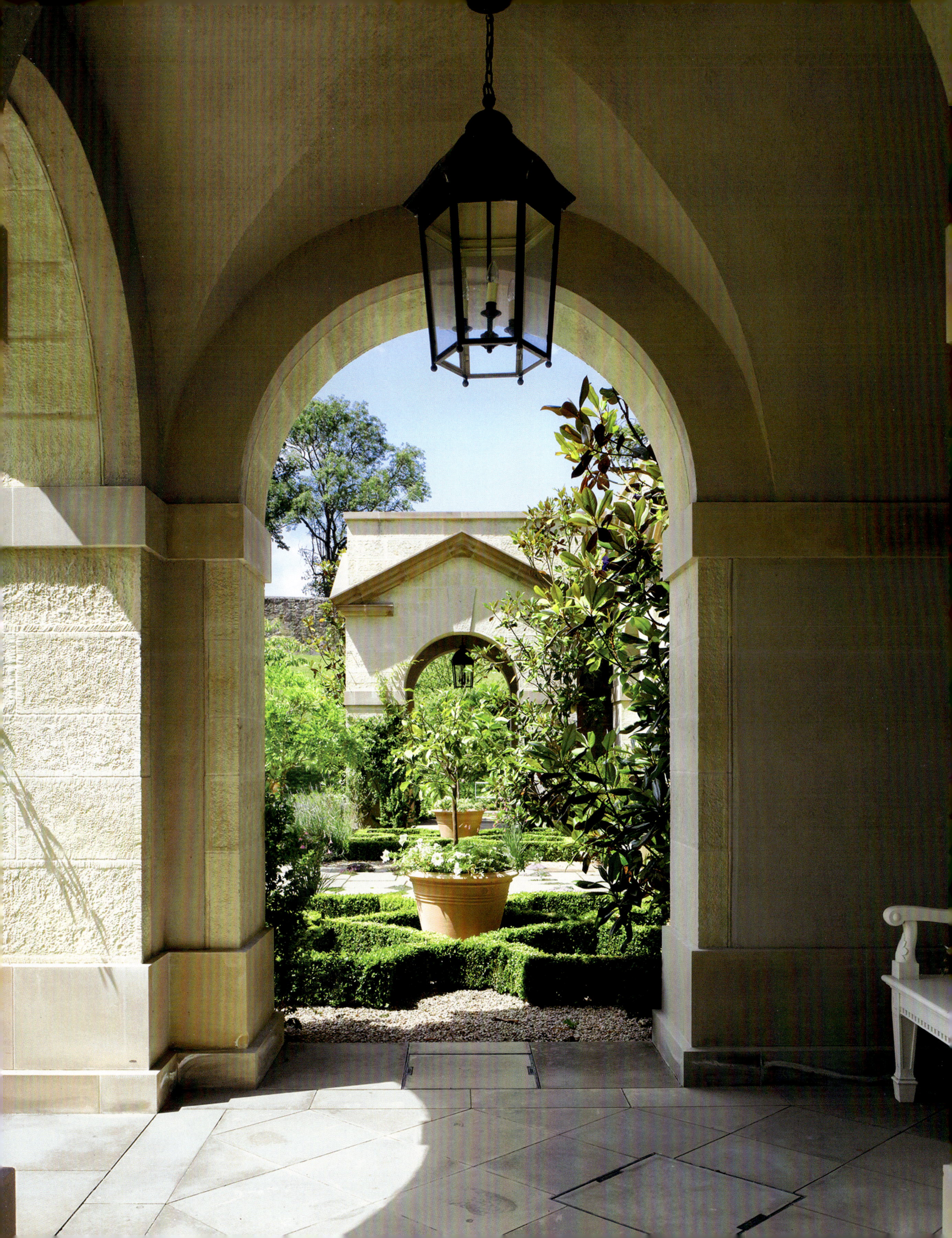

RECENT HOUSES IN THE USA AND THE BAHAMAS

From the late twentieth century a remarkable revival of the Classical country house has taken place in the United States of America. This has been marked by a return to the kind of respect for local materials and traditions that the Modern Movement thought it had abolished. A significant feature of the Classical Revival on both sides of the Atlantic is that this new respect for the past has included a revival of the tradition of architects writing books on historical aspects of architecture to serve as a model for current design. This is true of Allan Greenberg, Demetri Porphyrios, Thomas Gordon Smith, Peter Pennoyer, Robert Adam, George Saumarez Smith and Hugh Petter. A pioneer from the 1980s is the distinguished Classicist, Allan Greenberg, architect of numerous country houses, many in New England and Connecticut, including Huckleberry House, New England (1982–85), with a two-storeyed circular ballroom, projecting as a domed bow in the centre of the garden front. Greenberg has published *George Washington, Architect* (1999), *The Architecture of Democracy* (2006) and *Lutyens and the Modern Movement* (2007).

Gil Schafer, from a younger generation, built for himself Middlefield, New York State, in 1999, a house with a handsome, hexastyle, Greek Doric portico. He had hoped to buy one of the many nineteenth-century houses in a Greek Revival vernacular in the Hudson Valley, but finding them impossibly expensive created this one for himself. He used a local builder, designed the timber details in the local manner, and referred to source books used by nineteenth architects in the neighbourhood, such as Minard Lafever's *The Modern Builder's Guide* (1833). Though Middlefield looks externally traditional, it is internally wholly modern, centering on a large 'family room' and a generous kitchen for eating, all opening into each other in a great spatial flow. In the drawing room is a handsome chimneypiece, of *c.*1835, flanked by Ionic columns. The hilltop site of the house would also have been hardly possible in earlier periods when, before the arrival of the snow plough, it would need to have been sited near a road.

Schafer employed in the design of the house three assistants trained at the influential School of Architecture at the University of Notre Dame, South Bend, Indiana. Astonishingly, this is the only school in the world that teaches the practice of traditional and Classical architecture, with the result that its students are in enormous demand by clients throughout the USA. The Classical programme of the school was established by the architect, scholar and author, Professor Thomas Gordon Smith, during his chairmanship of the school from 1989–99. His Vitruvian House, South Bend (1990), led to other commissions for Classical country houses, such as Kulb House, Central Illinois, inspired by Mid-Western houses of *c.*1840, with its portico of limestone Ionic columns.

Middlefield, New York State, built for himself by Gil Schafer has a Greek Doric portico and timber details, derived from local nineteenth-century models.

182 · INTO THE TWENTY-FIRST CENTURY

CLASSICISM REBORN · 183

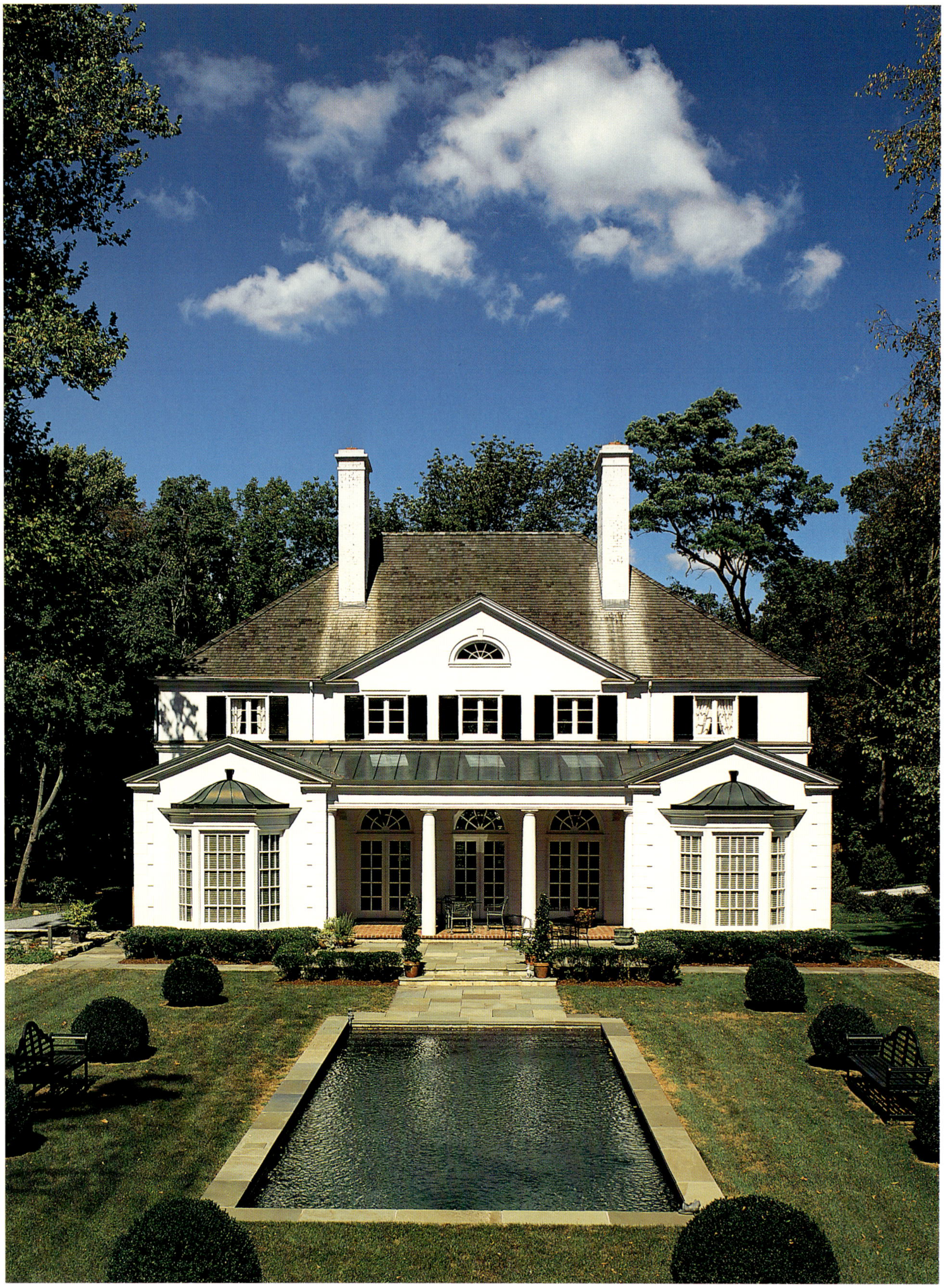

Thomas Gordon Smith's books include an edition of Vitruvius; a reprint of *The Builder's Guide* (1838) by Asher Benjamin, a Boston architect who was a powerful influence on late-Colonial architecture; and *John Hall and the Grecian Style in America* (1996), which includes reprints of three pattern books of 1840 by John Hall. It was with the help of such pattern books that the Classical architecture of Georgian England spread in America in the first half of the nineteenth century. With the current revival of the Classical language they are once again influential.

The prolific practice of Fairfax & Sammons, specializing in country houses, was established by Richard Sammons, who taught at The Prince of Wales's Institute of Architecture in London, and his wife, Anne Fairfax. Their recent work includes Lilliefields, Virginia, influenced by pattern books such as Asher Benjamin's *The American Builder's Companion* (1806). Its relatively austere entrance front, perhaps faintly echoing the rear façade of Palladio's Villa Malcontenta, is in contrast to the livelier garden front with a Doric loggia sheltering a trio of French windows like those in the hall at Thomas Jefferson's house, Monticello. Fairfax and Sammons both graduated at the University of Virginia School of Architecture, and have thus long been familiar with Jefferson's work, including Edgemont, Virginia, a largely timber house of *c.*1796, which has been a source of inspiration to them.

Lilliefields is of clapboard painted white with bottle green shutters, following a local tradition; the flush-boarded centrepiece is lined out to resemble ashlar and the wooden quoins also imitate stone work. The house has a compact six-room plan, its proportions following a perfect geometric system. To the right of the hall is the octagonal dining room, which echoes at the patron's request the octagonal room at Jefferson's Monticello.

Peter Pennoyer worked in the office of the leading Classical and traditional architect, Robert Stern, from 1981–83, before establishing his own practice in 1984. His country houses include Mishaum Point, Massachusetts, a summer house clad in local shingle, bleached silver in the salty air. The principal interiors lead on to a colonnaded portico or verandah with a mahogany deck floor. The main architectural heroes of Pennoyer are Latrobe, Soane, Lutyens and William Adams Delano.

Left: *The busy garden front of Lilliefields, Virginia, designed by Fairfax & Sammons, has the white painted clapboard of much American domestic architecture.*

Below: *The three round-headed windows of the drawing room in the centre of the garden front behind the loggia are inspired by a similar feature at Thomas Jefferson's Monticello, Virginia.*

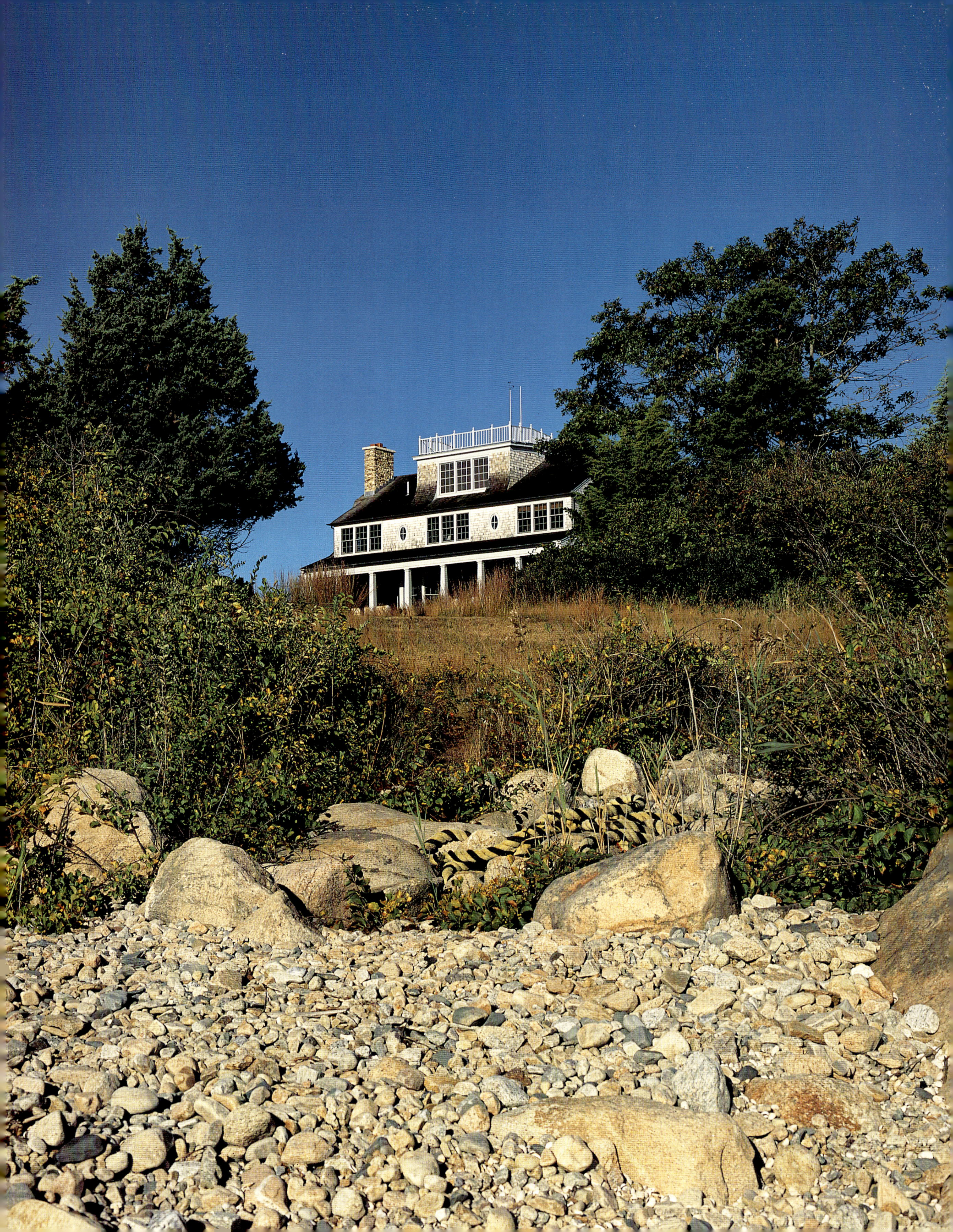

He has published books, with Anne Walker, including *The Architecture of Delano and Aldrich* (2003) and *The Architecture of Warren and Wetmore* (2006). The current Classical movement is thus no passing fashion but is rooted in scholarship, as in the academic journal, *The Classicist*. This is published by the influential Institute of Classical Architecture & Classical America, which was established in 2002 to unite two institutions founded respectively in 1991 and 1968.

Pembroke House, Paradise Island, Bahamas, (2000–2004) was designed in the Colonial style for a British client, who wisely employed three distinguished British artists: the architect, Hugh Petter, the sculptor, Dick Reid, and the landscape designer, Kim Wilkie. One of the five directors of the firm, ADAM Architecture, Hugh Petter was Senior Tutor of the Foundation Course at The Prince of Wales's Institute of Architecture for six years in 1990s, and architect of the addition to the British School at Rome. His publications include *Lutyens in Italy* (1992) and articles on the archaeology of Rome and on Beresford Pite.

Left: *Mishaum Point, Massachusetts, designed by Peter Pennoyer, hugs its superb rocky site above the sea.*

Below: *The colonnaded loggia at Mishaum Point, a summer residence.*

Built of concrete blocks and yellow-coloured stucco with a shingle roof, the house is placed 30-foot above the ocean to avoid hurricanes, while all the wood trim inside and outside is of mahogany, painted externally to withstand the effects of the sea. The garden front of Pembroke House, on the landward side, is dominated by a two-storeyed, pedimented portico. Petter explains that this was designed to give a Colonial spirit because it stacks two different Doric Orders on top of each other, both of which can be found in Fréart de Chambray's *Parallèle de l'architecture antique et de la moderne* (1650), of which a translation by John Evelyn was published in 1664. The Doric columns on the ground floor of Petter's portico have the unusual base incorporating two convex torus mouldings which is that of Vignola, as illustrated in his *Regola* (1562), translated as *Vignola: Or the Compleat Architect. Shewing in a plain and easie way the Rule of the Five Orders*, published in 1665.

The Order on the upper storey, by contrast, has no base at all, for it takes as its model Ancient Roman examples of Doric as at the Theatre of Marcellus in Rome. Thus, antiquity sits on top of the Renaissance at Pembroke House. From the upper storey of the portico a barrel-vaulted passage leads to a landing within the house. A vital part of the composition of the garden side of the house is that the portico is flanked by a pair of lower, two-storey dependencies, with bougainvillea-clad pergolas. On the ocean side of the house there is a two-storeyed verandah of baseless Doric columns. The tympanum over the entrance door was carved by Dick Reid, whose work can also be seen at Hampton Court Palace and Windsor Castle, but Pembroke House was one of his last commissions before his retirement in 2004.

What might appear at first sight to be a simple and light-hearted summer house is the product of careful attention to the Classical Orders and also of a harmonious proportional system, based on a 6-foot module. This creates an overall unity in which the principal interiors are all 12-foot high and either 18-foot square, or 18 by 36 foot. Individual touches include a striking tapered chimney stack and also tapering pilasters, which are relatively rare in architecture, though Vignola illustrated them in his treatise. Inigo Jones, who annotated his own copy of Vignola, used these pilasters in his design of 1621 for a Doric gateway at Beaufort House, Chelsea, and flanking his Tuscan portico at St Paul's, Covent Garden (1631–33). As a student, Petter had studied the way in which Lutyens had wrestled with the integration of columns and pilasters in the one-storeyed entrance portico at Tigbourne Court, Surrey (1899). Petter found that the use of tapered pilasters assists in uniting the bases of the columns with the geometrical patterns of paving.

It is a pleasure that in the present book, which has aimed to stress the continuity of the Classical tradition, Inigo Jones should appear once more in the final chapter, as he did in the first.

Above: *The sea front of Pembroke House, Paradise Island, Bahamas, an American Colonial-style house designed by the British architect, Hugh Petter.*

Right: *Petter's scholarly knowledge of the subtleties of the Classical Orders is demonstrated here in the superficially light-hearted garden front of Pembroke House with its two-storeyed portico.*

188 · INTO THE TWENTY-FIRST CENTURY

CLASSICISM REBORN · 189

BIBLIOGRAPHY

Primary Sources

Adam, Robert and James, *Works in Architecture* (1773–1822), reprinted Tiranti, London, 3 vols, 1931.

Alberti, Leo Battista, *On the Art of Building in Ten Books* (1486), transl. by Joseph Rykwert, *et al.*, MIT Press, Cambridge, Mass., and London, 1988.

Campbell, Colen, *et al.*, *Vitruvius Britannicus* (1717–71), reprinted Benjamin Blom, New York, 2 vols, 1967.

Castell, Robert, *The Villas of the Ancients Illustrated*, Printed for the Author, London, 1728.

Chambers, William, *A Treatise on the Decorative Part of Civil Architecture* (1791), reprinted Gregg, Farnborough, 1969.

Desgodetz, Antoine, *Les édifices antiques de Rome*, Coignard, Paris, 1682.

Palladio, Andrea, *The Four Books of Architecture* (1570), transl. Robert Tavernor and Richard Schofield, MIT Press, Cambridge, Mass., and London, 1997.

Pliny, the Younger, *Letters*, transl. Betty Radice, Penguin, Harmondsworth, 1963 etc.

Richardson, George, *New Vitruvius Britannicus* (1802–08), reprinted Benjamin Blom, New York, 1970.

Scamozzi, Vincenzo, *The Idea of a Universal Architecture* (1615), transl. P. B. Garvin *et al.*, Architectura & Natura Press, Amsterdam, 2 vols, 2003–08.

Scott, Geoffrey, *The Architecture of Humanism* (1914), reprinted Architectural Press, London, 1980, with foreword by David Watkin.

Serlio, Sebastiano, *On Architecture* (1537–75), transl. by Vaughan Hart and Peter Hicks, Yale University Press, New Haven and London, 2 vols, 1996–2001.

Stuart, James, and Nicholas Revett, *The Antiquities of Athens* (1762–1830), reprinted Acanthus Press, New York, 2007.

Vitruvius, *The Ten Books of Architecture*, transl. M. H. Morgan, Dover Publications, New York, 1960 etc.

Watkin, David, ed., *Sir John Soane: The Royal Academy Lectures*, Cambridge University Press, 2000.

Winckelmann, Johann Joachim, *History of the Art of the Antiquity* (1764), transl. Harry Francis Mallgrave, Getty Research Institute, Los Angeles, 2006.

Wood, Robert, *The Ruins of Palmyra* (1753), reprinted Gregg, Farnborough, 1971.

—, *The Ruins of Balbec* (1757), reprinted Gregg, Farnborough, 1971.

Wotton, Henry, *The Elements of Architecture* (1624), reprinted Gregg, Farnborough, 1969.

Secondary Sources

Aslet, Clive, *The Last Country Houses*, Yale University Press, New Haven and London, 1982.

Chaney, Edward, *The Evolution of the Grand Tour: Anglo-Italian Cultural Relations since the Renaissance*, Cass, London, 1998.

—, ed., *The Evolution of English Collecting: The Reception of Italian Art in the Tudor and Stuart Courts*, Yale University Press, New Haven and London, 2004.

Coltman, Viccy, *Fabricating the Antique: Neoclassicism in Britain, 1760–1800*, Chicago University Press, Chicago and London, 2006.

—, *Classical Sculpture and the Culture of Collecting in Britain Since 1760*, Oxford University Press, 2009.

Colvin, Howard, *A Biographical Dictionary of British Architects, 1600–1840*, 4th ed., Yale University Press, New Haven and London, 2008.

Farrar, Linda, *Ancient Roman Gardens*, Sutton Publishing, Stroud, 1988.

Girouard, Mark, *The Victorian Country House*, Yale University Press, New Haven and London, 1970.

Hill, Oliver, and John Cornforth, *English Country Houses: Caroline 1625–1685*, Country Life, London, 1966.

Hussey, Christopher, *English Country Houses: Early Georgian, 1715–1760*, Country Life, London, 1955, rev. ed. 1965.

—, *English Country Houses: Mid Georgian, 1760–1800*, Country Life, London, 1956.

—, *English Country Houses: Late Georgian, 1800–1840*, Country Life, London, 1958.

—, *English Gardens and Landscapes, 1700–1750*, Country Life, London, 1967.

Ingamells, John, ed., *A Dictionary of British and Irish Travellers in Italy, 1701–1800*, Yale University Press, New Haven and London, 1997.

Jenkins, Ian, *Archaeologists and Aesthetes in the Sculpture Galleries of the British Museum 1800–1939*, British Museum, London, 1992.

Lees-Milne, James, *Earls of Creation: Five Great Patrons of Eighteenth-Century Art*, Hamish Hamilton, London, 1962.

—, *English Country Houses: Baroque 1685–1715*, Country Life, London, 1970.

Robinson, John Martin, *The Latest Country Houses*, The Bodley Head, London, 1984.

—, and David Neave, *Francis Johnson Architect: A Classical Statement*, Oblong, Otley, 2001.

—, *The Regency Country House: From the Archives of Country Life*, Aurum Press, London, 2007.

Scott, Jonathan, *The Pleasures of Antiquity: British Collectors of Greece and Rome*, Yale University Press, New Haven and London, 2003.

Wilton, Andrew, and Ilaria Bignamini, eds., *Grand Tour: The Lure of Italy in the Eighteenth Century*, Tate Gallery, London, 1996.

Worsley, Giles, *Classical Architecture in Britain: The Heroic Age*, Yale University Press, New Haven and London, 2007.

Introduction

BELSAY HALL

Hewlings, Richard, 'Belsay Hall and the Personality of Sir Richard Monck, *Late Georgian Classicism*, Georgian Group Symposium, 1987.

Hussey, Christopher, 1958, *op. cit.*, pp.83–90.

FOOT'S CRAY PLACE

Colvin, Howard and John Harris, 'The Architect of Foot's Cray Place', *Georgian Group Journal*, VII, 1997, pp.1–8.

Vitruvius Britannicus, IV, 1767, pls.8–10.

MEREWORTH CASTLE

Vitruvius Britannicus, III, 1725, pls.35–8

MERKS HALL

Watkin, David, *Radical Classicism: The Architecture of Quinlan Terry*, Rizzoli, New York, 2004.

NUTHALL TEMPLE

Vitruvius Britannicus, IV, 1767, pls.56–7.

SHERINGHAM HALL

Repton, Humphry, Red Book for Sheringham, July 1812, reprinted in facsimile by Edward Malins ed., in *The Red Books of Humphry Repton*, Basilisk Press, London, 1976.

WIVENHOE NEW PARK

Archer, Lucy, *Raymond Erith Architect*, Cygnet Press, Burford, 1985, pp.171–2.

Raymond Erith: Progressive Classicist 1904–1973, exhib. cat., Sir John Soane's Museum, London, 2004, pp.60–1.

Robinson, John Martin, 1984, *op. cit.*, pp. 158–61.

Chapter I

WILTON HOUSE

Baker, Malcolm, '"For Pembroke, Statues, Dirty Gods and Coins": The Collecting, Display, and Uses of Sculpture at Wilton House', Nicholas Penny and Eike Schmidt, eds., *Collecting Sculpture in Early Modern Europe*, Yale University Press, New Haven and London, 2008.

Bold, John, *John Webb: Architectural Theory and Practice in the Seventeenth Century*, Clarendon Press, Oxford, 1989, reprinted with corrections, 1990.

—, and John Reeves, *Wilton House and English Palladianism: Some Wiltshire Houses*, HMSO, London, 1988.

STOKE BRUERNE PARK

Vitruvius Britannicus, III, 1717, pl.9.

Worsley, Giles, *Inigo Jones and the European Classicist Tradition*, Yale University Press, New Haven and London, 2007.

COLESHILL HOUSE

Gunther, R. T., *The Architecture of Sir Roger Pratt*, Oxford University Press, 1928.

Silcox-Crowe, Nigel, 'Sir Roger Pratt, 1620–1685, The Ingenious Gentleman Architect', in Roderick Brown, ed., *The Architectural Outsiders*, Waterstone, London, 1985, pp.1–20.

Vitruvius Britannicus, V, 1771, pls.86–7.

Chapter II

CHISWICK HOUSE

Barnard, Tony, and Jane Clark, eds., *Lord Burlington: Architecture, Art and Life*, The Hambledon Press, London and Rio Grande, 1995.

Harris, John, *The Palladian Revival: Lord Burlington, His Villa and Garden at Chiswick*, Yale University Press, New Haven and London, 1995.

—, 'Chiswick: A "Palladian" Garden?', *Garden History*, vol. 32, no. 1, Spring 2004, pp.124–36.

Pound, Ricky, 'The Master Mason Slain: The Hiramic Legend in the Red Velvet Room at Chiswick House', *English Heritage Historical Review*, 4, 2009, pp.154–61.

Rosman, T. S., 'The decoration and use of the principal apartments of Chiswick House, 1727–70', *Burlington Magazine*, October 1985, pp.663–77.

HOLKHAM HALL

Angelicoussis, Elizabeth, *The Holkham Collection of Classical Sculpture*, Philipp von Zabern, Mainz am Rhein, 2001.

Brettingham, Matthew, *The Plans, Elevations and Sections of Holkham in Norfolk* Haberkorn, London, 1761; enlarged ed., 1773.

Hassall, W. O., 'The Library at Holkham', *Connoisseur*, 133, 1954, pp.18ff, 87ff, 168ff.

Hiskey, Christine, 'The Building of Holkham Hall: Newly Discovered Letters', *Architectural History*, 40, 1997, pp.144–58.

Kenworthy-Browne, John, 'Matthew Brettingham's Rome Account Book 1747–1754', *The Walpole Society*, vol 49, 1983, pp.37–132.

Schmidt, Leo, ed., *Holkham*, Prestel, London, 2005.

WEST WYCOMBE PARK

Knox, Tim, 'Sir Francis Dashwood of West Wycombe Park, Buckinghamshire, as a Collector of Ancient and Modern Sculpture', in Nicholas Penny and Eike Schmidt, eds., *Collecting Sculpture in Early Modern Europe*, National Gallery of Art, Washington: Yale University Press, New Haven and London, 2008, pp.397–419.

KEDLESTON HALL

Vitruvius Britannicus, IV, 1767, pls.45–51.

Harris, Eileen, *The Genius of Robert Adam: His Interiors*, Yale University Press, New Haven and London, 2001.

—, *The Country Houses of Robert Adam: From the Archives of Country Life*, Aurum Press, London, 2007.

Harris, Leslie, *Robert Adam and Kedleston*, The National Trust, 1987.

Kenworthy-Browne, John, 'Designing around the Statues: Matthew Brettingham's Casts at Kedleston', *Apollo*, April 1993, pp.248–52.

Paine, James, *Plans, Elevations and Sections of Noblemen and Gentleman's Houses*, Printed for the Author, London, 2 vols., 1767–83, II, pls.42–52.

PACKINGTON HALL

Fitz-Gerald, Desmond, 'The Pompeiian Gallery, Packington Hall,' *Connoisseur*, September 1972, pp.8–9.

Watkin, David, 'Bonomi at Packington', *Georgian Group Journal*, 1989, pp.102–5.

PITZHANGER MANOR

de Divitis, Bianca, 'Plans, Elevations and Perspective Views of Pitzhanger Manor-House', *Georgian Group Journal*, XIV, 2004, pp.55–74.

Ewing, Heather, 'Pitzhanger Manor', in Margaret Richardson and MaryAnne Stevens, eds., *John Soane Architect: Master of Space and Light*, Royal Academy of Arts, London, 1999, pp.142–9.

Soane, John, *Plans, Elevations and Perspective Views of Pitzhanger Manor-House, and of the Ruins of an Edifice of Roman architecture … in a letter to a friend*, London: The Author, 1802 [published 1833].

Chapter III

GRANGE PARK

Brock, David, 'John Webb, William Samwell and the Grange', *English Heritage Historical Review*, 4, 2009, pp.98–121.

Crook, J. Mordaunt, 'Grange Park Transformed', in Howard Colvin and John Harris, eds., *The Country Seat*, Penguin, London, 1970, pp.220–8.

Geddes, James, 'The Grange, Northington', *Architectural History*, 26, 1983, pp.35–48.

Watkin, David, *The Life and Work of C. R. Cockerell*, Zwemmer, London, 1974.

KINGSTON LACY

Bankes, Viola, *A Dorset Heritage: The Story of Kingston Lacy*, Richards, London, 1953.

Cleminson, Antony, 'The Transition from Kingston Hall to Kingston Lacy', *Architectural History*, vol. 31, 1988, pp.120–35.

James, T. G. H., 'Egyptian Antiquities at Kingston Lacy, Dorset: William John Bankes as a Collector', *Apollo*, May 1994, pp.29–33.

Maclarnon, Kathleen, 'William Bankes and his Collection of Spanish Paintings at Kingston Lacy', *Burlington Magazine*, CXXXII, February 1990, pp.114–25.

Mitchell, Anthony, *Kingston Lacy*, The National Trust, 1990.

Ray, John, *The Rosetta Stone and the Rebirth of Ancient Egypt*, Profile Books, London, 2007.

Sebba, Anne, *The Exiled Collector: William Bankes and the Making of an English Country House*, John Murray, London, 2004.

PRESTWOLD HALL

Girouard, Mark, 1970, *op. cit.*, pp.138–42.

BRODSWORTH HALL

Brodsworth Hall and Gardens, English Heritage guide book, 1995 etc.

Girouard, Mark, 1970, *op. cit.*, pp.236–42.

GOSFORD HOUSE

Richardson, George, *The New Vitruvius Britannicus*, Bulmer & Co., London, vol. II, 1802, pp.13–14 & pls.43–8.

Chapter IV

NASHDOM

Butler, A. S. G., *The Lutyens Memorial, The Architecture of Sir Edwin Lutyens*, vol. I, *Country Houses*, Country Life, London, 1950, pp.36–7.

O'Neill, Daniell, *Sir Edwin Lutyens: Country Houses*, Lund Humphries, London, 1980.

Percy, Claire, and Jane Ridley, *The Letters of Edwin Lutyens to his wife Lady Emily*, Collins, London, 1985, pp.113, 122, 128.

Ridley, Jane, *The Architect and his Wife: A Life of Sir Edwin Lutyens*, Chatto & Windus, London, 2002.

GLEDSTONE HALL

Butler, A. S. G., 1950, *op. cit.*, pp.54–6.

O'Neill, Daniell, 1980, *op. cit.*, pp.143–8.

Stamp, Gavin, *Edwin Lutyens, Country Houses: From the Archives of Country Life*, Aurum Press, London, 2001.

VILLA VIZCAYA

Aslet, Clive, *The American Country House*, Yale University Press, New Haven and London, 1990.

Rybczynski, Witold, and Laurie Olin, *Vizcaya: An American Villa and its Makers*, University of Pennsylvania Press, Philadelphia, 2007.

Chapter V

ASHFOLD HOUSE

Binney, Marcus, *The Times Magazine*, 28 January 1995, pp.22–6.

Howard, Henrietta, *House and Garden*, September 1993, pp.69–74.

John, Richard, and David Watkin, *John Simpson: The Queen's Gallery and Other Works*, Papadakis, London, 2002, pp.104–25.

FERNE PARK

Watkin, David, 2004, *op. cit.*, pp.206–17.

RECENT HOUSES IN THE USA AND THE BAHAMAS

Dowling, Elizabeth M., *New Classicism: The Rebirth of Traditional Architecture*, New York, Rizzoli, 2004.

Miers, Mary, *American Houses: The Architecture of Fairfax & Sammons*, New York, Rizzoli, 2006.

INDEX

Page numbers in *italics* refer to illustrations

Acton family 140
Adam, James 75
Adam, Robert (1728–92) 12, 68–72, 75, 76, 117, 119, 121, 125, 129
Adam, Robert 163, 164
Adam brothers 12, 75, 76, 86, 19
Addison, Joseph 14
Albani, Cardinal 58, 84
Alberti, Leon Battista 11, 98
Algarotti, Count 51
Amesbury Abbey 105
Arch of Constantine, Rome 68, 72, 82
Argenti, Giosuè 114
Arrol, Sir William 121
Arundel, Earl of 7, 19, 24, 38, 58
Arundel House 58
Arundel Park House 167
Arundell, 8th Lord, of Wardour 12
Ashburnham Place, Sussex 170
Ashdown House, Berkshire 36
Ashfold House, Sussex 156–61, *156, 157, 158, 159, 161*
Asprucci, Antonio 76
Astor, William Waldorf 140
Aubrey, John 20, 24, 29, 30
Aylesford, Earls of 76, 81

Bankes family 101
Bankes, William 9, 101–2, 105, 107, 109, 137–8, 169
Banqueting House, Whitehall 19, 24, 34
Barbaro, Daniele 11, 33, 34, 45, 57, 62
Barbaro brothers 33
Barbet, Jean 30
Baring, Alexander 92
Baring, Sir Francis, Baronet 91–2
Barry, Sir Charles 89, 93, 97–8, 101, 105, 107, 109
Bartoli, Domenico 79
Bartoli, Francesco Santi 65
Basevi, George 98
Basilica, Vicenza 121
Basilica of Maxentius, Rome 49, 58, 75
Beach House, Sussex 9
Beaufort House, Chelsea 188
Beaumont, Sir George 76
Beckford, William 102
Belcher, John 167
Belsay Hall, Northumberland *88*, 89
Benjamin, Asher 185
Berain, Jean 178
Bernini, Giovanni 169
Bianchini, Francesco 66
Bicester, Lords 167, 170
Bicknell, Julian 12
Binney, Marcus 138
Bolton, Edmund 20, 29
Bonomi, Joseph 76, 79, 81
Borgnis, Giovanni 79
Borgnis, Giuseppe 62–5, 79
Borra, Battista 12
Brettingham, Matthew (elder) 68, 76, 79
Brettingham, Matthew (younger) 53–4, 57–8, 71, 101–2
Brettingham, Robert Furze 101
Bridges, Henry 33
British Embassy, Washington 148–53, *148–9, 150–1, 152–3*
Britton, John 160, 176
Brodsworth Hall, Yorkshire 14, 110–15, *110, 111, 112, 114, 115*
Brown, Lancelot 'Capability' 11, 43, 66, 81, 170
Bryce, David 97
Burlington, Lord 7, 12, 16, 34, 40, 43, 45–51, 53–4, 160
Burn, William 94, 97, 98, 167
Bute, Marquess of 126
Buti, Camillo 86
Butler, A. S. G. 14, 142, 144, 148
Byron, Lord 14, 102, 105, 10

Cairness House, Aberdeenshire 14, *14*
Calder, A. Stirling 140
Came House, Dorset 174
Campanella, Angelo 86
Campbell, Colen 7, 11, 12, 30, 32, 43, 45, 62
Campo Vaccino, Rome 72
Canova, Antonio 14, 114
Ca'Pesaro, Venice 174
Carlyle, Thomas 90
Carracci, Annibale 62, 65
Carter, Harold 163
Cartwright, Francis 174
Casentini, Giovanni 111, 113, 114
Castell, Robert 51, 72, 86
Castletown Cox, Co. Kilkenny 174
Caylus, Comte de 79
Chalfin, Paul 137, 138, 140
Chambers, William 43, 54, 76, 169
Charles, Prince of Wales 185
Charles I, King 24, 29, 30, 32, *103*
Chatsworth 30, 34, 51, 71
Cheere, Henry 65
Chelsea Hospital, London 148
Chiari, Giuseppe 58
Chiswick House, Middlesex 7, 11, 12, 16, 44–51, *44–5, 46, 47, 48, 49, 50, 51*
Christ Church, Spitalfields 164
Choragic Monument of Lysicrates, Athens 75, 91
Clarendon, Lord 20
Claude Lorrain 92, 98
Cleave, Richard 40
Clérisseau, Charles-Louis 76
Clerk, Sir John of Penicuik 45, 49
Cockerell, Charles Robert 92, 93, 98
Cockerell, Samuel Pepys 92
Coke, Thomas 53–4, 57–8
Coleshill House, Berkshire 9, 12, *18*, 36–41, *36, 37, 38–9, 40, 41*, 101, 107
College of William and Mary, Colonial Williamsburg 148
Colvin, Howard 66, 170
Conservative Club, St James's Street 98
Cook, Ernest 40
Cook, Thomas 66
Cornforth, John 107
Cortona, Pietro da 58
Cranbury Park, Hampshire 84
Crane, Sir Francis 32, 33
Croome Court 129
Cubitt, Thomas 89
Cuitt, George 75
Curzon, Hon. Eveline 125
Curzon, Nathaniel 68, 71, 72, 75

Dance, George 43, 82, 84, 91, 92
Daniell, Thomas 66
Dashwood, Sir Francis, 2nd Baronet 60, 62, 65–6
de Caus, Isaac 20, 24, 29, 51
de Caus, Salomon 24
de Critz, Emmanuel 25, 30
de' Ficorini, Francesco 54
de Vries, Vredeman 19
de Wolfe, Elsie 137
Debay, Auguste-Hyacinthe 114
Deepdene, The, Surrey 89, 93
Deering, James 16, 137, 138, 140
Deglane, Henri-Adolphe-Auguste 137
Desgodetz, Antoine 57, 58, 72
Diocletian, Emperor 29, 75, 76
Dixon, Cornelius 102
Dodd, John 20
Dodington Park 160
Doge's Palace, Venice 30
Dolgorouki, Her Highness Princess Alexis 131, 133, 135
Domus Aurea 79, 81
Donington Hall, Leicestershire 94
Donowell, John 62, 66
Downing College, Cambridge 90, 92
Drummond, Henry 90, 92
Ducal Palace, Mantua 51
Ducart, David 174
Durham House, London 30

Eccles, David 40
Edgemont, Virginia 185
Erechtheion, Athens 84
Erith, Raymond 16, 155, 173
Escorial, Palace of the 29
Evelyn, John 30, 187
Eydon Lodge, Northamptonshire 126

Fairfax, Anne 185
Fane, Hon. John 62
Favenza, Vincenzo 107
Ferne Park, Dorset 16, 172–81, *172, 173, 175, 176–7, 178–9, 180, 181*
Ferrari, Domenico 57
Flitcroft, Henry 45
Fonthill Abbey 102
Foots Cray Place, Kent 12
Forum of Trajan 84
Franchi, Pietro 114

Gabriel, Ange-Jacques 129
Gandy, Joseph Michael 84, 86
Generalife, Granada 140
Gérôme, Jean-Léon 137
Gibbons, Grinling 107
Gibbs, James 51
Giordano, Luca 75
Giorgione 107, 109
Glasgow Municipal Chambers 119
Gledstone Hall, Yorkshire 14, 142–7, *142, 143, 144–5, 146–7*, 153, 180
Golby, Rupert 176, 178, 180
Gordon, Charles 14
Gosford House, East Lothian 9, *114, 115*, 116–21, *118, 119, 120*
Grange Park, Hampshire 14, 89, 90–3, *90–1, 92, 93*, 105, 107
Greenberg, Allan 182
Grove, Thomas 173
Guarini, Guarino 46
Guernsey, Lord 76

Hadrian's Villa, Tivoli 57, 58, 65
Hagley Hall, Worcestershire 43, 89
Hall, John 185
Hamilton, Dowager Duchess of 169
Hammerwood Lodge, Sussex 89
Hannan, William 65, 66
Hardwick, Thomas 86
Harlaxton Manor, Lincolnshire 97
Haverfield, John 86
Hawksmoor, Nicholas 164
Haycock, Edward 14
Heathcote, Yorkshire 131, 142
Henbury Hall, Cheshire 12, *13*
Henley, Lord Chancellor 92
Henley, Sir Robert 90
Henrietta Maria, Queen 25, 29, 30, 49
Henry VIII, King 7
Hephaesteion, Athens 91
Herbert, Henry, 9th Earl of Pembroke 9, 11
Hermogenes of Priene 66
Hever Castle, Kent 140
Hicks, David 12
Highland Park House, Dallas 9
Hiolin, Louis 142
Hoffman, Francis Burrall, Jnr 137–8, 140
Holkham Hall, Norfolk 12, 19, 52–9, *52–3, 54–5, 56–7, 58–9*, 71, 79, 101, 113, 117
Home House, Portman Square 169
Hope, Thomas 81, 84, 86, 89, 93, 160
Hôtel de Salm, Paris 16
Houghton Hall, Norfolk 81
Huckleberry House, New England 182
Hugues, Pierre-François 79
Hunt, John 117

Isola Bella, Lake Maggiore 140

Jacques, Richard 142
James I, King 20, 24, 32
Jebb, Philip 167
Jefferson, Thomas 14, 16, 185
Jekyll, Gertrude 147, 174, 180
Johnson, Francis 155
Jolivet, Maurice-Louis 66
Jolli, Antonio 81
Jones, Inigo 7, 11, 14, 16, 19–20, 25, 29–30, 32–4, 36, 38, 40, 43, 45, 49, 51, 58, 105, 153, 170, 188
Jones, Thomas 86

Kant, Immanuel 180
Kedleston Hall, Derbyshire 12, 19, 68–75, *68, 69, 70, 71, 72–3, 74, 75*, 129
Kelly, Felix 12
Kent, William 11, 30, 45, 51, 53–4, 57, 179–80
King's Walden Bury, Hertfordshire *154*, 155, 173
Kingston Lacy, Dorset 9, 38, 100–9, *100, 101, 102, 103, 104, 105, 106–7, 108, 109*, 169
Kinross, John 126, 129
Knoblock, Edward 9
Kulb House, Central Illinois 182

Lafever, Minard 182
Latrobe, Benjamin 89
Lazzerini, Giuseppe 113
Ledoux, Claude-Nicolas 14, 81, 165
Lees Court, Kent 105, 109
Leicester, Lord 58
Leoni, Giacomo 12, 45
Lewis, James 126
Ligorio, Pirro 75
Lilliefields, Virginia, *184*, 185, *185*
Lincoln's Inn Fields 84, 86, 157, 159, 160
Linnell, John 72
Longhena, Baldassare 38, 57, 137, 174
Longhi, Martino, the younger 107
Lothbury Arch 82
Lowther Castle, Westmorland 71
Luti, Benedetto 75
Lutyens, Sir Edwin 7, 11, 14, 123, 131, 133, 135, 142, 144, 147, 148, 153, 174, 180

Mackennal, Bertram 123
Maderno, Carlo 140
Magni, Pietro 113
Major, Thomas 81
Maltravers House, Lothbury 36
Manderston, Berwickshire 124–9, *124, 125, 126, 127, 128*, 167
Mariari, Giacomo 53
Market Hall, Chipping Camden 179
Marot, Daniel 178
Mausoleum of Augustus, Rome 66
Maw, Ray 163
Medicis 20, 84
Mereworth Castle, Kent *2, 10*, 45, 62
Merks Hall, Essex 9, *12*, 36, 155
Michelangelo Buonarroti 32, 34, 159
Middlefield, New York State 182, *182–3*
Middleton Park, Oxfordshire 144
Miller, James 58,
Miller, Sir James 125–6, 129
Miller, Lady 86
Millichope Park, Shropshire 14, *14*, 162
Mishaum Point, Massachusetts 185, *186, 187*
Mitchell, Robert 91
Monck, Sir Charles, Baronet 89
Montagu, George 75
Montesquieu 60
Monticello, Virginia 14, 16, *16*, 185
Montrésor, Michelangelo 107, 109
Moore, Charles 148
Moore, John 81
Morris, John 170
Morris, Robert 16
Morris, Roger 9, 11
Müntz, J. H. 79
Murray, John 102
Muse, Lyn 9
Mylne, Robert 43, 81, 167

Nashdom, Buckinghamshire 7, 14, 130–5, *130, 131, 132, 134, 135*
Nelson, Sir Amos 142, 147
Nesfield, William Andrews 93
Newby Hall, Yorkshire 129
Newfield House, Yorkshire 155
Northumberland, Duke of 9
Nostell Priory, Yorkshire 71
Nuthall Temple, Nottinghamshire *11*

Osborne House, Isle of Wight 89

Packe, Charles William 94, 97
Packington Hall, Warwickshire 12, 76–81, *76–7, 78–9, 80, 81*, 86
Paestum 14, 53, 81
Paine, James 7, 9, 12, 69, 71–2, 75, 107, 169
Palazzo Chiericati 62
Palazzo Contarini degli Scrigni 109
Palazzo dei Conservatori 33, 34
Palazzo Farnese 65
Palazzo Massimo 7, 40, 49, 131
Palazzo Mocenigo 105
Palazzo Pandolfini 89, 98, 105
Palazzo Pisani 109
Palazzo Ruspoli 107
Palazzo Thiene 49
Palazzo Torlonia 138
Palazzo Trissino al Corso 33
Palazzo Valmarana 33
Palladio 11, 12, 16, 19, 30, 32, 33, 34, 38, 43, 45, 46, 49, 51, 54, 57, 62, 69, 72, 75, 86, 153, 174
Pantheon 30, 72, 75
Pastorini, Benedetto 79
Pegrassi, Salesio 107
Pembroke, Earls of 20, 24, 25, 29, 30
Pembroke House, Bahamas 187, *188–189*
Pennoyer, Peter 185, 187
Peruzzi, Baldassare 7, 40, 65, 131
Petit Trianon, Versailles 129
Petter, Hugh 187, 188
Phillimore, Claude 167, 169
Pierce, Edward 25
Piranesi, Giambattista 12, 66, 81, 84
Pite, Beresford 167, 187
Pitzhanger Manor, Middlesex 82–7, *82, 83, 84–5, 86, 87*, 157
Playfair, James 14
Pleydell, Sir Mark 36, 40
Pliny the Elder 57, 79
Pliny the Younger 9, 11, 72
Ponte Sant'Angelo, Rome 11
Pope, Alexander 147
Portico of Octavia, Rome 144
Poussin, Nicolas 92, 97
Powell, Hughie 178
Pratt, Sir George 36
Pratt, Sir Henry 36
Pratt, Sir Roger 19, 38, 101, 105
Prestwold Hall, Leicestershire 94–9, *94, 95, 96, 97, 98, 99*
Price, Uvedale 76

Quarenghi, Giacomo 12, 14
Queen's House, Greenwich 30, 38, 49, 105

Raphael 65, 75, 89, 94
Rayleigh, Lord and Lady 174
Redentore, church of the, Venice 57
Reid, Dick 187, 188
Repton, John Adey 9, 11
Repton, Humphry 9, 11, 43, 66
Revett, Nicholas 43, 60, 66, 89
Rialto bridge, Venice 11, 12
Rigaud, Jean-François 79, 81
Roberts, Thomas 12
Roman Forum 49, 58, 174
Romano, Giulio 51
Rose, Joseph, Jnr 79
Rothermere, Lady 173–4, 176, 178–9, 180
Rothermere, Lord 173
Rousham, Oxfordshire 179, 180, *180*
Rousseau, Pierre 16
Royal Academy 12, 82, 94
Royal Gardens, Richmond and Kew, 86

Saïd, Wafic 167, 169
Salvi, Nicola 72
Salvin, Anthony 97
Sammons, Richard 185
Samwell, William 90, 91
San Francesco, Rimini 98
San Giorgio Maggiore,Venice 38, 57, 174
Sanmichele, Michele 131
Sansovino, Jacopo 46
Sarcophagus of Marcus Agrippa 72
Scamozzi, Vincenzo 11, 19, 20, 29, 33, 45, 109
Schafer, Gil 182
Schloss Glienicke, 164
Scott, Geoffrey 14, 140
Serliana 25, 29, 45
Serlio, Sebastiano 20, 25, 29, 34, 38, 49
Settrington House, Yorkshire 155
Sheringham Hall, Norfolk *8*, 11
Shrubland Park, Suffolk 89
Simpson, John 155, 157, 159, 160
Sleter, Francesco 11
Smirke, Robert 34, 92, 94
Smirke, Sydney 98
Smith, Thomas Gordon 185
Smith, Vivian Hugh 167
Smiths of Warwick 68
Soane, Sir John 12, 34, 43, 69, 79, 81, 82, 84, 86, 89, 101, 137, 155, 157, 159–60, 185
Solar House, Wakeham, Sussex 162–5, *162, 163, 165*
Somerset House, London 25, 51
SS Apostoli, Rome 84
St James, Packington 81
St John Lateran, Rome 72
St Mark's Library, Venice 46
St Paul's, Covent Garden 34, 144, 188
St Paul's Cathedral, London 19
Stern, Robert 185
Stoddart, Alexander 180
Stoke Park, Northamptonshire 32–5, *32–3, 34–5*
Stoke Rochford House 97
Stone, Nicholas, the elder 30
Stowe House, Buckinghamshire *42*
Strafford, Lord 29
Stratton Park, Hampshire 91
Stuart, James 'Athenian' 43, 68, 75, 89
Stukeley, William 20
Suarez, Diego 138, 140
Syon House, Middlesex 9, 129

Talman, John 51
Tansey, Andrew 174
Taylor, Sir Robert 159, 170
Teatro Olimpico, Vicenza 51
Temple, 2nd Earl 43
Temple of Antoninus and Faustina, Rome 54, 58
Temple of Apollo Epicurius, Bassae 92, 93
Temple of Bel, Palmyra 65
Temple of Castor and Pollux, Rome 81
Temple of Deified Hadrian 72
Temple of Dionysus, Teos 66
Temple of Fortuna Virilis, Rome 57, 58
Temple of Hephaestus, Athens *93*
Temple of Isis, Philae 101
Temple of Isis, Pompeii 86
Temple of Mars Ultor, Rome 46
Temple of Romulus, Rome 51
Temple of Venus and Roma 49, 57, 58, 75
Temple of Vesta, Tivoli 72
Terling Place, Essex 174
Terry, Francis 174, 179, 180
Terry, Quinlan 9, 16, 66, 155, 170, 173–4, 176, 179–80
Thellusson, Charles Sabine 111, 113
Thomson, Alexander 'Greek' 164
Tigbourne Court, Surrey 188
Tijou, Jean 178
Tomb of Bacchus, Rome 65
Tower of the Winds, Athens 66, 164
Travellers' Club, Pall Mall 89, 98, 105
Treasury Buildings, Horse Guards Parade 54
Trentham Hall, Staffordshire 89
Trevi fountain, Rome 72
Tusmore Park, Oxfordshire 9, 166–71, *166, 167, 168, 170–1*
Tyringham Hall, Buckinghamshire 89, 159

Valadier, Luigi 12
Van Dyck, Sir Anthony 20, 25, 30
Veneto, The 16, 45, 46, 138
Veronese 62, 109
Vertue, George 40
Viceroy's House, New Delhi *122*, 123, 144, 147, 148, 153
Vignola, Giacomo Barozzi da 187, 188
Villa Albani 84, 86
Villa Barbaro 33
Villa Capra ('La Rotonda') *11*, 12, 45, 46, 153, 174
Villa Cornaro 62
Villa d'Este 89, 93
Villa Farnesina 65
Villa Gamberaia 140
Villa La Pietra 138
Villa Madama 51
Villa Malcontenta 46
Villa Medici 82, 89
Villa Mocenigo 54, 69, 71
Villa Molin 45
Villa Negroni 86
Villa Rezzonico 137
Villa Rocca Pisani 11, 12, 45, 46
Villa Torlonia 140
Villa Trissino 32
Villa Valmarana 45
Villa Verde, Algarve 12, *12*
Villa Vizcaya, Florida 16, 136–141, *136–7, 138, 139, 140–1*
Vitruvius 11, 14, 30, 34, 36, 40, 45, 46, 49, 51, 53, 57, 62, 65, 79, 129, 164, 182
Vulliamy, Lewis 98

Walker, Anne 187
Walpole, Horace 14, 75
Walpole, Sir Robert 53
Wanstead House 30
Wardour Castle, Wiltshire *6–7*, 9, *9*, 12, 14, *15*, 107, 169, 173, *178*
Ware, Isaac 12, 40
Waverton House, Gloucestershire 155
Webb, John 30, 36, 51
Webster, John 126
Wemyss, Earls of 9, 117, 121
West Wycombe Park, Buckinghamshire 11, 60–7, *60, 61, 62, 63, 64, 65, 67*
Westmacott, Richard 30
Whitehall Palace 29, 30
Whitfield, Sir William 9, 155, 167, 169
Wilkie, Kim 187
Wilkins, William 89–92, 94
Wilkinson, Philip 111
Williams-Wynn, Sir Watkin, 5th Baronet 102, 129
Wilton House, Wiltshire 9, 11, 12, 16, 20–31, *20–1, 22–3, 24–5, 26–7, 28–9, 31*, 36, 38, 54
Winckelmann, Johann 14, 84, 89, 90
Wivenhoe New Park, Essex 16, *17*
Wollaton Hall, Nottinghamshire 19
Wood, Robert 58, 65
Woronzow, Catherine 30
Wotton, Henry 11
Wren, Christopher 40, 123, 148
Wright, Stephen 170
Wright, Thomas 11, 12
Wyatt, James 12, 43, 81, 102, 109, 117, 160

York House, Pall Mall 169
Young, Rory 164
Young, William 9, 117, 119, 121

Zucchi, Antonio 76

192 · THE CLASSICAL COUNTRY HOUSE